W9-AQB-624

WOMEN OF
VALOR

The Struggle Against the Great Depression
As Told in Their Own Life Stories

WOMEN
OF VALOR

Edited with Commentary by
Bernard Sternsher and Judith Sealander

Chicago
IVAN R. DEE
1990

Drawings by Jorge Colombo

Grateful acknowledgment is made to the following publishers and individuals for permission to reprint copyrighted materials included herein: Excerpts from *Neighborhood: My Story of Greenwich House* by Mary K. Simkhovitch, copyright 1938 by W. W. Norton and Co., reprinted by permission of Helena Simkhovitch (Mrs. Frank Didisheim). Excerpts from *Windows on Henry Street* by Lillian D. Wald, copyright 1933, 1934 by Lillian D. Wald. Excerpts from *This I Remember* by Eleanor Roosevelt, copyright 1949 by Anna Eleanor Roosevelt, reprinted by permission of Harper & Row, Publishers. Excerpts from *The Long Loneliness: The Autobiography of Dorothy Day*, copyright 1952 by Harper & Row, Publishers, reprinted by permission of Harper & Row, Publishers. Excerpts from *Portrait of Myself* by Margaret Bourke-White, copyright 1963 by Simon and Schuster, reprinted by permission of the author's estate and the agents for the estate, Scott Meredith Literary Agency, 845 Third Avenue, New York, NY 10022. Excerpts from *The Roosevelt I Knew* by Frances Perkins, copyright 1946 by Frances Perkins, reprinted by permission of Viking Penguin, Inc. Excerpts from *Woman at Work: The Autobiography of Mary Anderson as Told to Mary Winslow* by Mary Anderson, copyright 1951 by the University of Minnesota, reprinted by permission of the University of Minnesota Press. Excerpts from *Arena: The History of the Federal Theatre* by Hallie Flanagan, copyright 1940 by Hallie Flanagan. Excerpts from *Red Ribbon on a White Horse* by Anzia Yezierska, copyright 1950 by Anzia Yezierska, afterword copyright 1987 by Louise Levitas Henriksen, reprinted by permission of Louise Levitas Henriksen and Persea Books. Excerpts from *The Third Door: The Autobiography of an American Negro Woman* by Ellen Tarry, copyright 1955 by Ellen Tarry, reprinted by permission of David McKay Co., a Division of Random House. Excerpts from *We Too Are the People* by Louise V. Armstrong, copyright 1938 by Louise V. Armstrong. Excerpts from *A Radical Life* by Vera Buch Weisbord, copyright 1977 by Indiana University Press, reprinted by permission of The Albert and Vera Weisbord Foundation. Excerpts from *We Are Many: The Autobiography of Ella Reeve Bloor* by Ella Reeve Bloor, copyright 1940 by International Publishers Co., reprinted by permission of International Publishers Co. Excerpts from *Salute to Spring* by Meridel Le Sueur, copyright 1940, 1977 by International Publishers Co., reprinted by permission of International Publishers Co. Excerpts from *To Win These Rights: A Personal Story of the CIO in the South* by Lucy Randolph Mason, copyright 1952 by Harper & Row, Publishers, reprinted by permission of Harper & Row, Publishers. Excerpts from *Rebel Pen: The Writings of Mary Heaton Vorse* by Mary Heaton Vorse, edited by Dee Garrison, copyright 1985 by Dee Garrison, reprinted by permission of the Monthly Review Foundation.

Library of Congress Cataloging-in-Publication Data:

Women of valor : the struggle against the great depression as told in their own life
  stories / edited with commentary by Bernard Sternsher and Judith Sealander.
     p.   cm.
  Includes bibliographical references.
  ISBN 0-929587-34-0
  1. Women social reformers—United States—Biography. 2. Women in politics—United States—Biography. 3. Women—Employment—United States—Biography. 4. Depressions—1929—United States. I. Sternsher, Bernard, 1925–   . II. Sealander, Judith.
HQ1412.W66   1990
303.48′4′09730922—dc20   90-37350

CONTENTS

WOMEN OF
VALOR

DURING THE 1930S AMERICANS BECAME RADIO SOAP OPERA ADDICTS.
Millions tuned in each week to the dozens of fifteen-minute shows
sponsored largely by soap and cleaning-agent companies. Procter &
Gamble and other sponsors discovered a new advertising gold mine.
Their listeners not only adjusted their weekly schedules in order to
hear each new serial installment, they also dutifully bought the
advertised products.

While the "soaps" sold detergent, they also sold an image of the
American woman. Invariably she was the strong anchor who held her
family together, the one who kept her man from despair. Helen
Trent's life embodied her motto that "romance can live in life at
thirty-five and even beyond." If so, Helen's romance rarely owed to
her legions of male admirers, who were forever confessing weakness,
only to be propped up by the stalwart Helen. Molly Goldberg had
sense and strength enough to run her own family and much of the
neighborhood to boot. Mother Barbour and Ma Perkins likewise
pulled the family strings, solving problems and soothing crises.[1]

Historians who have examined the roles played by women during
the Depression, if they have not found Ma Goldberg herself, certainly have found evidence in thousands of letters, diaries, and printed
accounts of strong women doing their best to hold their families

together. But, unlike the heroines whose stories boosted the sales of Rinso, real-life American women experienced far fewer happy endings. In fact, most scholars who have studied the matter depict women during the Depression era chiefly as victims of the economic crisis. They not only struggled to keep their families and homes together but also bore the brunt of unemployment and lost status in the professions and public life. Feminism went on the defensive or died out altogether.

Squeezed between the supposed liberation of the post-suffrage flapper and the wartime service of Rosie the Riveter, women in the 1930s have until recently drawn relatively little attention from historians. This older neglect is being supplanted by a broad new interest in twentieth-century women's history. Although historians have yet to reach a consensus on the situation of women between the winning of suffrage in 1920 and the revival of feminism in the 1960s, the emerging picture of the 1930s is far more rich and varied than previously suggested. In this new view, historians see women helping to pull the country through the Depression rather than solely as victims of the economic crisis. By highlighting women's positive roles in their families, communities, and public life, historians have actually returned to the interpretation put forth in 1933 by Eleanor Roosevelt in her aptly titled book *It's Up to the Women*: "The women know that life must go on and that the needs of life must be met, and it is their courage and determination which, time and again, have pulled us through worse crises than the present one." The United States could never have survived the Depression without the collective contributions of American womanhood.

I

During this time of severe economic crisis, when many established values were under assault, most Americans, men and women, clearly supported traditional family roles. And this despite economic hurdles to marriage and family brought on by hard times. Women married at a slightly older age between 1930 and 1940, with women of all ages a bit more likely to be single than married at decade's end. Even if they married, women often postponed their first babies. But neither they nor their men challenged the view that marriage and child-rearing were women's primary goals. In fact, the overwhelming majority of adult women continued to marry and have children. According to polls, most Americans believed that wives who did not devote themselves exclusively to husband and home threatened the stability of the American family, and that wives who worked stole employment from deserving men. Only the most dire financial circumstances could justify a married woman's taking a position outside the home.

As the Depression deepened and jobs became even more scarce, both private and public employers sought to deny work to women, especially to married women. Section 213 of the 1932 Federal Economy Act, for instance, required that one spouse resign if both worked for the federal government. More than three-fourths of the spouses forced to quit under this law were wives. The law could have been used to fire more husbands, but most bosses correctly understood "spouse" to be a euphemism for wife. At some time during the 1930s more than half the states made the attack on working wives more explicit, passing laws or issuing executive orders that removed married women from state employment and specified that qualified males with families be given preference over single women. The private sector was no different. Many thousands of industrial firms across the country fired women.[2]

Still, at a time when work was so difficult to find and society so strongly disapproved of women wage-earners, the number of married women at work increased by almost 15 percent. By 1940 married women made up about one-third of the female labor force. More young women married but stayed at work until the birth of a first baby. Older wives returned to work, sometimes when husbands lost jobs, often, in less trying circumstances, to maintain family spending patterns established in the more prosperous twenties. The Depression decade thus saw a discrepancy between disapproval based on tradition and practice dictated by hard times.

If contemporary polls have any substance, women themselves thought they should concentrate on the home. Yet in the 1930s the percentage of women working for pay outside the home increased slightly—from 24.3 to 25.4. The work world that most women encountered, whether they were single or married, professional or manual workers, was one of diminished opportunities and pay. The proportion of women in professional fields declined, even in some traditionally female occupations such as teaching, as employers held jobs open for men—and as men, with no other options, took them. Thousands of women with college degrees and professional or managerial work experience found themselves grateful to find any kind of job. Former supervisors, professors, and librarians took jobs as salesgirls or factory laborers. Throughout the spectrum of employment, women faced pay cuts, heavier work loads, and hostility. At the top, professionals often found themselves responsible for the work of two people, with no increase in salary, as employers retrenched; at the bottom, women hoping for day work as maids earning nine to fifteen cents an hour stood on corners, waiting for housewives to drive by and choose them.[3]

Women faced formidable burdens as victims of social prejudice, discrimination, and their own ambivalence. Society told women at home that they were responsible for keeping their families cheerful, even as they bought less meat at the grocery, mended rather than purchased clothing, curtailed recreation, and moved to cheaper housing—or, in even more drastic circumstances, begged for charity to feed their children. Society told women at work that they did not belong and punished them with lowered status, fewer opportunities, and diminished pay. And women responded in the end by lowering their expectations. Discouraged and confused, American women during the Depression retreated. Proportionally, fewer sought higher education. Fewer believed, as had their sisters and mothers during the prosperous twenties, that they could combine a challenging career with a happy marriage. The jobs they found, in general, were menial: clerical, factory, or semi-professional work. In hard times, women made fewer big plans. Instead they nourished smaller hopes of just a little more security.[4]

II

These reduced aspirations notwithstanding, to view women during the Depression only as victims, as historians have usually done, is to look through a narrow lens and fail to see an important development. The Depression narrowed opportunity for the average woman as it did in many ways for the average man. But for a remarkable minority the thirties brought chances for leadership as social activists both conservative and radical, as government officials, and as union organizers.

As social activists women continued to lead reform movements in roles many had played for decades. They were often the first to observe the Depression at close range, and they doubled their efforts to help those whom the Depression left down and out. Many managed religious charities, soup kitchens, or settlement houses, whose aid became increasingly critical to their often desperate recipients. The view of the Depression from the bottom up was so devastating that these social activists were among the most powerful voices calling for federal action to meet the problems of relief and unemployment. Social workers, most of whom were women, also benefited from other people's misfortunes. As Lillian Wald observed in 1932, "I think this is a good time for social workers; the only people who seem to be employed—alas!"[5] Meanwhile, more radical female social activists argued that the crisis signaled a need not for relief efforts but for drastic social and economic change. As editors, writers, or street-corner agitators, they demanded an end to capitalism and the restructuring of American politics.[6]

The creation of the modern welfare state in response to the Depression was one of the factors which encouraged a flowering of women's talents in the New Deal administration of Franklin D. Roosevelt, an area richly represented in this collection. The President's own support for women's social welfare initiatives, the constant prodding of his wife Eleanor, and the experimental climate of the early New Deal combined to open up the governmental process to women in an unprecedented way. Women came to the New Deal not so much as feminists but as reformers eager to solve the crisis of the Depression.

The Depression thus witnessed the growth of a "woman's network" of female federal officials whose numbers and influence would not be matched again until the 1960s. These several dozen highly placed officials made important contributions to the creation and administration of New Deal social welfare programs.

While the formation of the welfare state gave women opportunities in government, it is also possible to say, as historian Susan Ware has argued, that "women founded the modern welfare state."[7] The National Industrial Recovery Act, the Social Security Act of 1935, and the Fair Labor Standards Act of 1938 in important ways represented victories for women officials. Such women as First Lady Eleanor Roosevelt, Secretary of Labor Frances Perkins, Molly Dewson, director of the Women's division of the Democratic party, and Ellen Sullivan Woodward, director of Women's and Professional Projects for the Works Progress Administration (WPA), were shapers of policies to combat the Depression, not its diminished victims.

In addition to this powerful group of major policymakers, greater numbers of women served in the lower levels of federal agencies. The Federal Writers' Project, for instance, employed fourteen women state administrators. Even the infamous Section 213, not rescinded until 1937, did not prevent percentage increases for women in new agencies and programs. Few women found new jobs in federal departments such as War, Navy, or Commerce, but by 1939 new bureaucracies, like that established for the Works Progress Administration, included large percentages of women employees. In most of these agencies, women made up at least a third of the work force. And these women, too, shaped New Deal programs, as social workers, relief administrators, or writers and artists on the federal payroll.[8]

Finally, women shared the benefits of the New Deal's endorsement of workers' right to organize. Under the umbrella of New Deal legislation such as Section 7(a) of the National Industrial Recovery Act and the National Labor Relations Act of 1935, union membership surged. This story has been told many times, but women are almost invisible in the usual accounts. By the onset of World War II, more than 800,000 women belonged to unions, three times their number in 1929. Women organizers, especially in the CIO and radical labor groups, played important roles in this growth.[9]

III

One fruitful way to understand the contributions of this remarkable minority of American women is through their own testimony. While published autobiographies do not exist for some of the most influential and interesting women, a significant number did write about their lives. Others produced books, articles, or materials focusing on other topics but containing a great deal of autobiographical detail.[10]

Since 1970, scholars influenced by trends in social and labor history have demanded investigation of history from "the bottom up," as opposed to top-down or "elite" history, and they have produced a great many collections of first-person history from the Depression: interviews conducted decades after the Depression ended,[11] interviews conducted across the country in the 1930s by Federal Writers' Project personnel,[12] and hundreds of reports filed by investigators for relief agencies such as the Federal Emergency Relief Administration and the WPA.[13] Finally, millions of Americans wrote letters to public officials—letters that praised, condemned, or begged for help.[14] These materials often provide brief but powerful glimpses into the daily lives of ordinary women. They wrote of lives lacking "plesure [sic] of any kind" and an inability to pay the mortgage "with seven little children + no place to go."[15] They reported that "...Lights have been Cut off and Credit stopped and furniture houses are taking the furniture away."[16] Some wistfully pleaded with Eleanor Roosevelt for a little money or clothing. One urged the First Lady to remember her if she had "a few old discarded dresses among the ones that you have tired of that you would like to get rid of, and do some good at the same time."[17]

Collections of first-person history from the Great Depression help to reclaim the "nameless masses," men and women, and treat them as individuals. But among nonordinary folk, the hundreds of biographies and numerous autobiographies of influential political, economic, and social leaders at national, state, and local levels nearly all concern men. Social history about "ordinary" women is not counterbalanced or complemented by a substantive literature of "elite" history, and many Depression-era women await biographies. Meanwhile, scholars have neglected published autobiographies of women activists. Indeed, literary scholar Estelle Jelinek has argued that most critics have ignored women's autobiographies because "they do not fit their criteria of a 'proper' autobiography, one that has the characteristics found in men's autobiographies." Such characteristics, traditionally, have included a focus on career and contemporary events in contrast to the emphasis often seen in women's autobiographies on family and personal issues.[18]

In fact, critics may not have bothered to read enough women's autobiography. The authors of the works excerpted here, it is true, often reveal intimate details of their personal lives. We learn of joy in a good marriage and near death from a botched abortion. But they also write about their lives and their work, as have many of the best autobiographers of both sexes, in the context of the times. These excerpts reveal not just self-assessments but perspectives on the politics and culture of the decade. They show resourceful professionals trying to cope with all sorts of challenges and threats—to their budgets, to their self-esteem, to their lives.

Their own words attest that although some of these women suffered, certainly none of them was silent, and whatever their economic circumstances, they certainly were not down and out. Rather, in the important areas of social activism, government service, and labor organization, they helped to create the agendas of the era. They were not victims but shapers. This does not mean they were all well known, although some women represented here, such as Eleanor Roosevelt and Frances Perkins, were among the most famous in America. But whether they were national household names or known only within their own communities, these nonordinary women told life stories in which top-down and bottom-up history merged: they confronted problems that affected "ordinary" women, doing so with compassion and courage.

IV

The sixteen women represented here do not form a sufficient sample for a study in collective biography. Still, it seems appropriate to point to several characteristics which many of them share. Most were city-dwellers. In fact, just one city, New York, was the scene of activity of a distinct majority. Twelve of the sixteen women either lived or worked there at some time during their lives. Lillian Wald, director of a settlement house, grew up and remained in New York City. Frances Perkins, Franklin D. Roosevelt's Secretary of Labor, and Mary Kingsbury Simkhovitch, director of a settlement house, were born in Boston but began their careers in New York City. Mary

Heaton Vorse, labor journalist and activist, like Perkins and Simkhovitch, was a New Englander who moved to the city, where she became an editor of the socialist journal *The Masses*. Ellen Tarry, a native of Birmingham, Alabama, was an employee of the Federal Writers' Project in New York City, and Dorothy Day, born in New York City, returned to her birthplace as an adult and, like Vorse, became a socialist journalist, later founding, with Peter Marin, the Catholic Worker Movement. Anzia Yeziereska, like Tarry an employee of the New York City Division of the Federal Writers' Project, arrived in the city from Russia in 1890 when she was about ten years old. Eleanor Roosevelt lived most of her early life in the city. Like Perkins, she later moved to Albany and Washington. Margaret Bourke-White, photographer and social activist, was a lifelong resident of New York City. Vera Buch Weisbord and Ella Reeve Bloor were New Yorkers whose careers as labor organizers took them to various locales in the United States. For decades, Hallie Flanagan, director of the Federal Theater Project, taught at Vassar College and maintained close contact with the New York theater world.

Only Louise Armstrong, Mary Anderson, Lucy Mason, and Meridel Le Sueur had little connection with New York City, but they too were urban women. Armstrong, a regional relief administrator, moved from Chicago to a rural locale in northern Michigan only after the Depression struck. Anderson, head of the Women's Bureau of the Department of Labor, spent most of her adult life either in Chicago or Washington. Mason, labor organizer, lived in Richmond, Virginia, until her work with the Congress of Industrial Organizations prompted her nearly constant travel across the South. Le Sueur, also a labor organizer, was born in a small town, Murray, Iowa, but lived at various times in Chicago, Los Angeles, and San Francisco.

Most of these women came from families whose economic status ranged from comfortable to very wealthy. Only three women were exceptions. Anderson was a poor immigrant from Sweden whose career as a labor organizer began with work as a teen-age shoe stitcher in Chicago. Yezierska, who worked as a young girl in the New York garment industry, grew up, along with Weisbord, in a working-class family. The fathers of Perkins, Flanagan, and Wald were successful businessmen, but this did not inhibit their daughters from becoming social activists or New Deal employees. On the other hand, the socialist views of Le Sueur's parents clearly influenced her, and an abolitionist, free-thinking uncle had an impact on Bloor. Others were parties to familial discord, Yezierska fleeing her orthodox, demanding father, and Vorse suffering disinheritance by her family.

Most of these women were white, native-born Protestants. The exceptions were Day, who converted to Catholicism; Yezierska and Wald, who were Jewish; and Tarry, who was black. Only Anderson and Yezierska were immigrants. Even two of the three Communists, Bloor and Le Sueur (Weisbord was the third), had the kinds of ancestral roots that, in other circumstances, might have delighted the Daughters of the American Revolution. Bloor's Dutch family had been in the country since the eighteenth century, while Le Sueur's mother was the descendant of Puritans.

The marital histories of these women suggest the difficulty of combining marriage and career. Anderson, Yezierska, Wald, and Mason avoided this dilemma by never marrying, although being single did not assure tranquility. Bourke-White divorced twice, as did Bloor and Yezierska. Day and Le Sueur left common-law husbands, and Tarry renounced a brief, secret marriage. Vorse was twice widowed, and Flanagan's first husband died in 1919 after a prolonged illness. Perkins was married for decades to a mentally unstable and frequently hospitalized husband. The marriages of Armstrong, Roosevelt, Simkhovitch, and Weisbord were lasting but not necessarily harmonious, as was evident in the Roosevelts' relationship marked by private coolness and effective public alliance. Double standards clearly existed, and they made a combination of leadership and a stress-free personal life even harder to achieve for women than for men.

The women represented here nevertheless struggled on, bringing a special courage to the fight against the Great Depression. What follows are their own accounts, faithfully reproduced. That four of the five women in the section "In the Workplace" were on the radical left is not meant to discount the valor of such nonradical labor activists as Agnes Nestor, Rose Pesotta, or Margaret Robins (whose autobiographies are cited in note 10). Our selections, we felt, convey a more vivid impression of what labor historian Irving Bernstein has called *turbulent* years.

1. For a discussion of the 1930s soap operas see Louise Tanner, *All the Ways We Were* (New York, 1968), 68–85.

2. For a discussion of these patterns of discrimination see Judith Sealander, *As Minority Becomes Majority: Federal Reaction to the Phenomenon of Women in the Work Force, 1920–1963* (Westport, Conn., 1983), 58–65.

3. Some of the best works examining roles played by and social attitudes toward women are Leslie Tentler, *Wage Earning Women: Industrial Work and Family Life in the United States, 1900–1930* (New York, 1979); Lois Scharf, *To Work and to Wed: Female Employment, Feminism, and the Great Depression* (Westport, Conn., 1980); David Katzman, *Seven Days a Week: Women and Domestic Service in Industrializing America* (New York, 1978); Julia Kirk Blackwelder, *Women of the Depression: Caste and Culture in San Antonio, 1929–1939* (College Station, Tex., 1984); Blackwelder, "Women in the Work Force: Atlanta, New Orleans, San Antonio, 1930–1940," *Journal of Urban History*, 4 (Fall 1978), 331–358; Tamara Hareven, *Transitions: The Family and the Life Course in Historical Perspective* (New York, 1978); Frank Mott, *Women, Work, and the Family: Dimensions of Change in American Society* (Lexington, Mass., 1978); Jeanne Westin, *Making Do: How Women Survived the Thirties* (Chicago, 1976); Winifred Wandersee, *Women's Work and Family Values, 1920–1940* (Cambridge, Mass., 1981); Susan Ware, *Holding Their Own: American Women in the 1930s* (Boston, 1982); and Susan D. Becker, *The Origins of the Equal Rights Amendment: American Feminism Between the Wars* (Westport, Conn., 1981). See also Ruth Milkman, "Women's Work and the Economic Crisis: Some Lessons from the Great Depression," *Review of Radical Political Economics*, 8 (Spring 1976), 73–97; Winifred D. Wandersee Bolin, "The Economics of Middle Income Family Life: Working Women During the Great Depression," *Journal of American History*, 65 (June 1978), 60–74; Winifred Wandersee, "American Women and the Twentieth Century Work Force: The Depression Experience," in Mary Kelley, ed., *Women, Identity, and Vocation in American History* (Boston, 1979), 296–312; Wandersee, "A New Deal for Women: Government Programs, 1933–1940," in Wilbur J. Cohen, ed., *The Roosevelt New Deal: A Program Assessment Fifty Years After* (Austin, Tex., 1986), 185–197; Lois Rita Helmbold, "Beyond the Family Economy: Black and White Working-Class Women During the Great Depression," *Feminist Studies*, 13 (Fall 1987), 629–656; Helmbold, "Downward Occupational Mobility During the Great Depression: Urban Black and White Working-Class Women," *Labor History*, 29 (Spring 1988), 135–172; Sealander, *As Minority Becomes Majority*, 57–94; John Bishop, "Women in the Nation's Labor Market," *Quarterly Journal of Economics*, 54 (May 1940), 527–534; Dolores Janiewski, "Flawed Victories: The Experiences of Black and White Women Workers in Durham During the 1930s," in Lois Scharf and Joan M. Jensen, ed., *Decades of Discontent: The Women's Movement, 1920–1940* (Westport, Conn., 1983), 85–109; Ruth Schwartz Cowan, "Two Washes in the Morning and a Bridge Party at Night: The American Housewife Between the Wars," *Women's Studies*, 3 (1976), 147–172; and Mary W. M. Hargreaves, "Darkness Before the Dawn: Status of Women in the Depression Years," in Mabel E. Deutrich and Virginia C. Purdy, ed., *Clio Was a Woman: Studies in the History of American Women* (Washington, D.C., 1980), 178–188.

4. Scharf, *To Work and to Wed*, 90–111.

5. See Studs Terkel, *Hard Times: An Oral History of the Great Depression* (New York, 1970), 153–158 and 419–420, and Westin, *Making Do*, 183–187 and 191–195, for the recollections of case workers.

6. For discussions of women as agitators and reformers, see Bert Cochran, *Labor and Communism: The Conflict That Shaped American Unions* (Princeton, 1978); James Leiby, *A History of Social Welfare and Social Work in the United States* (New York, 1978); and Ware, *Holding Their Own*, 87–149.

7. Susan Ware, "Women and the New Deal" in Harvard Sitkoff, ed., *Fifty Years Later: The New Deal Re-evaluated* (New York, 1985), 119.

8. The best book exploring this subject is Susan Ware, *Beyond Suffrage: Women and the*

New Deal (Cambridge, Mass., 1981). See also George Martin, *Madam Secretary: Frances Perkins* (New York, 1976); Lois Scharf, *Eleanor Roosevelt: First Lady of Liberalism* (Boston, 1987); and Jerre Mangione, *The Dream and the Deal: The Federal Writers' Project* (Boston, 1972).

9. For good summaries of the work women did as labor organizers during this period, see Alice Kessler Harris, *Out to Work: A History of Wage Earning Women in the United States* (New York, 1982); Ware, *Holding Their Own*, 41–49; Ruth M. Milkman, "The New Deal, the CIO, and Women in Industry," in Cohen, ed., *The Roosevelt New Deal*, 167–183. See also Marjorie Penn Lasky, "'Where I was a person': The Ladies' Auxiliary in the 1934 Minneapolis Teamsters' Strikes," in Ruth Milkman, ed., *Women, Work, and Protest: A Century of U.S. Women's Labor History* (Boston, 1985), 181–205.

10. For an extensive listing of autobiographical materials available in print, see Patricia K. Addis, *Through a Woman's I: An Annotated Bibliography of American Women's Autobiographical Writings, 1946–1976* (Metuchen, N.J., 1983); Johnnetta B. Cole, "Black Women in America: An Annotated Bibliography," *Black Scholar*, 3 (December 1971), 42–53; Gary M. Fink et al., ed., *Biographical Dictionary of American Labor Leaders* (Westport, Conn., 1974); Louis Kaplan, compiler, *A Bibliography of American Autobiographies* (Madison, Wisc., 1961); Carolyn H. Rhodes, *First Person Female American: A Selected and Annotated Bibliography of the Autobiographies of Women Living After 1950* (Troy, N.Y., 1980); Barbara Sicherman et al., ed., *Notable American Women: The Modern Period, A Biographical Dictionary* (Cambridge, Mass., 1980); Esther Stineman, with the assistance of Catherine Loeb, *Women's Studies: A Recommended Core Bibliography* (Little, Colo., 1979), which includes a section on "Autobiography, Biography, Diaries, Memoirs, Letters," 41–134; Ora Williams, *American Black Women in the Arts and Social Sciences: A Bibliographic Survey*. Revised and expanded edition (Metuchen, N.J., 1978), 9–19; Estelle C. Jelinek, *The Tradition of Women's Autobiography: From Antiquity to the Present* (Boston, 1986), "Autobiographical Works," 212–221; James Craig Holte, *The Ethnic I: A Sourcebook for Ethnic Autobiography* (Westport, Conn., 1988); and Joanne M. Braxton, *Black Women Writing Autobiography: A Tradition Within a Tradition* (Philadelphia, 1989).

Many women in the fields of social activism, government, and labor organization, needless to say, did not write autobiographies, published or unpublished, while for a relatively small number of them autobiographies are available in manuscript. To mention only the category of public officials relevant here (many of whom are identified in *Notable American Women*; Emily Newell Blair, "A Who's Who of Women in Washington," *Good Housekeeping*, 102 [January 1936], 38–39; Elsie L. George, "The Women Appointees of the Roosevelt and Truman Administrations: A Study of Their Impact and Effectiveness," doctoral dissertation, American University, 1972; Lorena Hickok and Eleanor Roosevelt, *Ladies of Courage* [New York, 1954]; and Susan Ware, *Beyond Suffrage*), published autobiographies are not available for Grace Abbot, Children's Bureau, Department of Labor; Mary McLeod Bethune, director, Division of Negro Affairs, National Youth Administration; Emily Newell Blair, Consumers' Advisory Board, National Recovery Administration; Jane M. Hoey, Social Security Board; Katherine F. Lenroot, chief, Children's Bureau, Department of Labor; Mary H. Rumsey, Consumers' Advisory Board, National Recovery Administration; Hilda Worthington Smith, director, Workers Education, Works Progress Administration; Mary Switzer, director, Office of Vocational Rehabilitation, Works Progress Administration; Sue Shelton White, Consumers' Advisory Board, National Recovery Administration; and Ellen Sullivan Woodward, director, Women's and Professional Division, Works Progress Administration, among others.

Autobiographies in manuscript are available for Hilda Smith (Schlesinger Library, Radcliffe College); Clara M. Beyer, associate director, Division of Labor Standards, Department of Labor (Historical Office, Department of Labor); Mary A. Dewson, Social Security Board (Franklin D. Roosevelt Library); and Elinore M. Herrick, National Labor Relations Board (Schlesinger Library). Andrea Hinding, ed., *Women's History Sources: A Guide to Archives and Manuscript Collections in the United States*, 2 vols. (New York, 1979), is a comprehensive guide to unpublished materials.

Some women who were social activists, government employees, or labor organizers wrote autobiographies that do not contain passages appropriate for inclusion here (in some instances because they are a series of fragments): Louise de Koven Bowen (president, board of directors, Hull House), *Raymaster* (privately printed, 1944); Anna Arnold Hedgeman (Young Women's Christian Association, New York City Emergency Relief Administration), *The Trumpet Sounds: A Memoir of Negro Leadership* (New York, 1964); Rebekah B. Kohut (social welfare), *More Yesterdays: An Autobiography* (New York, 1950); Lucy Robins Lang (labor activist), *Tomorrow Is Beautiful* (New York, 1948); Agnes Nestor (labor organizer), *Woman's Labor Leader: An Autobiography of Agnes Nestor* (Rockford, Ill., 1954); Mary White Ovington (National Association for the Advancement of Colored People), *The Walls Came Tumbling Down* (New York, 1947); Rose Pesotta (labor organizer), *Bread Upon the Waters* (New York, 1944; reprinted, Ithaca, N.Y., 1987); Margaret Dreier Robins (Women's Trade Union League), *Margaret Dreier Robins: Her Life, Letters, and Work,* by Mary Dreier (New York, 1950); Rose Schneiderman (Labor Advisory Board, National Recovery Administration and Secretary, New York State Department of Labor) and Lucy Goldthwaite, *All for One* (New York, 1967); and Mary Church Terrell (National Association of Colored Women), *A Colored Woman in a White World* (Washington, D.C., 1940). A chapter in Margaret Sanger (birth control), *Margaret Sanger: An Autobiography* (New York, 1938), 418–427, recounts her dealings with Congress in which she expressed views similar to those she had expounded before the Great Depression.

11. Studs Terkel, *Hard Times,* fits this category, as does Alice Lynd and Staughton Lynd, *Rank and File: Personal Histories by Working Class Organizers* (Boston, 1973).

12. See Federal Writers' Project, *These Are Our Lives,* ed. by W. T. Couch (Chapel Hill, N.C., 1939); Tom Terrill and Jerrold Hirsch, ed., *Such as Us: Southern Voices of the Thirties* (Chapel Hill, N.C., 1978); Ann Banks, ed., *First Person America* (New York, 1980); John Robinson, ed., *Living Hard: Southern Americans in the Great Depression* (Washington, D.C., 1981); James Seay Brown, Jr., *Up Before Daylight: Life Histories from the Alabama Writers' Project, 1938–1939* (University, Ala., 1982); C. Edward Doty, ed., *The First Franco-Americans: New England Life Histories from the Federal Writers' Project* (Orono, Me., 1985).

13. See, for instance, Richard Lowitt and Maurine Beasley, *One Third of a Nation: Lorena Hickok's Report on the Great Depression* (Urbana, Ill., 1981).

14. See, for instance, Robert McIlvaine, *Down and Out in the Great Depression: Letters from the Forgotten Man* (Chapel Hill, N.C., 1983); Leila Sussman, *Dear F.D.R.: A Study in Political Letter Writing* (Totowa, N.J., 1963); and Gerald Markowitz and David Rosner, ed., *"Slaves of the Depression": Workers' Letters About Life on the Job* (Ithaca, N.Y., 1987).

15. Quoted in McIlvaine, *Down and Out,* 166.

16. *Ibid.,* 169.

17. *Ibid.,* 164.

18. Estelle Jelinek, *The Tradition of Women's Autobiography,* xii. For a discussion of the phenomenon of women's autobiography see also Jelinek, ed., *Women's Autobiography: Essays in Criticism* (Bloomington, Ind., 1980); Jelinek, "Disguised Autobiographies: Women Masquerading as Men," *Women's Studies International Forum,* 10 (No. 1, 1987), 53–62; Anna Walters, "Self Image and Style: A Discussion Based on Estelle Jelinek's "The Tradition of Women's Autobiography: From Antiquity to the Present," *Women's Studies International Forum,* 10 (No. 1, 1987), 85–93: Donna Stanton, ed., *The Female Autograph: Theory and Practice of Autobiography from the Tenth to the Twentieth Century* (Chicago, 1984); Sidonie Smith, *A Poetics of Women's Autobiography: Marginality and the Fictions of Representation* (Bloomington, Ind., 1987); Braxton, *Black Women Writing Autobiography*; and Katherine Jellison, "'Sunshine and Rain in Iowa': Using Women's Autobiography as a Historical Source," *Annals of Iowa,* 49 (Winter 1989), 591–599.

PART ONE

In Town and Country

MARY

KINGSBURY

SIMKHOVITCH

"We have all suffered together..."

While still a teen-ager during the 1890s, Eleanor Roosevelt was introduced to the problems of the less privileged as a volunteer teacher in the Rivington Street Settlement House on the Lower East Side in New York City. One of her mentors there was another wealthy young woman with a social conscience, Mary Kingsbury Simkhovitch. Unlike Roosevelt, Simkhovitch devoted the rest of her life to the settlement house movement, founding a famous New York institution, Greenwich House, and establishing herself as an influential social reformer.

Born in 1867 into the prominent Kingsbury family of Boston, Mary

Simkhovitch enjoyed the kinds of advantages available to the daughters of the rich in the nineteenth century—for example, she toured Europe often with her mother. But Simkhovitch, unlike many of her contemporaries who made debuts and socially correct marriages, continued her education. Her training in sociology and economics at the University of Berlin and Columbia University sparked for her a concern with the social disruption caused by rapid urbanization.

By 1899, when she married Russian-born Vladimir Simkhovitch, a professor of history at Columbia, Mary had become known in New York City as an advocate of public housing reform. After working with various settlement houses and reform organizations in the city, she founded Greenwich House in 1901. It was to become her life. She remained its director until her retirement in 1946 at age seventy-nine. The following excerpt is from her autobiography, Neighborhood: My Story of Greenwich House, *published in 1938. Simkhovitch describes the ways in which she and her staff at Greenwich House tried to help the residents of her Barrow Street neighborhood cope with the Depression while they themselves experienced major changes in their own activities, including greater involvement with the federal government.*

SOURCES: In addition to her autobiography, information about Simkhovitch can be found in Carroll Smith-Rosenberg's essay on her in *Notable American Women: The Modern Period*, edited by Barbara Sicherman and Carol Green (1980), 649–650. Allen Davis's *Spearheads of Reform: The Social Settlements and the Progressive Movement* (1967) discusses her work as a pioneering settlement house founder. Timothy McDonnell's *The Wagner Housing Act: A Case Study of the Legislative Process* (1957) mentions her work as a prominent advocate of low-cost public housing. Her settlement work is also discussed in Judith Ann Trolander's *Settlement Houses and the Great Depression* (1975). Simkhovitch's papers are at the Schlesinger Library, Radcliffe College.

MARY KINGSBURY SIMKHOVITCH

I WAS IN HARTFORD AT THE HOS-
pital during that October [1929]. My brother brought me back to his

house on the twenty-ninth. He said that the stock market had crashed and everything had gone to pieces. Somehow it didn't seem to mean much. It was like learning of a flood in China. We like to be sympathetic, but we rarely have the imagination and sensitiveness for what is remote. But my mother was far from indifferent. When eighty years of age some time before this, she had decided she would put her affairs in the hands of a trust company, for, as she said, "No knowing when I shall be incompetent." But when she learned that there was nothing less than a panic, for the first time she regretted that she was not handling her own securities. "Why?" said my brother. "Because I'd like to go down and buy 'United Fruit,'" she said. And sure enough, this stock held its own! My mother never lost either her charm or her intellectual acumen during all of her ninety-four years.

I convalesced in Litchfield with a friend and still didn't grasp the magnitude of the calamity. At first it was felt that this was a temporary panic and governable if only the financial forces would rally and pull together. It was thought that "morale" could win. But it didn't. For the crash of 1929 resulted in the most serious unemployment the country has ever witnessed. In 1907–8, 1914–15 and 1921–22, to be sure, there had been panics which were of economic importance. Students of these cycles, however, did not foretell this particular disaster. The panic of 1907–8 was precipitated by the failure of the Knickerbocker Trust Company. There were rent strikes on the East Side. Workingmen relied on their savings, secured other jobs and were helped out by friends. They did not ask for charity or welcome it. In December of 1914 Mayor Mitchel appointed a citizen's committee. Emergency workshops were established. The settlements of the city visited retail stores to discover they were carrying an increased number of customers on credit. The Citizens' Committee found unemployment in almost 25 per cent of the families covered. There were about thirty thousand people homeless, and four thousand of these were on bread lines. In 1921 President Harding called a conference on unemployment, but nothing really important resulted from the deliberations. Unemployment had in fact come to be recognized as one of the marks of a rapidly changing technology.

But the crash of 1929 grew worse as the months went by. Conferences increased and organizations multiplied. Money was raised by

Mary Kingsbury Simkhovitch

private charitable associations that attempted at first to cope with the mounting disaster. In New York the Welfare Council's Coordinating Committee, representing every type of social agency dealing with relief, was formed in order to effect some measure of joint thought and action. The distress of the unemployed showed itself in insufficient food and fuel. Credit disappeared. The use of milk was infrequent, and eggs disappeared from the diet of the unemployed. Starch and sugar became the leading articles of food. Moving to poorer quarters was inevitable, and an exodus to relations and friends was frequent. Doubling up became the rule—to such an extent that a Welfare Council report in 1932 spoke of the occupancy of three rooms by eight or ten as not uncommon. Rooms not used by members of family groups were rented to lodgers. Debt for back rent mounted, and property was lost for lack of ability to meet mortgage payments. Parents were forced to postpone dental care for themselves and their children. Of course excursions, new clothing, contemplated educational advance and all kinds of recreation were abandoned. And then came the tighter pinch of inability to buy ice or coal or even the use of electricity or gas.

Public relief—both "home relief" (that is, money aid which followed giving up the grocery orders), so embarrassing and openly shameful to the great masses of unemployed people, and "work relief," which as time went on assumed various names but which was, nevertheless, "relief"—was established both for humanitarian reasons and also as "priming the pump" to effect an increase in the consumption of goods. But at Greenwich House we felt it a neighbor's obligation to give emergency help when the wheels of public assistance moved too slowly. This was especially necessary in the case of moving families from one apartment to another, or in keeping the light and heat from being turned off. The large Italian church of the neighborhood, Our Lady of Pompeii, helped especially by giving out the blessed church candles to light the darkened tenements. This particular church believed that every human need ought to be met by it as far as it was possible. It was for this reason that they erected a great parish building with a hall where miracle plays were given and where preschool children could come as well as the young people and the older groups. It was a mark of true neighborliness that a prominent local Jewish businessman made a handsome contribution to the new

Pompeii church when they left the old building. That was in boom days, but it was genuine and it indicated the frequent examples of the interpenetration of one group by another in even the most heterogeneous of neighborhoods.

In the autumn of 1931 unemployment among homeless men became visible to even the most indifferent New Yorker. In various parts of the city where there were open spaces and vacant lots, "jungles" appeared. These villages of the unemployed built by them for shelter were as creditable to ingenuity as they were pitiful exhibits of the failure of organized society.

Our own local jungle* was located on West Street at the corner of Charlton Street. It occupied one of the blocks cleared by the New York Central Railroad for its tracks. The adjacent blocks were surrounded by high board fences.

On the side toward West Street were located the shacks of the white settlers. The Negroes were on the Washington Street side. The white and Negro communities kept quite separate from each other socially, although they were physically near. One or two of the Negroes, however, fraternized with the whites. There was also a group of Mexicans, and Central Americans, and South Americans, with whom the whites had little or nothing to do.

The houses were in large measure below the ground. Since the lot was originally covered with houses, the cellar holes formed a good base for construction. Many of the houses were at least three-quarters under ground, with only enough above the surface to permit a window and roof. Some of the houses located in the hollows made by cellar holes were not dugouts, their walls being entirely of board and a space existing outside of the walls. The shacks varied greatly in quality. Some, both of the dugouts and of the shacks which were above ground, were well built and snug as well as fairly roomy. Others were merely thrown together or scooped out; they were dark, cold and cramped.

The best house built above the ground was a two-room bungalow with well-matched boards, good flooring, beams and doorjamb true, good roofing and a good window. Inside, the wall was wainscoted

*I am indebted to a group of my associates for the detailed accuracy of this description: Miriam Oliver, Helen Johnson Small, Murray Sachs.

Mary Kingsbury Simkhovitch

halfway up. The wood used for this purpose consisted of very narrow lathes carefully cut and fitted together and stained green. The upper part of the walls was lined with cardboard and papered with white wallpaper, as was the low ceiling. The main room contained substantial shelves, the bedroom firm bunks. An old coal range, secured in return for assistance to a man who was moving, had been installed in one corner. A piece of linoleum covered the floor. At the windows, over the shelves and over the door to the second room were curtains. The walls were decorated with pictures drawn by one of the neighboring shack dwellers. This shack was shared by three men, and others came in to do their baking in the stove, as it was the only oven in this part of the jungle. It took one man about three days to build the main room, and when his friends joined him they built the addition.

The best dugout was constructed by three sailors. They lined the walls with stone chinked with clay, whitewashed over the stone, constructed firm shelves and three bunks, carpeted the floor, installed a skylight in the roof and a window on one side, wallpapered the ceiling and one part of one wall and curtained the window and bunks. For heat this house used a tin oil barrel laid on its side, with a piece of tin over the hole at one end; the top side was flattened so that a frying pan might be rested on it. A smokestack at the opposite end went out through the roof.

Furniture for these and other shacks had been secured from the city marshal. When furniture belonging to persons who have been dispossessed is not claimed within a certain period the city marshal has to get rid of it. From this source the shacks were well furnished with tables, chairs, and so forth, and also with dishes (from this or some other source). In some cases open fireplaces with a piece of tin over the top were used for heat, but most of the shacks used a tin barrel and stovepipe. Light was furnished by candles or lanterns in most shacks. One or two were dark, though at least one had an excellent kerosene lamp donated to it. In contrast to the shacks which were comparatively well built, there were a few very miserable hovels without heat, air or light. One of these looked like an overgrown coffin on stilts. It was raised about a foot off the ground, was hardly high enough for a man to sit up in, and was perhaps four or five feet wide and ten feet long. It had neither heat nor light. Another had only a hole through a flap of canvas for an entrance. Its owner crawled in with his coat off and then dragged his coat in after him. It had neither heat nor light. Another consisted of an overturned Ford with a fireplace where the engine was and a couple of packing boxes out behind. The occupant slept with his feet in the fireplace.

Food was secured by periodic trips to the downtown market when produce was coming in. Here it is always possible to pick up supplies. The rest of the food was purchased. Since wood for heat can be picked up in plentiful quantities and building materials also requisitioned, only food and candles or kerosene had to be purchased. Water was carried in pails or milk cans from a gas station near-by. Most of the white occupants were permitted by the gas station people to use the toilet facilities there.

The men went looking for work nearly every day. Someone stayed behind in each shack to see that it was not rifled while the other occupants hunted for an hour or two of work on the docks, helped load trucks or did other odd jobs. Some brought in funds by panhandling, but the "better element" did not approve of this. Panhandling was common among both Negroes and whites. The publicity given to the settlement brought a number of sight-seers, who left a contribution for food or cigarettes in the houses which they visited. A very few of the men worked regularly. Possessions were shared, according to one man on the assumption that "everything that I have is yours and everything that you have is yours also." This, he says, "worked fine." It did not work well enough, however, to make it unnecessary to guard the shacks.

The men who lived in this town were estimated, in the fall of 1931, at approximately fifty whites and three hundred blacks and Central Americans. New men came in every day, although it was difficult to see from the crowding of shacks just where newcomers would be able to stake their claims. Many of the whites came in from the sea, being sailors, stokers, firemen, engineers, and so forth, on the ships which docked near-by. Others were longshoremen. Among them, in numbers estimated by the "better element" as constituting a majority, were steady workingmen. The white group included mostly Americans, with a few miscellaneous characters described as "Polacks" and an occasional Italian. The blacks and mestizos included American Negroes, West Indian "spicks," "Cubians," and Central Americans. Most of them also came in on the boats. Among the West Indians there were many who habitually take ship at the end of the coffee season, to return in the spring. These have come in largely on the Clyde Line boats, having worked their passage one way and being unable to secure work on the boats going out or any work on shore.

There were only men in the jungle. Some had sent wife and children home to the wife's parents and had dug themselves in to take their chances on finding work. One engineer from one of the coast-wise steamship lines took his wife and children home to New England (from Fourteenth Street, where they had resided) and hitchhiked all the way to Texas looking for work along the way. When he got back he decided that the chances were better as a squatter in New York than working for six dollars a week in the New Bedford mills. He said that he thought the best thing to do if they got chased off this lot was to find another place where it was possible to squat in the same way. The men who occupied the better shacks kept their places clean and maintained their own personal appearance, being well washed and shaved and altogether upstanding in appearance and manner. One man was said to have his sons with him.

No one disturbed these men in the exercise of squatter privileges for many months. Depredations by a hoodlum gang along West Street were attributed to the jungle men, but when the marauders were caught they turned out to be mostly residents of Greenwich Street. . . .

Dr. Caroline Ware's study of our area in the postwar decade took place in 1930. About a hundred students, neighbors and associates from various racial and religious and political groups took part in the study, which brought to light valuable data to follow up. The exodus to other neighborhoods, so striking a feature of the immediately preceding years, was checked in the depression years. Initiative of any kind was in abeyance, and fear stopped new trends. The Old Age Pension Law, which was passed April 10, 1930, came at the right time to help with at least one of the distressing features of the period. Families who would otherwise have been added to the relief rolls were kept afloat by even the small amounts this law provided. Also, additional educational facilities were thrown open at this time both in the schools and through the various work relief projects resulting finally in the establishment of the Works Progress Administration.

There has been a vast amount of discussion on the merits of the WPA, but the main point to keep in mind as we have seen it in the settlements is that skills have been retained and also developed which otherwise would have been lost. The hopelessness and degradation of home relief in comparison with working for wages has seemed to us obvious. Many of the projects may have been foolish or wasteful. But the difference in spirit and attitude towards life which work brings to the unemployed as contrasted with receiving public money as charity is certainly incontrovertible. That public works should be organized to employ as far as may be those not absorbed by industry seems the logical way of meeting this difficulty. Public works plus relief for those not capable of being used in a public works program would still leave room for a middle group not able, perhaps, to be used in public works but who can do useful work in the community for which payment is just. While some of the arts program of the white-collar projects of the WPA may be open to criticism, there is a solid body of accomplishment which has been a very real social asset. The country needs more music, drama, crafts and art. Subsidies have been granted to keep afloat these spiritual interests in many countries. Even in our own country we have had here and there on the public pay roll, irrespective of relief needs, some of these activities. Bands in the parks, buildings provided by the taxpayers to house art treasures occur to one as examples. We felt in our neighborhood that it was good to preserve and intensify interest in these matters even where the excellence was questionable. And often the skills have been exceptionally good. There has been a true popular demand both for performance and for appreciative enjoyment which has been encouraging in communities where too little stress has been laid on these civilizing influences.

Naturally during these years a center like Greenwich House was crowded with those who enjoyed a happy life there even in the midst of the greatest economic stress. Sports attracted a large group. Club meetings and dances, week end trips, chess tournaments and bridge games brought others. Good patterns of behavior were maintained in this way which so easily slipped for those to whom such opportunities were unavailable. The use of our House was continuous; we were overcrowded. The concerts that our music school held at local schools or in the library were greatly appreciated. We sent away unusually large parties of children for the summer, and it was then that we noticed that children infested by mosquito bites or with other minor infections had such difficulty in throwing them off. This the nurses maintained was owing to the excessive use of starch in the current diet. . . .

During 1931 and 1932 there was a general deflation. All savings were spent, insurance cashed in, payment on mortgages not met, renewal of clothing abandoned, recreation given up. We were obliged to give emergency aid for carfare, for light, heat and sometimes shelter. The opening of the Eighth Avenue subway made our district still more accessible to the city at large. As government aid increased, our neighborhood was furnished with orchestral help, with block recreational activities. Painting classes were crowded. The evictions, the grocery orders, the general breakdown, all served to reinforce our conviction that civic organization would be far more effective if the city were divided into administrative districts.

It is not possible to do anything well from a distance. Just as we are all finding out that federal aid and standards are necessary but that administration is more efficient when carried on locally, so it is in large cities that central management would be greatly aided and humanized by local participation. Years ago the local school boards were shorn of any real power. As a whole the move toward centralization was good, but the school system would have developed in a more elastic way, suiting local needs more adequately, if a study had been made with a view to incorporating local opinion in local matters. It has been supposed that parents' associations would supply this function, but too often these parents' groups have turned out to be pressure or critical groups engaged in personalities rather than in fundamental improvements. However, these parents' organizations have great possibilities for good. With the new charter, it may be expected that provision for a city plan commission with large powers in coordinating central and local authority will treat these relationships in a more scientific way than in the past.

Local autonomy is impossible and undesirable, but still local sentiment can be mobilized for local improvement, and that has been our aim at Greenwich House throughout these years. During the most crowded part of 1933 the House had a weekly attendance of about ten thousand people—double the number that should be normally harbored in our space. During these years of depression we made many valuable tie-ups with city departments, especially with the Department of Education. Not only the change in the workshops administration but the opportunity to use public school teachers for the summer play school, the securing of credits by students of the continuation school in our nursery school and other departments, and numerous other connections have made our House a very real annex to the public schools of the neighborhood. Whereas the progressive schools have the advantage of having their children all day long, these schools obviously are not available to the great masses of the children. The progressive schools hope to influence public education and prevail upon the school authorities to adopt their methods. There are many teachers in the public schools who are as progressive as any outside these schools, but so far the size of the classes and the vastness of the problem allow of relatively little accent on those features which are of especial charm and interest to children. We have felt, therefore, that we should accent, in the activities we provide for children after school, painting, dancing, drama, music and crafts, including the household arts and sciences. Interest in science is intense when properly presented. The settlements as a whole, and certainly Greenwich House, have neglected this particular field.

At the music school in 1933–34 more than four hundred students received free group instruction from unemployed music teachers furnished by the WPA. The House during this period has used not only WPA leaders in recreation, adult and workers' education, drama, music, and arts and crafts, but when the National Youth Administration made assignments to the settlements, we accommodated about eighty of these young people as helpers also. The introduction of these government helpers has been in many ways a great aid to our work. We have been able to offer additional recreational and educational opportunities to our neighbors at no salary expense to our Society.

29
Mary Kingsbury Simkhovitch

There have been great qualitative difficulties, as would be expected. One genteel old lady taught crocheting to the girls and the making of knitted belts to a boys' group. Up to this time she had taught her craft in hospitals where her pupils were from the nature of things under more or less subjugation and incapable of deviltry. Our ten-year-olds were quite a shock to her. At the end of a long day, she toiled up to the office of the afternoon children's activities director and sank exhausted into a chair. She expressed a hope to be transferred soon and wound up with these words, "Oh, how I do long for the peace and quiet of an insane asylum." Many transfers have been made, some at the instance of the government bodies and some at our recommendation. These changes often presented the quiet continuity of dependable leadership which is the *sine qua non* of group work. In many instances, however, there has been marked leadership among the white-collar workers. At Pompeii church, which has the only good, very large auditorium in our neighborhood, *Joseph and His Brethren* was put on with a cast of two hundred under competent management, greatly to the delight of large audiences. Similar musical and educational events would have been impossible with our regular small staff. However, as these positions are liquidated, we face the necessary deflation in the number of activities which the neighborhood has enjoyed under the government white-collar projects. There is a widespread hope that many of these activities will be saved and incorporated into governmental educational programs under normal public auspices. The sifting both in leadership and in project choices must needs be very thorough if values of this work are to be permanently conserved.

Neighborhood forces, especially valuable in this period, have included the Greenwich Village Association activities and particularly the work of its Village Plan Committee, whose ideas, we hope, may be incorporated into the city plan the new charter ensures. The *Villager*, a local newspaper, presented its first issue on April 13, 1933. The local newspapers of the past had been either literary attempts, which had had really nothing to do with local life, or of the home news variety, which had centered their attention upon the older neighborhood groups with little reference to new growth and change.

This paper has been most useful in bringing about a common knowledge of Village activities. . . .

The depression years in our neighborhood tended to break up the group solidarities of the postwar decade. Distress struck every layer of Village life. We have all suffered together, and common disaster brings people close together. The social disintegration that came directly after the war was replaced by fears held in common during this time. As prewar radicalism gave way to the emphasis upon art and pseudo art after the war, so during the depression years the life of the region swung back to a re-emphasis on the social significance of current events. Why did the depression come about? What can we do about it now that it is here? How can the American standard of living be preserved at such a time? These were the questions that concerned the entire country and resulted in the election of President Roosevelt. Then came about the many federal measures taken as an attempt to answer these questions. The measures found their echo in the small urban districts, as elsewhere. And there grew up within these districts, for the first time perhaps, an attempt at self-education. Organizations of the unemployed sprang up, some of them dogmatically radical, others more factual in attitude. Locals have been formed throughout the country with a view to understanding the situation and securing action in defense of the American standard of living. Although such organizations are "pressure groups" with a view to securing benefits to the members, they are also a real attempt at bringing to light the social evils of the time and the administrative inequalities which naturally have clustered about so vast a calamity as that of the crisis from which we are now emerging.

And to what extent are we emerging? The unemployed are still with us in vast numbers. The benefits from the federal unemployment program are only beginning to be felt, and public housing has made only a small beginning with a hopeful but nevertheless an uncertain future; but like a person who has been very ill and who is now in need of convalescent care, so is our social situation. Many of the unemployed in our neighborhood will never find re-employment, owing to age, or lack of skill, or technological change. But dark as the situation is in a neighborhood like ours, it still is far brighter than it was in 1929. One of the good aspects of the depression has certainly

31
Mary Kingsbury Simkhovitch

been a very real liquidation of vanity, snobbery and pretense. Much has been taken away, but the residuum shows, perhaps especially in youth, a solid facing of the facts on which the future may be better built.

LILLIAN
WALD

"The devastation of homes without number..."

For many decades Mary Simkhovitch and Lillian Wald were colleagues in the New York City settlement-house world. They respected and praised each other. Lillian Wald, however, enjoyed the larger national reputation. Her settlement, the House on Henry Street, became internationally known, rivaled in influence only by Jane Addams's Hull House in Chicago.

Born in 1867 in Cincinnati, Ohio, Lillian Wald grew up in what she later described as an ideally happy German-Jewish family, which had migrated to America to escape the revolutions of 1848. When she was an adolescent, her father, whose optical-parts business prospered, relocated the family to New York.

In 1893, after receiving training at the New York Hospital school for nurses and at the Woman's Medical College of New York, Lillian Wald launched her career as a public health nurse on New York City's Lower East Side. Shocked by the terrible poverty she witnessed, she soon found herself allying with other middle-class social reformers. In 1895 she established a "nurses' settlement" at 265 Henry Street. Here people from the surrounding neighborhoods could receive adequate medical care regardless of their ability to pay. One of the nation's first settlements, Henry Street soon expanded its original goals. By the 1930s it had become a large and powerful institution, occupying many buildings, with branches throughout New York City. Wald by then was in her late sixties, a reformer who had been in the national spotlight for decades. Influential within the Democratic party and a personal friend of Eleanor Roosevelt and Frances Perkins, Wald was a major adviser to New Deal administrators on a variety of health care and social welfare issues. Although she never married and never had children of her own, her advocacy of legislation outlawing child labor and of better systems of medical care and education for children was a special life-long crusade.

Lillian Wald's two books about the Henry Street Settlement constitute a kind of serial autobiography. Her first book, The House on Henry Street, *published in 1915, has continued over the decades to enjoy a wide readership. The excerpt included here appears in its sequel,* Windows on Henry Street, *published in 1934. Wald's descriptions of the Depression's devastating impact on the people who used the services of Henry Street were among her last written words. After the publication of* Windows on Henry Street, *she suffered a massive cerebral hemorrhage. Incapacitated for several years, she died in 1940, never to see the return, with wartime, of prosperity to Henry Street.*

SOURCES: R. L. Duffus's overly romanticized and dated biography, *Lillian Wald: Neighbor and Crusader* (1938), still provides a great deal of information about her life. A more valuable biography is Doris Groshen, *Always a Sister: The Feminism of Lillian D. Wald* (1989). See also an extensively edited collection of Wald's letters and articles, Clare Coss, ed., *Lillian Wald: Progressive Activist* (1989), and Robert H. Bremner's essay on Wald in *Notable American Women, 1607–1950*, III, 526–529 (all other references in these Sources notes to *Notable American Women* are to Vol. IV, *The Modern Period*). Lillian Wald's papers are divided between the Butler Library Archives at Columbia University and the Manuscripts Room at the New York Public Library.

To WORKERS IN SETTLEMENTS, as to others in daily contact with wage earners, are first revealed the signs of the times affecting their security. As the periods of depression come over us, there is no sudden avalanche, but a creeping daily change—shortening hours of work, an increasing number of dismissals, wage cuts, and the uneasiness which none can comprehend unless they have learned to recognize and share it. It permeates a neighborhood like a thickening fog of anxiety and fear.

Increasingly in the winter of 1928–1929, months before the stock-market crash, we were made aware of the foreboding among our neighbors. In the kindergarten one morning, when the little ones were sitting around the table drinking their milk, I said, "What do you think you are going to be when you grow up?" There was no very active response, and to prod them I said, "When I was a little girl I thought I should like to be a carpenter—the shavings are so curly and the carpenters who came to our house were such nice folks." Whereupon a four-year-old who sat there, his head in his hand, a sober expression on his little face, answered, "Miss Wald, the carpenter that lives in our house ain't got any work."

The nurses' daily records are delicate barometers of conditions. This was brought home to me once as I watched our statistician sticking her pins in the map that shows the current cases of pneumonia, and observed an increasing number of blue pins in the Syrian quarter. Inquiring into this, I was told that the children of the kimono workers then on strike were probably getting less milk and good nourishment, and hence their resistance was lowered.

Signs of the gathering storm multiplied. Within a brief period a succession of individuals came to ask for work, and that stimulated us to further inquiry. In January 1928, we discussed this with our intimate circle. In February 1929, eight months before the "boom" collapsed, we summoned our colleagues to a meeting, just as, on the first declaration of war in August 1914, we called a group to come together in solemn conference.

There was general agreement that times were increasingly hard in the neighborhoods where small wage earners lived, with mounting numbers of men and women "laid off." But at that time the public was absorbed in "the greatest period of prosperity the world has ever seen," and the storm signals were unheeded.

As troubles grew, we realized that in respect to the disaster to individuals and to the community these desperate years were to prove even more serious to American workers than the War. Families were broken by war, and homes knew terrible griefs—the sacrifice of youth, the lost anchors of safety and security. But all these disasters also befall the people when there is no work, no family income, when youth is sacrificed because its hopes, its dignity, its ambitions, crumble away, and there is no sense of common cause, of a goal to be attained, to glorify the sacrifice. Homes were swept away during the War. Pitiful they were, those fallen roofs and broken walls that I saw in France. But, though less tragic to the onlooker, such depression as we have been experiencing has meant the devastation of homes without number, simple as well as luxurious, built up with high hope and with confidence in the ability of the breadwinner to support the family and to help the children to a higher estate. . . .

The House on Henry Street has seen five major depressions in its forty years—1893, 1907, 1914, 1921, and the years since 1929. No depression has touched in magnitude the situation of to-day, which must be described, not as critical, but as desperate. During different crises I have served on committees appointed to work out measures of protection against future disasters. The forces have never been so well organized as they are to-day to avoid waste motions, to mobilize resources, to prevent overlapping. But those who have been closest to the chief sufferers know best how inadequate have been even these heroic efforts to meet the most elementary need. And perhaps veterans of experience realize with special clarity the price that must be paid for a break of such magnitude in our economic and social life.

As one sums up the effects of unemployment on the individual and the community, it seems to me that the loss of the dignity of man is the first and most tragic. With this are bound up the loss of home, of ties, of position, the humiliation of the long bread lines, the appeal to relief agencies, the overwhelming sense of failure.

Next I should put, as a result of loss of home, a further break in housing standards, with families herding together for shelter rather than for a home. From that comes loss of family unity, of self-respect, of ambition and pride.

Under the strain of prolonged unemployment, irritations and loss of personality are inevitable even among the heroic.

The people most troubled are often marked by an inexplicable patience, or, it may be, apathy. Perhaps because of lack of leadership, the little groups which have assembled to protest against delay in relief or against methods of relief have had little to contribute. If there is willingness to discuss with them the difficulty of satisfactory relief methods with available resources, their protest melts away. This was illustrated in the attitude of Washington authorities toward the "armies" which demanded relief through the bonus payment in two successive winters—a menace to public health and public dignity, a tragic and absurd display of armed brutality one year; and the next, 1933, the remnant of the "army" well ordered and immediately responsive to considerate treatment.

Finally, this prolonged period of unemployment has forced upon young people the conviction that society, which helped rear and educate them, has no place for them.

The most obvious antisocial effect of unemployment is the breaking up of the family. Social workers long familiar with the vicissitudes of those whose margin between income and expenditure is narrow are impressed by the passionate desire, even from unexpected sources, to cling together that they may maintain family life, that the household may go on. One instance to illustrate:—

A neighbor, a teamster with good wages, was a man of questionable habits until he married a girl of exemplary character. When their baby came, no one who owns a shooting lodge in Scotland or a villa in Florida could feel more pride and satisfaction that this young couple evidenced in moving into an apartment with a bathroom. The room was not only a modern convenience to them, but a long step forward in standard of living and self-respect. The housekeeping was immaculate, but special care was lavished on the bathroom, and no visitor departed without being shown its glories. In the winter of 1930–1931, there was no work for the teamster, and, hoping against hope, we lent the young people rent each month for three months. But recovery did not come, and they were forced to move to cheaper rooms, of course with unkept halls and unkempt janitor. Quickly came the next step down—the demoralization of overcrowding under the necessity of sharing with another couple the rent of the miserable little place. The whole level, not only of housing, but of cleanliness, recreation, personal pride, manners, slumped—as in the days of the Terror in France, when so many heads went under the guillotine, and no to-morrow seemed likely or worth anyone's waiting for.

During that same winter we knew of many instances of three families herded into one apartment. In one such household there were in three rooms seven children and five adults, among them two pregnant women.

And yet our neighbors never hesitated to share their meagre quarters when need arose. The day after a young mother came home from the hospital with her first-born, the nurse called to teach her how to give the baby its bath. To her amazement, she found two newborn babies and a second mother, a young girl who was a stranger to her. This girl had occupied the bed next to the nurse's patient in the ward, and had confided to her that she had no home and no friends to whom she could go when she left the hospital. Her neighbor in the ward therefore invited her to share her tiny tenement quarters. "I can't do much for her," she said apologetically to the nurse, "but I can put a roof over her head." The husband gave up his half of the family bed to the stranger and slept on a narrow couch, and the extra baby slept in the kitchen in the carriage proudly provided for the child of the house. But there was only good will shown to the guest, and a determination to "make out the best we can." I am glad to add a cheering footnote to this story. The husband, so long out of work, has at last obtained a good job, and the young girl also secured employment and has been able to go her way.

When we first lived in a neighborhood of small wage earners, to see on the sidewalk the furniture of a family dispossessed for nonpayment of rent was an everyday affair. Gradually the welfare agencies freed one neighborhood after another from that humiliating evidence of inadequate and tardy relief. It is a matter of pride in the Settlement that there was only one such instance in the winter of 1931–1932 in our immediate neighborhood, and that was through an unforeseeable slip in procedure. But during the continued depression this problem has grown beyond the power of the relief agencies in some sections, and it is now beyond us. The frequent sight of the belongings of the shattered household could, without great stretch of imagination, be compared with the ruined homes we saw in the occupied territory of France. But in this emergency, as in so many others, cooperation is forthcoming from the neighbors whenever possible.

Mrs. D———went to the hospital to be delivered of her first child. In her absence the "dispossess" was served. Her husband disappeared, taking most of the household goods with him. This, let me hasten to add, was not an example of the "shiftless poor." The wife had taken a four-year commercial course after graduating from a Chicago high school; the husband was a licensed teacher. Desperate would have been the plight of the young mother when she returned from the hospital had it not been for a neighbor who opened her door to Mrs. D———and the baby. The neighbor herself was receiving relief, but she shared what she had with the deserted, homeless wife and child. The nurse secured such supplementary help as she could for the household. The most delicate consideration is being shown Mrs. D———by her hostess. But we hope the kind neighbor will soon be relieved of this burden, which she ought not to bear; the initiative will not come from her.

The folk feeling, always at first limited to immediate kith and kin, is widened through sympathy, and the recent years have brought forth, as does every time of stress and strain, not only quick sympathy, but immediate sharing. No ceremonial or convention waits upon the act. Compassion is a basic element when people are thrown together, and too much cannot be said of the simplicity with which our neighbors give and take.

It is at the opposite social pole that one most frequently finds those who frankly refuse to be involved in other people's troubles. At a dinner party in the second winter of the depression I found myself sitting beside a man who told me that he did not care to hear stories of need, that he never read the appeals which came to his bank or to him personally, that he was deaf to their urgency. And when examples of the help of the needy to one another were cited, he complacently retorted that this was inevitable, "because they see it around them all the time." He seemed to pride himself on his deafness, and to be all unaware of the death of the spirit within him.

Under the strain of unemployment and the anxiety and hardship it brings into the home, the wage earner's rebellion against his predicament or his boredom with the long, empty days not infrequently expresses itself in outbursts of temper. In one such home, the ambulance doctor, summoned by our nurse, diagnosed the mother's illness as "starvation complicated by follicular tonsillitis." And the kindly young physician added, "If I have to make many more diagnoses like this I'll be a chicken-hearted fool." The husband, a skilled artisan, had been with the same firm for nine years. Then his employers failed, and for nearly a year he had had no job except a few weeks of "work relief" at a third of his former wage rate. In apologizing to the nurse for rudeness to her and to his family, the man said, "I don't mind being hungry myself, but it's hard to see the wife and kids without enough to eat. And sometimes you get mad and holler just because you feel so bad."

These trying days have been a challenge to the settlements to keep life as balanced as possible, particularly for young people who, having sometimes been educated at great sacrifice, find themselves unwanted. Home conditions have gone beyond reasoning, and they are often reproved for not finding work, with barbed reminders of what others have done. Henry Street has participated in and initiated measures to serve the people, particularly youth, in danger of quagmires from which it might be impossible to bring release. The dances, the music, the club meetings, the gayeties, have never been so strenuously pursued as during these lean years.

One evening, a hot August night, when the children of the neighborhood were playing games and singing in the street, I stopped to talk with three girls walking arm in arm. Young and at the romantic age, it seemed there must be something better for them to do than to walk up and down this hot and crowded street, where children and garbage cans on the sidewalk made even a stroll difficult. I knew there was a dance on the roof of our Playhouse to which ten cents would admit them. To these young girls of dance age I said, "Why aren't you at the party to-night?" In chorus they answered, "We're out of work. We haven't got ten cents." There was a committee meeting at eight-thirty the next morning, and the price of the dances was adjusted to conform to the means of those who most needed the pleasure.

Because of urgent pressure for the most primitive needs of the people, food and shelter, the essentials of recreation are in danger of being overlooked or even considered indecorous when family cupboards are bare of bread. One truly anxious friend questioned the time and money, however reasonable in amount, allocated to pleasure and recreation in the Settlement budget. But she readily withdrew her objections when the plight of the unemployed boys and girls was described. Few people who have brought up their young under comfortable circumstances have failed to see the importance of a wholesome atmosphere for youth, but they have not always realized that the same rules of control and protection they know to be essential apply to those who live in congested rooms, who hear the doleful tales of their kinsfolk and neighbors, and who may not have even the cheapest movie as a release. . . .

The problem of the large family with a small and irregular income is not, of course, reserved for periods of depression. Sometimes the personality of the wage earner, sometimes the nature of his occupation, causes sharp and not infrequent ups and downs in the family fortune, and a general slump only serves to accentuate this difficulty. "Ah, yes," sighed a Scotch acquaintance, "Robbie is a grand roofer, but he's more out o' work nor in."

The resident in charge of the relief office at Henry Street reported the usual pleas varied one morning by the appearance of an Oriental-looking man who pressed for attention: "No work—no work in my trade."

"What is your occupation?"

"Lady, I am a professional mourner."

"But people die as usual."

"Yes, lady, but they do not mourn—they just bury them."

Though the mothers feel the brunt of unemployment and the real sacrifice of giving up even pennies and nickels to the children, they have a protective instinct which enables them to comprehend the price youth may pay if entirely deprived of natural outlets for fun and comradeship. In the face of dire need, it is oftentimes startling to find how deeply embedded in the mothers is the urge to save the young from hardship or from discredit with their comrades.

A mother in the last month of her pregnancy slept on the floor, that her two little children might occupy the only bed in the house. Another mother dragged home a packing box she found on the street and helped her young son make of it a chair to use at table. "He's got to learn manners," she explained. Another mother removed the outer cretonne covering from a mattress supplied her by the Red Cross, and turned it into curtains to hang at the two windows, "so home will seem nicer to my girl."

Sometimes this instinct to protect expresses itself in overindulgence that defeats efforts toward character training. I cannot forget one boy who had obtained employment in the circulation department of a New York newspaper. The office reported to the Settlement that the boy had been dishonest. He came to see me, and far into the night I tried to make him agree to take back to his employers the shoes and new suit he had bought with the money he had stolen. He fought hard. When he left me, however, I was sure that he saw the ethical point and that he would pack up the clothing and make restitution as far as was in his power. As I watched him go down the steps, thought I to myself, "I hope his grandmother [who took the place of his dead mother] does not frustrate this wholesome discipline." I was sure of the boy if she did not do so. But she did. What she said in extenuation was, "The boy is a good boy. He promised never to do it again. I didn't want him shamed." . . .

A man who has worked and supported his family does not take his first dismissal as a doom. He has always been on good terms with his boss and his foreman, and he feels sure that he will get work again soon. But, after an actual experience, unemployment is to him a constant threat and terror. Inadequate as it is under any scheme now put forward, unemployment insurance offers a measure of protection against this vast indignity that even in good times threatens millions of the wage earners of the Machine Age. Perhaps only such assurance of some degree of security could free from fear men like the skilled furniture finisher, whose story, though I have told it before, bears retelling, I think.

The man had had no steady work for more than two years. His wife had succeeded in getting part-time factory work. Except for the husband's occasional odd jobs, this small wage was the sole family support. One of our nurses was called in to see the wife. The diagnosis was "pregnancy complicated by underfeeding." The nurse suspected that the parents were giving to the two children most of what food they had, and were slowly starving themselves. The husband, who was over six feet tall, weighed one hundred and twenty pounds. The nurse urged the wife to give up her job and apply for aid. This the woman refused to do. "We want work. I've got to keep my job till labor pains begin." Before she returned to her home for the night, the nurse purchased the suburban papers and found to her delight a Long Island firm's advertisement for a furniture finisher. She telephoned the employer and he promised to interview the man if he came to the office at eight the next morning. That evening the nurse went back to see the anxious man, told him the good news, and gave him carfare. But the next morning she was disappointed to find him waiting at her office, already half an hour late for the possible job. "You'll never get it now!" she exclaimed. "I couldn't help it," he replied dully. "After you left, my wife's pains began. I had no money to get a doctor, so I went for a policeman and he got an ambulance. The ambulance surgeon delivered her. But the baby died and he took my wife back to the hospital. I couldn't leave the children or the dead baby. During the night I made a little coffin with some nice wood I had. But I don't know what to do next." The nurse accompanied him to the morgue. "He had the look of Lazarus," she said. . . .

It was a disheartening experience, in preparing this chapter, to go back to the report of the unemployment committee appointed by

Mayor John Purroy Mitchel, in December 1914, of which I was a member. On the basis of the experience gained in that terrible winter, the committee in its final report, submitted in 1917, stated its conviction that unemployment is a problem calling for constant study and attention, and for a permanent organization to lead the community in forestalling and mitigating its effects. The committee outlined eight major factors in a community attack on the problem: fact finding; stabilization of seasonal industries; adequate public employment service; public works planned ahead to take up the slack when private industry sags; unemployment insurance; vocational guidance and training; relief; and emergency employment. There is something almost prophetic in a sentence from the foreword to the report, written by Henry Bruère, who, as Chamberlain in the Mitchel administration, took the initiative in setting up the committee. Mr. Bruère observed, "Always industrial crises find American communities unprepared to deal with the crucial social problems which they develop."

Even as the report was submitted we began to feel the stir and lift of better times, and this valuable contribution was left to gather dust in the files. The report was reprinted and given wide circulation in 1921. But it was only in the fourth winter of the next depression that some of the recommendations of fifteen years before were embodied in legislation and in administrative machinery....

Most people now realize that there is no single remedy for unemployment. There is widespread conviction that measures to correct our failures must be many and coordinated.... From the old fear of "socialism" we have progressed to a sense of the obligation of a democracy to uphold its people....

There is no one panacea to bring about a saner and more balanced security. The intent of the people in the settlements may seem bewildered, scattered, and, indeed, irrelevant. And yet the pressing message to which the community is now ready to listen does have a part in the movement toward a better-ordered society. What is urged on the basis of knowledge and experience has weight in furthering a reasonable provision for days when business and industry slow down, for old age, when life ceases to function strenuously; and preparations for right living are as essential as the stirring of conscience which, in the last quarter of a century, has brought about our gains in the direction of widows' pensions, old-age pensions, preventive medicine, vocational guidance, the establishment of the visiting nurse to serve and to educate. The millennium is not yet in sight, but the success that has been achieved is a challenge to every right-minded person to become interested, to study, to understand, and to participate. Those who are despondent lest our vigilance be weakened can stiffen their courage by a backward look over the way we have come.

ELEANOR
ROOSEVELT

"I had a point of view of my own..."

During the Depression, Eleanor Roosevelt was as omnipresent a force in American political life as her husband President Franklin Roosevelt. Redefining the role of First Lady, she acted as a kind of unofficial cabinet minister without portfolio in the four Roosevelt administrations. Although she held no paid position, she exercised significant influence within the federal government and certainly within the Democratic party. Millions followed her whirlwind activities and read her books and columns. Clearly she was the most famous woman in America; when she died in 1962, she was the most famous woman in the world.

Born in 1884 into a prominent New York family, Eleanor Roosevelt was a member of the "Oyster Bay" Republican branch of the Roosevelt family and a niece of President Theodore Roosevelt. She grew up with financial privilege and emotional poverty. By the time she was ten, her alcoholic, emotionally unstable father and her weak, abused mother were dead, along with a younger brother. The orphan girl lived with a series of relatives and reached young adulthood painfully insecure. Her marriage in 1905 to her distant cousin Franklin Roosevelt brought her within the domestic sphere of his domineering mother, Sarah. For the next fifteen years she placated her mother-in-law, bore six children, one of whom died, and managed a large, wealthy household.

It is important to note, however, that by the time Eleanor Roosevelt became First Lady in 1933 the period of subservience to an implacable mother-in-law was already long in her past. By then she was herself a grandmother in her fifties. More important, during the previous decade she had established an independent identity. In 1921, polio paralyzed Franklin, already a rising political star who had run on the unsuccessful Democratic presidential ticket in 1920 as James Cox's vice-presidential running mate. During his long years of recovery, Eleanor Roosevelt became her husband's eyes and ears, traveling constantly, giving speeches, organizing women within the Democratic party. By 1928, when Franklin won the first of two terms as New York's governor, his wife had become a Democratic political leader, not just a Democratic political wife.

During her years in the White House, Eleanor Roosevelt expanded the range of public activities she had engaged in as the governor's wife. She was Democratic party partisan, social welfare advocate, civil rights crusader, champion of the poor, best-selling author. The following excerpts from her autobiography, This I Remember, *afford a flavor both of her formidable personality and the wide span of her interests. In the pages reprinted here she also discusses her relationship with Franklin and how both viewed her role. Theirs was a unique political alliance. One of Eleanor Roosevelt's favorite stories helps sum it up. One day she left very early in the morning without informing her husband, so that she might fit a trip to a prison workshop into her already crowded daily schedule. When Franklin asked his wife's secretary where she was, the reply came, "In prison." To which the President answered, "I'm not surprised, but what for?"*

SOURCES: Eleanor Roosevelt wrote several volumes of autobiography. In addition to *This I Remember* (1949) which focuses on the White House years, she also wrote *This Is My Story* (1937), *Autobiography* (1961), and *It's Up to the Women* (1933). Of the many biographies of Eleanor Roosevelt, among the best are Joseph

Lash, *Eleanor and Franklin* (1971) and Joseph Lash, *Eleanor: The Years Alone* (1972). See also Tamara K. Hareven, *Eleanor Roosevelt: An American Conscience* (1968); Lois Scharf, *Eleanor Roosevelt: First Lady of American Liberalism* (1987); J. William T. Youngs, *Eleanor Roosevelt: A Personal and Public Life* (1985); and William H. Chafe's essay in *Notable American Women*, 595–601. Eleanor Roosevelt's papers are housed at the Franklin D. Roosevelt Presidential Library, Hyde Park, New York.

ELEANOR ROOSEVELT

D URING THE EARLY WHITE
House days when I was busy chiefly with getting settled and organizing my side of the household, my husband was meeting one problem after another. I think it had a most exhilarating effect on him. Decisions were being made, new ideas were being tried, people were going to work and businessmen who ordinarily would have scorned government assistance were begging the government to find solutions for their problems, willingly accepting almost anything that was suggested.

What was interesting to me about the administration of those days was the willingness of everyone to cooperate with everyone else. As conditions grew better, of course, people's attitude changed, but fundamentally it was that spirit of cooperation that pulled us out of the depression. Congress, which traditionally never has a long honeymoon with a new president, even when the political majority is of his party, went along during those first months, delegating powers to the president and passing legislation that it would never have passed except during a crisis.

All this meant, however, that Franklin was very busy and had no time for any personal interests. Consequently very soon after we went to Washington I realized that if I wanted friends and members of the family to visit us in the White House I would have to take the initiative. My husband, I knew, would be delighted to see them and would never question whom I invited, or when they came, but they could not be permitted to interfere with the work he had to do, and their comfort and pleasure would have to be solely my responsibility.

I planned all the family reunions and parties and tried to remember to invite to the White House old friends and other people to whom I thought it would mean a great deal to come at least once into that historic mansion. This applied not only to those who came to stay, but to those who came to meals. If anyone was neglected or overlooked, the blame is wholly mine. Franklin arranged his own times for seeing the people who worked with him, but except for the purely formal, official entertainments to which people came by right of position, the social invitations were always left to me.

As Miss LeHand lived in the White House she very often, when I was not there, invited people she thought my husband would enjoy, or whom she personally wanted, but he never gave this type of social gathering a thought.

Soon after the inauguration of 1933, however, we began to have a succession of visitors whom after dinner Franklin would take upstairs to his study, where he expected not to be disturbed, unless he specifically asked us to join him.

There were two very simple reasons why these particular people were invited to the White House these first years. One was that the economic and political situation in the world made it necessary for him to establish contacts with the leaders of other countries; the other was his desire to build new contacts for better understanding in this continent and abroad.

The routine of the visits was always similar. Sometimes we had a quiet family dinner, after which Franklin took the visitor or visitors up to his study in the oval room for a talk. Later there was usually an official dinner, and when there was a lady in the visiting party we included the ladies of the cabinet or the wives of the government officials whom we were inviting. If the guest was a man alone, Franklin had an official stag dinner or an official stag luncheon.

For the heads of nations, Franklin worked out a reception which he thought made them feel that the United States recognized the importance of their government. On rare occasions we went together to meet people in the presidential reception room at the railroad station; then drove in two cars, he with the gentleman and I with the lady or ladies, back to the White House. More often the Secretary of State met the visitors. If they were heads of states, they drove up to the south portico of the White House, where an honor guard and military band, assembled on the lawn, paid them military honors. My husband greeted them in the diplomatic reception room and received the members of their party; then he introduced them to the cabinet members and such Supreme Court Justices, senators and representatives from the Foreign Affairs Committee as were present.

When no military honors or immediate receptions were scheduled, Franklin and I together sometimes met the guests at the front door; but whether Franklin could or not, I always made it a point to greet the guests at the door, and to see them off when they left.

If the guests arrived in the afternoon we had tea for the entire party; afterward, all but the most important guests went to a hotel or to their own embassy. Later Blair House across Pennsylvania Avenue was acquired by the government and arranged for the use of important visitors. The head of a government spent one night in the White House, accompanied by his wife if she was with him. There usually was a state dinner with conversation or music afterwards. The following morning Franklin and his guest would often have another talk before the guest went over to Blair House or to his embassy.

On one or two occasions important visitors came when I could not be there, and Franklin had to do all the honors. However, visits were as a rule planned far enough ahead for my schedule to be arranged accordingly. Most of my plans were as flexible then as they have been the rest of my life. Only when I had signed a contract to speak or had made an engagement many weeks beforehand, did I feel I could not change them. . . .

Aside from one recreation, riding, my time was entirely taken up with the life of the White House. The president's wife does not go out informally except on rare occasions to very old friends. Now and then in the spring Elinor Morgenthau and I stole away in my car or hers, and stopped in at some little place for lunch or tea.

Driving my own car was one of the issues the Secret Service people and I had a battle about at the very start. The Secret Service prefers to have an agent go with the president's wife, but I did not want either a chauffeur or a Secret Service agent always with me. I never did consent to having a Secret Service agent, but during the last years at the White House, life became so busy that I did less and less driving myself and took fewer and fewer trips by automobile, either for pleasure or for business. I always had my own car, however, and during the first years I covered a good many miles driving myself.

After the head of the Secret Service found I was not going to allow an agent to accompany me everywhere, he went one day to discuss this very serious question with Louis Howe. Finally he plunked a revolver down on the table before Louis and said: "Well, all right, if Mrs. Roosevelt is going to drive around the country alone, at least ask her to carry this in the car." I carried it religiously, and during the summer I asked a friend, a man who had been one of Franklin's bodyguards in New York State, to give me some practice in target-shooting so that if the need arose, I would really know how to use the gun. After considerable practice, I finally learned to hit a target. I would never have used it on a human being, but I thought I ought to know how to handle a revolver if I had to have one in my possession.

I told this story once in front of a small boy when I was on a lecture trip. The story became very glamorous under the small boy's repetition, and he was reported to have said he had seen the gun. This created great excitement, because in the city where I was going next to lecture, it was against the law to carry firearms, and an official of that city threatened to arrest me on arrival. Our son, James, who was at that time one of his father's secretaries, called me from the White House and I had to explain that since I was not driving, I did not have the gun and therefore would not be arrested. The Secret Service, feeling I should be protected against such possibilities, gave me a badge to carry everywhere which entitled me to have a gun as part of my luggage. Needless to say, I never had to use it. Episodes like this used to bother my friends much more than they did me. So far as I was concerned, they were simply part of the whole picture....

Always, when my husband and I met after a trip that either of us had taken, we tried to arrange for an uninterrupted meal so we could hear the whole story while it was fresh and not dulled by repetition. He had always asked me questions, even before [my trip to the Gaspé peninsula in Quebec], but now his questions had a definite purpose.

After this trip he asked about life in northern Maine, and very quickly the pattern for reporting on future trips evolved. It was extremely good training for me, though my trips with Franklin during his governorship had already given me some experience as a field reporter. That I became, as the years went by, a better and better reporter and a better and better observer was largely owing to the fact that Franklin's questions covered such a wide range. I found myself obliged to notice everything. For instance, when I returned from the trip around the Gaspé, he not only wanted to know what kind of fishing and hunting was possible in that area, but what the life of the fisherman was, what he had to eat, how he lived, what the farms were like, how the houses were built, what type of education was available and whether it was completely church-controlled like the rest of the life of the village.

When I spoke of Maine, he wanted to know about everything I had seen on the farms I visited, the kinds of homes and the types of people, how the Indians seemed to be getting on and where they came from. I told him I thought they were of the same tribe as old Tomah Josef, who used to visit Campobello Island for many years. That interested him.

Franklin never told me I was a good reporter nor in the early days were any of my trips made at his request. I realized, however, that he would not question me so closely if he were not interested, and I decided this was the only way I could help him, outside of running the house, which was very soon organized and running itself under Mrs. Nesbitt. . . .

In the autumn I was invited by the Quakers to investigate the conditions that they were making an effort to remedy in the coal mining areas of West Virginia. My husband agreed that it would be a good thing to do, so the visit was arranged. I had not been photographed often enough to be recognized, so with one of the social workers I was able to spend a whole day going about the area near Morgantown, West Virginia, without anyone's discovering who I was or that I was even remotely connected with the government.

The conditions I saw convinced me that with a little leadership there could develop in the mining areas, if not a people's revolution, at least a people's party patterned after some of the previous parties born of bad economic conditions. There were men in that area who had been on relief for from three to five years and who had almost forgotten what it was like to have a job at which they could work for more than one or two days a week. There were children who did not know what it was to sit down at a table and eat a proper meal.

One story which I brought home from that trip I recounted at the dinner table one night. In a company house I visited, where the people had evidently seen better days, the man showed me his weekly pay slips. A small amount had been deducted toward his bill at the company store and for his rent and for oil for his mine lamp. These deductions left him less than a dollar in cash each week. There were six children in the family, and they acted as though they were afraid of strangers. I noticed a bowl on the table filled with scraps, the kind that you or I might give to a dog, and I saw children, evidently looking for their noon-day meal, take a handful out of that bowl and go out munching. That was all they had to eat.

As I went out, two of the children had gathered enough courage to stand by the door, the little boy holding a white rabbit in his arms. It was evident it was a most cherished pet. The little girl was thin and scrawny, and had a gleam in her eyes as she looked at her brother. Turning to me she said: "He thinks we are not going to eat it, but we are," and at that the small boy fled down the road clutching the rabbit closer than ever.

The pathos of poverty could hardly have been better illustrated. It happened that William C. Bullitt was at dinner that night; and I have always been grateful to him for the check he sent me the next day, saying he hoped it might help to keep the rabbit alive.

This trip to the mining areas was my first contact with the work being done by the Quakers. I liked the Quaker people I met, Clarence Pickett particularly, and I liked the theory of trying to put people to work to help themselves. There was a chair factory which was equipped with some of the most remarkable makeshift machinery I had ever seen, but it taught the men to do something in addition to mining and it also bolstered their hope. The men were started on projects and taught to use their abilities to develop new skills. Those who worked on chairs made furniture for their own scantily furnished homes. The women were encouraged to revive any household arts they might once have known but which they had neglected in the drab life of the mining village.

This was only the first of many trips into the mining districts but it was the one that started the homestead idea. The University of West Virginia, in Morgantown, had already created a committee to help the miners on the Quaker agricultural project. With that committee and its experience as a nucleus, the government obtained the loan of one of the university's people, Mr. Bushrod Grimes, and established the Resettlement Administration. Louis Howe created a small advisory committee on which I, Mr. Pickett, and others served. It was all experimental work, but it was designed to get people off relief, to put them to work building their own homes and to give them enough land to start growing food.

It was hoped that business would help by starting on each of these projects an industry in which some of the people could find regular work. A few small industries were started but they were not often successful. Only a few of the resettlement projects had any measure of success; nevertheless I have always felt that the good they did was incalculable. Conditions were so nearly the kind that breed revolution that the men and women needed to be made to feel their government's interest and concern.

I began to hear very serious reports of conditions in Logan County, West Virginia, where for many years whole families had been living in tents because they had been evicted from company houses after a strike. All the men had been blacklisted and could not get work anywhere; they were existing on the meager allowance that the state of West Virginia provided for the unemployed.

For many years I had been sending a small contribution to this area through the Women's Trade Union League, but I had never seen what the conditions were. I began to hear that the tents were worn out, that illness was rampant and that no one had any medical care. Finally Mrs. Leonard Elmhirst and I established a clinic to take care of the children. When I told my husband of the conditions there he told me to talk to Harry Hopkins and to tell him that whatever should be done must be done, and that these families must be out of tents by Christmas. It was done; and for two years, out of my radio money and Mrs. Elmhirst's generosity, we tried to remedy among the children the effects of conditions which had existed for many years.

I came to know very well a stream near Morgantown called Scott's Run, or Bloody Run because of the violent strikes that once occurred in the mines there. Some of the company houses, perched on hills on either side of the Run, seemed scarcely fit for human habitation. In one place the Quakers had established a self-help bakery and a nursery school.

I took many, many people to see the village of Jere, West Virginia, along Scott's Run, for it was a good example of what absentee ownership could do as far as human beings were concerned. The coal mines of West Virginia are owned largely by people not living in the state. The money goes out and does not come back, leaving the state poorer in cash and in personal interest than before. Most of the people living along the Run, which flows into a broader stream below, worked no more than two or three days a week. Some of the children were sub-normal, and I often wondered how any of them grew up.

The Quakers tried to improve conditions by getting the children off the floors at night. It was quite usual to find all the older children sleeping on bags or rags on the floor and the mother and father and youngest children in the only bed, which might or might not have a mattress. Sometimes there was just a blanket over the springs. The WPA mattress project helped considerably, as did the building of sanitary privies. The welfare commissioner who authorized them, Miss Alice Davis, nearly landed herself in jail because they were built on private mine-owned property and she had not known it was against the law to improve privately owned property.

However, breaking rules or even laws saved a good many lives. Every spring and every autumn in this area there had been an outbreak of typhoid fever; only after several people died would the company doctor appear and inoculate the rest of the population. No efforts were made to eliminate the cause of the disease. The Run in Jere, like all the others that ran down the gullies to the larger, main stream, was the only sewage disposal system that existed. At the bottom of the hill there was a spigot from which everyone drew water. The children played in the stream and the filth was indescribable.

You felt as though the coal dust had seeped into every crack in the houses and it would be impossible to get them or the people clean. When you walked into a kitchen, you were struck by the scarcity of cooking utensils. Though the families were almost always large, it was rare to see more than two or three cups and plates on the shelves, most of them chipped or broken.

Some of the older miners still could speak only enough English to understand the orders given by the mine boss. Nobody had taken the trouble to help the adults, who were going to live and work in this country, learn English and understand our government. The children went to school when they had clothes. Unexplained absences could often be attributed to the fact that if one child in the family went to school, the other children had to stay at home because there was only one dress or one pair of pants or one pair of shoes in the family, although shoes did not matter much since all the children went barefooted most of the time.

Where there was a company store every family always owed a bill; as they were thus kept permanently in debt, they could never move away.

After the homesteads were started, I persuaded many people to go down to visit them. On all my early visits I stayed at the home of the project superintendent, Mr. Glenn Work, who had been a mine foreman and knew the conditions under which the miners and their families lived. The homestead project started near Morgantown was called Arthurdale and took in people from all the near-by mining villages.

One of the first people to go to Arthurdale was Bernard M. Baruch, who helped me to establish the original school and always took a great interest in the project, even visiting it without me on some occasions. I have always hoped that he got as much satisfaction as I did out of the change in the children after they had been living on the project for six months.

Miss Elsie Clapp, a fine teacher and a follower of Dr. John Dewey, whom Mr. Pickett knew, was asked to come and start the school. Once before she had done a similar job of creating a community where none had existed, and she now rendered a remarkable service to Arthurdale. Later the state of West Virginia took over the school. Though for some time we continued the nursery school, we finally realized that the kind of experimental school which Miss Clapp established was really not satisfactory to the people. It did its job of creating a community feeling by drawing the people together, but it was a new idea and the people wanted what other communities had. Eventually Miss Clapp moved on and the school became completely state supported.

I remember one gentleman, whose home is in New York City, whom I took into one of the houses along Scott's Run. He came out very rapidly indeed, having found two of the children sick in bed and living conditions such as he had never seen before. When I joined him outside he said: "I will give you any money you want to help remedy these conditions, but please do not ask me to go into any more houses. I feel contaminated and it makes me really ill."

Some of the people who went with me during these years were Mr. Baruch, Mrs. Henry Morgenthau, junior, Mr. and Mrs. Frederick B. Adams, Mr. and Mrs. Allee Freed, Mr. and Mrs. George T. Bye, Mrs. Henry Goddard Leach, Mr. and Mrs. Robert Deans and Major Henry S. Hooker. All of them, at one time or another, helped some specific project, but our most constant helpers were Mr. Baruch, Mrs. Morgenthau and Mr. and Mrs. Freed. After Mr. Freed's death, Mrs. Freed still maintained her interest.

The homestead projects were attacked in Congress, for the most part by men who had never seen for themselves the plight of the miners or what we were trying to do for them. There is no question that much money was spent, perhaps some of it unwisely. The projects were all experimental. In Arthurdale, for instance, though the University of West Virginia recommended the site, apparently nobody knew what was afterwards discovered—that there was a sub-stratum of porous rock which finally caused great expense in making the water supply safe. Nevertheless, I have always felt that many human beings who might have cost us thousands of dollars in tuberculosis sanitariums, insane asylums, and jails were restored to usefulness and given confidence in themselves. Later when during the last war I met boys from that area, I could not help thinking that a great many of them were able to serve their country only because of the things that had been done to help their parents through the depression period.

At the time of an act, one is not likely to realize its future ramifications. My trips to this area, as well as my lecture trips, turned out to have an unsuspected value when I visited the men in hospitals during the war. Frequently a boy in a hospital bed would say: "I come from———. You made the commencement address at my school." Then I would try to remember something about his town, because a lonely boy in a hospital bed in some far off place will often feel better about the world if somebody remembers the town square or the court house in his home town.

Nothing we learn in this world is ever wasted and I have come to the conclusion that practically nothing we do ever stands by itself. If it is good, it will serve some good purpose in the future. If it is evil, it may haunt us and handicap our efforts in unimagined ways.

I have been getting rather far away from my original story, but perhaps what I have said will help make clear why Arthurdale and the other homestead projects held so much interest for me for so many years. I shall never be able to forget some of the people or some of the things I saw there.

For instance, just before Christmas Day after the first people moved into their houses, I went to call on a young woman who had just had a baby. Her two other children were perhaps four and six years old, little girls. The baby was a boy. As I went in I remarked that I was afraid it was going to be difficult for her to do much about Christmas. She looked at me, her face alight, and said: "This will be a wonderful Christmas. Do you know what Christmas last year was like? We were in rooms which had no windows; the only light came through the door. We did not dare tell the children it was Christmas but when they went out they came back and said: 'Mother, it must be some kind of a day, some children have new toys.' All we had for Christmas dinner was some raw carrots for them to chew on. This year they will each have a toy and we have a chicken, one of our own, that we are going to eat. It will be wonderful."

There was another family, a family of thirteen. The father worked in the furniture factory which the Quakers had started. He made most of the furniture for his own house on his own time, including a table large enough for the whole family of thirteen to gather around. One morning when I went to see them at about nine o'clock, I found the house in immaculate order and smelling of freshly baked bread. The mother told me she and her husband were going off for the week end, and she was up early baking bread because she did not want her eldest daughter to have to do it while she was away. This couple were among those who particularly seemed to enjoy the square dances; the woman looked young in spite of her eleven children. I have heard good things of their sons' war service and I hope they now own their house and land.

There was one elderly man whom I particularly liked. He was rather a problem because his wife was old and sick and the only person he had at home to help him was a grandson of about thirteen. The old man worked as janitor of the administration building, kept himself and his house and grounds clean, and took care of his wife like a trained nurse.

Oh, yes, the human values were most rewarding, even if the financial returns to the government were not satisfactory.

Years later after the Social Security Act was passed, I saw how it worked in individual cases in this area. There was a mine accident in which several men were killed, and my husband asked me to go down and find out what the people were saying. One man received the Carnegie medal posthumously because he had gone back into the mine to help rescue other men. His widow had several children so her Social Security benefits would make her comfortable. In talking to another widow who had three children and a fourth about to be born, I asked how she was going to manage. She seemed quite confident and told me: "My sister and her two children will come to live with us. I am going to get Social Security benefits for nearly sixty-five dollars a month. I pay fifteen dollars a month on my house and land, and I shall raise vegetables and have chickens and with the money from the government I will get along very well. In the past probably the mine company might have given me a small check and often the other miners took up a collection if they could afford it, but this income from the government I can count on until my children are grown."...

As time went by, I found that people no longer considered me a mouthpiece for my husband but realized that I had a point of view of my own with which he might not at all agree. Then I felt freer to state my views. However, I always used some care, and sometimes, for example, I would send Franklin one of my columns about which I was doubtful. The only change he would ever suggest was occasionally in the use of a word, and that was simply a matter of style. Of course, this hands-off policy had its advantages for him, too; for it meant that my column could sometimes serve as a trial balloon. If some idea I expressed strongly—and with which he might agree— caused a violent reaction, he could honestly say that he had no responsibility in the matter and that the thoughts were my own.

Though Franklin himself never tried to discourage me and was undisturbed by anything I wanted to say or do, other people were frequently less happy about my actions. I knew, for instance, that many of my racial beliefs and activities in the field of social work caused Steve Early and Marvin McIntyre grave concern. They were afraid that I would hurt my husband politically and socially, and I imagine they thought I was doing many things without Franklin's knowledge and agreement. On occasion they blew up to him and to other people. I knew it at the time, but there was no use in my trying to explain, because our basic values were very different, and since I was fond of them, I thought it better to preserve the amenities in our daily contacts.

One afternoon, I remember, I gave a garden party at the White House for the girls from the reform school in Washington—most of them were colored. Steve thought that was very unwise, politically, and I did get some bad publicity in the southern papers. Steve felt the same way about my work with the members of the American Youth Congress. Franklin, however, never said anything to me about it. I always felt that if Franklin's re-election depended on such little things that I or any member of the family did, he could not be doing the job the people in the country wanted him to do.

I know Franklin felt the same way. Many of his political advisers, as well as some of the family, were deeply troubled over Elliott's and Anna's divorces, feeling that they would react unfavorably on my husband's political career. In each case, Franklin had done what he could to prevent the divorce, but when he was convinced that the children had made up their minds after careful reflection, it never occurred to him to suggest that they should subordinate their lives to his interest. He said that he thought a man in politics stood or fell by the results of his policies; that what the children did or did not do affected their lives, and that he did not consider that their lives should be tied to his political interests. He was quite right. I think the majority of the people in the country regretted that he had to undergo any anxiety of this kind, but realized that his family was much like other families. And many families, during this period of uncertainty, experienced stresses and strains which were, perhaps, a part of the times.

It is possible that sometimes Franklin carried his disregard of criticism too far. I was appalled when, in 1937, he asked James to come to Washington as one of his secretaries. James of course was delighted, for he had always been interested in politics and thought the opportunity to help his father a great chance to learn much and be really useful in the administration. I, however, could foresee the attacks that would be made on his father for appointing him, and on James himself, and I could imagine all kinds of ways in which, through his necessarily political activities, he might get himself and his father into trouble. I protested vehemently to Franklin and told him he was selfish to bring James down. I talked to James and tried to persuade him not to come, but he could see no objections. Finally I was silenced by my husband's saying to me: "Why should I be deprived of my eldest son's help and of the pleasure of having him with me just because I am the president?" It did seem hard, and what he said had a point. Nevertheless, I was unhappy, and I think my fears were justified by what actually happened.

Jimmy did a good job and it meant a great deal to Franklin to have him, but he was more vulnerable to the jealousies and rivalries than were the other secretaries, and he did get into trouble when he began to work with people in Congress. As a result of the work and anxiety, he developed ulcers of the stomach and eventually had to go out to the Mayo Brothers hospital for an operation. Franklin, with his usual necessary entourage, arrived the morning of the operation. He was very calm, as he usually was in a crisis, and chatted as though nothing were on his mind. I can be calm and quiet, but it takes all the discipline I have acquired in life to keep on talking and smiling and to concentrate on the conversation addressed to me. I want to be left alone while I store up fortitude for what I fear may be a blow of fate. However, I have learned to feel one way inside at such times and outwardly to go on like an automaton. I still remember waiting through the operation that morning and then waiting some more until the doctors came with the laboratory report and said nothing malignant had been found. They told

James the nervous strain was bad for him, and he accepted their advice not to return to his duties at the White House.

In 1937, about the time he brought Jimmy to Washington, Franklin became much troubled over the decisions that the Supreme Court was rendering. His advisers were divided, some of them feeling that it was very unwise to have any change made in the court. Franklin, felt, however, that if it was going to be possible to pass progressive legislation only to have it declared unconstitutional by the Supreme Court, no progress could be made. He also felt that people became too conservative as they grew older and that they should not be allowed to continue indefinitely to wield great power.

The defeat of the Supreme Court bill seemed to me to be a real blow to Franklin, but he spent no time in regrets and simply said: "Well, we'll see what will happen." Later he was able, little by little, to change the complexion of the court. He remarked one day that he thought the fight had been worth while in spite of the defeat, because it had focused the attention of the public on the Supreme Court and its decisions, and he felt that aroused public interest was always helpful. He had a firm belief in the collective wisdom of the people when their interest was awakened and they really understood the issues at stake.

Though I had been in complete sympathy with what he was trying to do, I used to think that he might have saved himself a good deal of trouble by just waiting a while, since it was death and resignations that really gave him the opportunity to appoint new people to the Supreme Court. However, if he had not made the fight, perhaps fewer people would have resigned. . . .

I have said before that of the cabinet people Henry and Elinor Morgenthau were the two closest to us; and Mrs. Morgenthau and I had many interests in common. For one thing, we were both much interested in the woman's prison at Alderson, West Virginia, where a remarkable woman, Dr. Mary Harris, was the superintendent. She was doing notable work with the women, many of whom had been committed for being drug addicts or for helping their husbands to run stills in the mountains. The training was largely in housework, all of which in the prison was done by inmates, but they were given opportunities to learn to read and write. We found many women who, having come in with practically no education and no knowledge of how to live decently, were appreciative of the chance to return to their families better equipped to cope with the responsibilities of a home. Many of them, particularly the mountain women, had not only a husband but a large number of children as well.

Once when Dr. Harris told her cook that I was coming, the cook asked her how many soldiers were coming with me and if she had to prepare enough food for them. When Dr. Harris told her that no one but Mrs. Morgenthau was coming with me, the cook said: "Lawdy me, does that man in the White House trust us down here enough to send his wife alone?"

I was introduced to a very gentle-looking colored woman who was mowing the lawn, and when I asked later what her offense was, I was told she had committed a murder and was in for life. Of course, murder that is committed from an emotional impulse does not necessarily indicate criminal tendencies; it may not even mean that the person is likely to murder again. In any case, this particular woman was one of the most trusted inmates, and I never heard that she showed any further signs of violence. Years afterward I came to know quite well, and to count as a friend, a woman who had been in this prison for mailing drugs to another drug addict. She had known one of the cabinet wives, and wrote asking if she could come to see me to talk over conditions in Alderson and similar prisons for drug addicts. She pointed out to me that the sentences imposed on the prisoners were much too short to effect real cures and that the drastic measures used in abruptly removing the drugs to which they were accustomed were particularly hard on women.

On one occasion, Elinor Morgenthau and I drove in my car down into Virginia where, somewhere near Williamsburg, we met Sanford Bates, who was then head of federal prisons. He took us over a number of prison camps where he was trying to introduce industries under moderate security conditions to provide for the inmates an intermediate step between regulated prison life and the business of earning a living in normal society. We also visited the prison in Richmond and were shocked to find how poor were both the educational system and the opportunities for keeping the men busy.

I am reminded here of a story Miss Thompson tells about the time during the war when I visited one of the prisons in Baltimore with

Mr. Maury Maverick who was in charge of prison industries during the war and wanted me to see the salvage work being done there. In order to fit the trip into my schedule, I had had to leave the White House very early without saying good-morning to Franklin. On his way to the office, he called to Tommy and asked where I was: "She's in prison, Mr. President," Tommy said. "I'm not surprised," said Franklin, "but what for?"

Another old friend in the cabinet was Frances Perkins, in whose work I was extremely interested. Notwithstanding the very unfair treatment meted out to her by the press and many other people—especially some women's groups—who should have known better, it was a remarkable achievement. . . .

Another person I saw often was Aubrey Williams. He was an idealist who, I think, never lost his sense of values as Harry [Hopkins], in certain ways, did. A fine administrator and organizer, he was not always politically wise. On one occasion when we were both attending a meeting in Birmingham, Alabama, he said some things to the newspaper reporters which he felt so miserable about afterwards that he came to my suite in the hotel and asked if I thought he should resign. I told him I did not believe my husband would think that he had made too serious a mistake. While Franklin often wished that people would think before they spoke, he understood that it is a habit hard to acquire, and his only remark about this particular incident was: "Of course I don't want Aubrey to resign. He's much too valuable. He'll learn and this will blow over." It did.

The meetings of the Southern Conference of Human Welfare in Birmingham were attended by both colored and white people, although they were segregated in the meeting places. Aubrey and I were late at one session and dashed into the church where the meeting was being held and sat down on the colored side. At once the police appeared to remind us of the rules and regulations on segregation. I was told that I could not sit on the colored side. Rather than give in I asked that chairs be placed for us with the speakers facing the whole group. At a later meeting word came to us that all the audience was to be arrested and taken to jail for breaking one of Birmingham's strongest laws against mixed audiences. However, nothing happened and the meetings for the rest of the day went off well.

Two women of whom I am very fond and whom I am always happy to see now are Mrs. Florence Kerr and Mrs. Ellen Woodward, who worked on relief with Harry Hopkins and later in Social Security, doing remarkable work in spite of the handicap of being women. Other women in government service whom I came to know and to admire were Katharine Lenroot, head of the Children's Bureau, Dr. Martha Eliot, her associate, Hilda Smith, whose life's work has been in workers' education, Mary Anderson, head of the Bureau of Women in Industry, and the late Mrs. Mary McLeod Bethune, educator and head of the Negro Youth Division of the National Youth Administration. And there were many others. I think of them all with affection and am happy when our paths cross now.

In my work with Farm Security I came to know Dr. Milburn L. Wilson very well and to have a great admiration for him as a person and as an able government official. Dr. Thomas Parran did remarkable work in the Public Health Service, on one or two occasions bringing wrath down upon his head by daring to touch on certain tabooed subjects that no one before had dared to speak of openly. By speaking out, he did a great service to our men in the military forces.

I made one or two rather fruitless efforts to work with the wives of the cabinet members outside the purely official social functions. One attempt I remember very well. I had from the first been interested in housing conditions in the District of Columbia, feeling that improved housing was basic to all other efforts for better living conditions. At one point in the early years I asked the cabinet wives whether they would come and listen to a talk by someone who was an authority on Washington housing and then go with me to see some of the alleys and slums. I suggested that it might be a good thing if they and I could leave behind us as our contribution some improvement in living conditions in the capital city.

We went on our housing trip, but I could see that they had no great enthusiasm for any contact with slum conditions. The women who drove with me politely got out of the car and observed the conditions, but those with Elinor Morgenthau stayed in the car and suggested that she report to them since "she was accustomed to seeing such conditions." When we met again I was told that their husbands took a great deal of time and that, after all, the care of her husband and her official duties were a wife's most important job. They were busy with the social life of Washington and they did not feel they could undertake any work of this kind, and besides their husbands would not approve. I never made any further effort to work with the cabinet wives on anything but our joint social duties. They were most cooperative in that field, which they felt was safe and correct.

Though I liked all these women, I never came to know many of them well. That, I think, was largely because I had reached an age when making real friends was becoming more difficult; also my preoccupation with young people and many other problems, as well as the amount of time I had to spend on my own social obligations and my mail and writing, made it difficult for me to arrange the kind of everyday contacts that might have drawn us closer together.

I have never known what it was to be bored or to have time hang heavily on my hands. It has always been difficult to find time to do the things I want to do. When I was young I read a great deal, but during these last years I have had to read so many things that those I should like to read are too often neglected. Sometimes I think it would be delightful if an afternoon or evening could actually be given to uninterrupted reading for pure pleasure. In the White House I often left a movie in order to work on my mail and went back just before the end, hoping that my guests did not know I had deserted them in between. I practically never found time to go to the movies outside the White House....

DOROTHY DAY

"It is a permanent revolution, this Catholic Worker Movement..."

Their experiences as members of circles of New York social critics and reformers in the early twentieth century proved to be an important catalyst for all the women included in this section. Dorothy Day was no exception, but her career as an activist was to take a dramatically different turn when she converted to Catholicism. Like Roosevelt, Simkhovitch, and Wald, she was a champion of the poor, the ill-housed, and the politically oppressed. Like them, she fought for a fairer society and a more equitable legal system. Beginning in the thirties, however, Day, one of the founders of the Catholic Worker Movement, grounded all her efforts within a deeply religious context.

Born in 1897, Dorothy Day was the daughter of a free-lance journalist *who constantly moved his large family around the country as work beckoned. A scholarship to Urbana College in Illinois gave Day the opportunity for higher education and her first exposure to left-wing politics. She became a socialist and, after graduation, drifted to New York City, where she found work as a writer for such publications as the* New York Call, *a daily socialist newspaper.*

During the twenties, Day lived the life of a New York bohemian. Her friends were socialists, anarchists, and artists in the avant garde. With them, Day joined picket lines and went to jail. She entered into a common-law marriage with an English radical, Forster Bannerman, and in 1927 bore a child. By her own account, the birth of her daughter spurred Day towards a wrenching time of spiritual soul-searching.

Day's own family background had been only nominally Episcopalian. Her friends and co-workers, including her husband, were scornful of religion. But in 1927 Day experienced a fierce and mystical longing to be a Catholic. She began to pray and attend mass daily. Leaving Bannerman, whom she still loved passionately, she moved to New York's Lower East Side and continued to work as a journalist. Her search for a new direction in life ended in 1933. In that year, as she informs us in this segment from her autobiography, The Long Loneliness, *she met a French-Canadian priest, Peter Maurin. Together Day and Maurin founded the Catholic Worker Movement, which she continued to lead until her death in 1980. In the following pages Day describes how the journal they founded,* The Catholic Worker, *agitated for social justice and the rights of the urban poor during the Depression.*

SOURCES: In addition to her autobiography, first published in 1952, several excellent books about Dorothy Day have recently appeared. Among the best are Mel Piehl, *Breaking Bread: The Catholic Worker and the Origin of Catholic Radicalism in America* (1982); William Miller, *Dorothy Day: A Biography* (1984); Anne Klejment and Alice Klejment, *Dorothy Day and the "Catholic Worker": A Bibliography and Index* (1985); and Robert Coles, *Dorothy Day: A Radical Devotion* (1987). See also Daniel Berrigan's introduction to the 1981 reprint edition of *The Long Loneliness*, vii–xxiii.

I WAS LIVING IN A "RAILROAD flat," or a "dumb-bell apartment" as they are called, with a large room in front, a kitchen in the back and the two dark airless bedrooms in between. It was on the first floor and narrower than those upstairs and noisier, what with tenants going in and out and the milkman starting the long parade early in the day. But the house was spotlessly clean. The Riedel family lived on the third floor rent free and received a salary to keep the place clean, to dispose of the garbage and refuse from the other seven families who lived there. It was an Italian and German neighborhood in a section of the East Side where the houses have been torn down since, to make way for an immense housing project. I was attracted to the house on Fifteenth Street because of the beautiful back yards, separated by wooden fences. Each house had its flower garden, divided by a home-built wire fence from a cement-paved yard where the children could play without trampling flowers. There were tall untrimmed privet hedges against the back fences. When these were in bloom there was a pleasant acrid odor in the air. Beds of perennials grew in profusion, and kept increasing every year. Between borders of ice plant and widows' tears there were brick walks, and in the center of each plot there was, wonder of wonders, a fig tree which had to be well corseted in winter with straw and bound up to keep warm. There were many of these in New York, in the back yards of the Italians.

There was no heat in the house, so we used the gas stove in the kitchen for both heating and cooking. In the coldest months, this meant that the bill would come to twenty dollars a month. The rent of the apartment was also twenty. I felt that the four rooms with their cross ventilation from street to back garden gave me air and breathing space, and I settled down to work and writing with great peace and joy.

I was writing a novel. I have always been a journalist and a diarist pure and simple, but as long as I could remember, I dreamed in terms of novels. This one was to be about the depression, a social novel with the pursuit of a job as the motive and the social revolution as its crisis. There was to be the struggle between religion and otherworldliness, and communism and thisworldliness, replete with a heroine and hero and scores of fascinating characters. I put my own struggle and dreams of love into the book and was very happy writing it.

But my life was too full. I progressed slowly. I had to work for a living. I walked to and from my work. I arose early for Mass, and I began to go to daily communion for the first time in the four years I had been a Catholic. This was at the urging of a priest whom I never happened to see, to whom I spoke in the confessional, to whom I confided my struggles from week to week. . . .

After I had become a Catholic I began little by little to lose track of my friends. Being a Catholic, I discovered, put a barrier between me and others; however slight, it was always felt. . . .

Since I could leave my daughter, I decided I would go to Washington as a reporter for *The Commonweal*, the first Catholic publication for which I had written. . . .

Getting an advance from *The Commonweal* to cover expenses, I took the bus with Mary Heaton Vorse, that valiant labor reporter, whom I had known in the days when I worked for the old *Masses* and the *Liberator*. She knew all the reporters in Washington and we went to the home of one of them when we arrived to get the latest news on the demonstrators [hunger marchers from New York]. Mary was always helping support her children and her children's children, so she traveled and lived as cheaply as she could, in lodging houses all over the world. She had worked for the labor movement in America in addition to writing stories for *Collier's* and the women's journals, stories which she called lollipops; but her real love was "Labor."

She had covered every major strike in the country. She knew the aristocrat of New England as well as the radical and the Bohemian; in her family there had been a long tradition of high thinking for generations back. Her first two husbands had died, and she had married Robert Minor, who took Earl Browder's place when he was imprisoned during the early years of World War II, as general secretary of the Communist party. Bob had struggled through from a faith in the I.W.W., the anarcho-syndicalist, to that of the Communist, with much soul-searching and study, Mary said, and was a sincere though a rather dull revolutionist. Later they separated, he to marry a younger woman (one with no career of her own) and Mary to continue her work as a world reporter.

I had had such a peaceful summer and fall. Now at the beginning of December, I was in the thick of the struggle again, writing not the nice leisurely novel but the immediate flash story of revolt. That was how the newspapers interpreted it. It was an impressive demonstration. Leaving New York, the procession of old trucks and cars, such as the Joad family in *Grapes of Wrath* traveled in some years later in quest of land and work, paraded through various cities, and, where they could, stopped to hold meetings in Protestant churches and labor halls. In one such church in Wilmington, Delaware, the police broke up the meeting by throwing tear-gas bombs through the windows and when the marchers broke out from the church in disorderly fashion, clubbed and arrested those whom they suspected of being the leaders.

In spite of such incidents, and there were others, the hunger marchers persisted and went on to Washington. We had been late in starting, Mary and I, and when we arrived, they were there before us.

This was not long after the tear-gassing and routing of the veterans, who had encamped for a while in Washington to bring their plight before the legislators of the country. Now the papers were full of the Communist menace. There were scare headlines, and as a result of the hysteria built up by the press, police had stopped the procession of trucks as it entered Washington on Route One; there the men remained encamped for three days and nights. The road was closed and all other traffic was rerouted. On one side was a park of sorts and on the other railroad tracks; the police hemmed in the demonstrators, keeping them there with threats of tear gas and machinegunning. The demonstrators slept in trucks and on the roadside those first days of December when the weather was already bitter, while the respectable citizen slept in his warm bed and read comfortably of the "reds" who had come to take over Washington. I do not think the people themselves were frightened. Left to themselves they would reasonably have permitted the demonstration, have listened to the complaints, passed on the recommendations to the proper authorities, expecting in due course that something might be done.

But the newspapers had to have their story. With scare heads, yellow journalism, and staccato radio, the tense, nervous stories built up, of communism at home and Communist atrocities in the rest of the world.

If there was not a story, the newspapers would make a story. If there was not a war, the press would see to it that there was a class war, a war in which all the weapons were on the side of the authorities. The newspaper reporters were infected by their own journalism and began to beg city editors to give them tear-gas masks before they went out to interview the leaders of the unemployed marchers. They knew what they were building up to.

Mary Vorse and I stayed in a tourist house on Massachusetts Avenue, and ate cheaply in lunch wagons. We felt that when people were enduring the hardships these men and women were suffering, it was not the time for us to be comfortable. We ate frugally and we put up in dollar-a-night lodgings so there was something left over to contribute to the food fund of the strikers. Mary had always been that kind of a reporter. Her brand of journalism was different.

And then, after three days of mounting hysteria, suddenly permission was given to the marchers to proceed. On a bright sunny day the ragged horde triumphantly with banners flying, with lettered slogans mounted on sticks, paraded three thousand strong through the tree-flanked streets of Washington. I stood on the curb and watched them, joy and pride in the courage of this band of men and women mounting in my heart, and with it a bitterness too that since I was now a Catholic, with fundamental philosophical differences, I could not be out there with them. I could write, I could protest, to arouse the conscience, but where was the Catholic leadership in the gathering of bands of men and women together, for the actual works of mercy that the comrades had always made part of their technique in reaching the workers?

How little, how puny my work had been since becoming a Catholic, I thought. How self-centered, how ingrown, how lacking in sense of community! My summer of quiet reading and prayer, my self-absorption seemed sinful as I watched my brothers in their struggle, not for themselves but for others. How our dear Lord must love them, I kept thinking to myself. They were His friends, His comrades, and who knows how close to His heart in their attempt to work for justice. I remembered that the first public act of our Lord recorded in the New Testament was the overthrowing of the money-changers' tables in the temple. The miracle at Cana, when Christ was present at the wedding feast and turned water into wine, has been written of as the first public act of our Lord. It was the first miracle, it was the sanctifying of marriage, but it was not the social act of overturning the tables of the money changers, a divine courage on the part of this obscure Jew, going into the temple and with bold scorn for all the riches of this world, scattering the coins and the traffickers in gold.

The demands of the marchers were for social legislation, for unemployment insurance, for old-age pensions, for relief for mothers and children, for work. I remember seeing one banner on which was inscribed, "Work, not wages," a mysterious slogan having to do with man's dignity, his ownership of and responsibility for the means of production.

The years have passed, and most of the legislation called for by those workers is on the books now. I wonder how many realize just how much they owe the hunger marchers, who endured fast and cold, who were like the Son of Man, when He said, "The foxes have holes, and the birds of the air have nests but the Son of man hath not where to lay his head."

When the demonstration was over and I had finished writing my story, I went to the national shrine at the Catholic University on the feast of the Immaculate Conception. There I offered up a special prayer, a prayer which came with tears and with anguish, that some way would open up for me to use what talents I possessed for my fellow workers, for the poor.

73
Dorothy Day

As I knelt there, I realized that after three years of Catholicism my only contact with active Catholics had been through articles I had written for one of the Catholic magazines. Those contacts had been brief, casual. I still did not know personally one Catholic layman.

And when I returned to New York, I found Peter Maurin—Peter the French peasant, whose spirit and ideas will dominate the rest of this book as they will dominate the rest of my life....

We started publishing *The Catholic Worker* at 436 East Fifteenth Street in May, 1933, with a first issue of 2,500 copies. Within three or four months the circulation bounded to 25,000, and it was cheaper to bring it out as an eight-page tabloid on newsprint rather than the smaller-sized edition on better paper we had started with. By the end of the year we had a circulation of 100,000 and by 1936 it was 150,000. It was certainly a mushroom growth. It was not only that some parishes subscribed for the paper all over the country in bundles of 500 or more. Zealous young people took the paper out in the streets and sold it, and when they could not sell it even at one cent a copy, they gave free copies and left them in streetcar, bus, barber shop and dentist's and doctor's office. We got letters from all parts of the country from people who said they had picked up the paper on trains, in rooming houses. One letter came from the state of Sonora in Mexico and we read with amazement that the reader had tossed in an uncomfortable bed on a hot night until he got up to turn over the mattress and under it found a copy of *The Catholic Worker*. A miner found a copy five miles underground in an old mine that stretched out under the Atlantic Ocean off Nova Scotia. A seminarian said that he had sent out his shoes to be half-soled in Rome and they came back to him wrapped in a copy of *The Catholic Worker*. These letters thrilled and inspired the young people who came to help, sent by Brothers or Sisters who taught in the high schools. We were invited to speak in schools and parishes, and often as a result of our speaking others came in to help us. On May Day, those first few years, the streets were literally lined with papers. Looking back on it, it seemed like a gigantic advertising campaign, entirely unpremeditated. It grew organically, Peter used to say happily, and not through organization. "We are not an organization, we are an organism," he said.

First there was Peter, my brother and I. When John took a job at Dobb's Ferry, a young girl, Dorothy Weston, who had been studying journalism and was a graduate of a Catholic college, came to help. She lived at home and spent her days with us, eating with us and taking only her carfare from the common fund. Peter brought in three young men from Columbus Circle, whom he had met when discussing the affairs of the world there, and of these one became bookkeeper (that was his occupation when he was employed), another circulation manager, and the third married Dorothy Weston. Another girl came to take dictation and help with mailing the paper, and she married the circulation manager. There were quite a number of romances that first year—the paper appealed to youth. Then there were the young intellectuals who formed what they called Campion Committees in other cities as well as New York, who helped to picket the Mexican and German consulates and who distributed literature all over the city. Workers came in to get help on picket lines, to help move dispossessed families and make demonstrations in front of relief offices. Three men came to sell the paper on the street, and to eat their meals with us. Big Dan had been a truck driver and a policeman. The day he came in to see us he wanted nothing more than to bathe his tired feet. That night at supper Peter indoctrinated him on the dignity of poverty and read some of Father Vincent McNabb's *Nazareth or Social Chaos*. This did not go over so well, all of us being city people, and Father McNabb advocating a return to the fields, but he made Dan Orr go out with a sense of a mission, not worrying about shabby clothes or the lack of a job. Dan began to sell the paper on the streets and earned enough money to live on. He met others who had found subsistence jobs, carrying sandwich signs or advertising children's furniture by pushing a baby carriage, a woman who told fortunes in a tea shop, a man who sold pretzels, which were threaded on four poles one on each corner of an old baby carriage. He found out their needs, and those of their families, and never left the house in the morning without bundles of clothes as well as his papers.

Dan rented a horse and wagon in which to deliver bundles of the paper each month. (We had tried this before he came but someone had to push the horse while the other led it. We knew nothing about driving a wagon.) Dan loved his horse. He called it Catholic Action, and used to take the blanket off my bed to cover the horse in winter. We rented it from a German Nazi on East Sixteenth Street, and sometimes when we had no money he let us have the use of it free for a few hours. It rejoiced our hearts to move a Jewish family into their new quarters with his equipment.

Dan said it was a pious horse and that when he passed St. Patrick's Cathedral, the horse genuflected. He liked to drive up Fifth Avenue, preferably with students who had volunteered their help, and shout, "Read *The Catholic Worker*" at the top of his lungs. He was anything but dignified and loved to affront the dignity of others.

One time he saw me coming down the street when he was selling the paper in front of Gimbel's and began to yell, "Read *The Catholic Worker!* Romance on every page." A seminarian from St. Louis, now Father Dreisoner, took a leaf from Dan's book and began selling the paper on the corner of Times Square and at union meetings. He liked to stand next to a comrade selling *The Daily Worker*, and as the one shouted "Read *The Daily Worker*," he in turn shouted, "Read *The Catholic Worker* daily." Between sales they conversed.

Another of Peter's friends was an old Armenian who wrote poetry in a beautiful mysterious script which delighted my eyes. He carried his epic around with him always. He was very little and wore a long black overcoat which reached to his heels and a black revolutionary hat over his long white hair. He had a black cat whom he called Social Justice, mimicking Big Dan. She was his constant companion. He used my washrag to wipe her face with after eating. He prepared dishes for us with rice and meat wrapped in grape leaves, held together with toothpicks. He slept on a couch in the kitchen for a time. Once when Tamar was tearing around the house playing with Freddy Rubino, the little boy who lived upstairs, and I told her to be a little more quiet, that Mr. Minas was asleep in the next room, she said mischievously, "I don't care if the Pope is asleep in the next room, we want to play and make noise." Day and night there were many meetings in the converted barber shop which was our office, and Tamar heard plenty of noise from us. When someone asked her how she liked *The Catholic Worker* she wrinkled up her nose and said she liked the farming-commune idea, but that there was too much talk about all the rest.

Peter, the "green" revolutionist, had a long-term program which called for hospices, or houses of hospitality, where the works of mercy could be practiced to combat the taking over by the state of all those services which could be built up by mutual aid; and farming communes to provide land and homes for the unemployed, whom increasing technology was piling up into the millions. In 1933, the unemployed numbered 13,000,000.

The idea of the houses of hospitality caught on quickly enough. The very people that Peter brought in, who made up our staff at first, needed a place to live. Peter was familiar with the old I.W.W. technique of a common flophouse and a pot of mulligan on the stove. To my cost, I too had become well acquainted with this idea.

Besides, we never had any money, and the cheapest, most practical way to take care of people was to rent some apartments and have someone do the cooking for the lot of us. Many a time I was cook and cleaner as well as editor and street seller. When Margaret, a Lithuanian girl from the mining regions of Pennsylvania came to us, and took over the cooking, we were happy indeed. She knew how to make a big pot of mashed potatoes with mushroom sauce which filled everyone up nicely. She was a great soft creature with a little baby, Barbara, who was born a few months after she came to us. Margaret went out on May Day with the baby and sold papers on the street. She loved being propagandist as well as cook. When Big Dan teased her, she threatened to tell the "pasture" of the church around the corner.

To house the women we had an apartment near First Avenue which could hold about ten. When there were arguments among them, Margaret would report them with gusto, giving us a blow-by-blow account. Once when she was telling how one of the women abused her so that she "felt as though the crown of thorns was pressing right down on her head" (she was full of these mystical experiences), Peter paused in his pacing of the office to tell her she needed to scrub the kitchen floor. Not that he was ever harsh, but he was making a point that manual labor was the cure of all such quarreling. Margaret once told Bishop O'Hara of Kansas City that when she kissed his ring, it was just like a blood transfusion—she got faint all over.

Jacques Maritain came to us during these early days and spoke to the group who were reading *Freedom and the Modern World* at that time. He gave special attention to the chapter on the purification of means. Margaret was delighted with our distinguished guest, who so evidently loved us all, and made him a box of fudge to take home with him when he sailed for France a few weeks later.

Ah, those early days that everyone likes to think of now since we have grown so much bigger; that early zeal, that early romance, that early companionableness! And how delightful it is to think that the young ones who came into the work now find the same joy in community. It is a permanent revolution, this Catholic Worker Movement.

In New York we were soon forced by the increasing rent of three apartments and one store to move into a house on the West Side. We lived on West Charles Street, all together, men and women, students and workers, about twenty of us. In the summer young college girls and men came for months to help us, and, in some cases, returned to their own cities to start houses of hospitality there. In this way, houses started in Boston, Rochester, Milwaukee, and other cities. Within a few years there were thirty-three houses of hospitality and farms around the country.

One of the reasons for the rapid growth was that many young men were coming out of college to face the prospect of no job. If they had started to read *The Catholic Worker* in college, they were ready to spend time as volunteers when they came out. Others were interested in writing, and houses in Buffalo, Chicago, Baltimore, Seattle, St. Louis and Philadelphia, to name but a few cities, published their own papers and sold them with the New York *Catholic Worker*. A *Catholic Worker* was started in Australia and one in England. Both papers are still in existence, but the New York *Catholic Worker* is the only one published in the United States. The English and Australian papers are neither pacifist nor libertarian in their viewpoint, but the Australian paper is decentralist as well as strongly pro-labor. The English paper concentrates on labor organization and legislation. "These papers have part of the program," Peter said, "but ours makes a synthesis—with vision."

The coming of war closed many of the houses of hospitality, but with new ones reopening there are still more than twenty houses and farms. When the young men in the work were released from service, most of them married and had to think in terms of salaries, jobs to support their growing families. The voluntary apostolate was for the unwilling celibate and for the unemployed as well as for the men and women, willing celibates, who felt that running hospices, performing the works of mercy, working on farms, was their vocation, just as definitely a vocation as that of the professed religious.

Voluntary poverty means a good deal of discomfort in these houses of ours. Many of the houses throughout the country are without central heating and have to be warmed by stoves in winter. There are back-yard toilets for some even now. The first Philadelphia house had to use water drawn from one spigot at the end of an alley, which served half a dozen other houses. It was lit with oil lamps. It was cold and damp and so unbelievably poverty-stricken that little children coming to see who were the young people meeting there exclaimed that this could not be a *Catholic* place; it was too poor. We must be Communists. They were well acquainted with the Communist point of view since they were Puerto Rican and Spanish and Mexican and this was at the beginning of the Spanish Civil War.

How hard a thing it is to hear such criticisms made. Voluntary poverty was only found among the Communists; the Negro and white man on the masthead of our paper suggested communism; the very word "worker" made people distrust us at first. We were not taking the position of the great mass of Catholics, who were quite content with the present in this world. They were quite willing to give to the poor, but they did not feel called upon to work for the things of this life for others which they themselves esteemed so lightly. Our insistence on worker-ownership, on the right of private property, on the need to de-proletarize the worker, all points which had been emphasized by the Popes in their social encyclicals, made many Catholics think we were Communists in disguise, wolves in sheep's clothing.

The house on Mott Street which we occupied for many years began to loom up in our lives as early as 1934, through Mary Lane. She was one of our readers, who lived in a small tenement apartment on the upper West Side on her telegrapher's pension. She was very holy, and when she first saw a copy of the paper with its stories of human misery, she who also saw poverty at first hand began collecting clothes for us. The first time she came down she stood at the door dramatically and said to me abruptly, "Do you have ecstasies and visions?" Poor dear, so hungry for mystical experience, even if secondhand, after a long life of faith.

I was taken aback. "Visions of unpaid bills," I said abruptly. Her warmth, her effusiveness, were embarrassing but I soon learned to take them for what they were, an overflowing of an ardent soul, ready to pour itself out in love.

She became our faithful friend. She was lame, half blind, old, yet she stinted herself and gave us five dollars a month of her pension. She had a well-to-do friend named Gertrude Burke, the only daughter of an invalid widowed mother. Gertrude took care of her mother until she died and then began to give her property away to the Church. She went to live at the House of Calvary, a cancer hospital for the poor, which was one of her pet charities. This had been founded by a small group of widows, a "lay institute" according to the terminology of the Church. They were not a religious order. Neither wife nor virgin could belong, though either could help. Miss Burke's uptown house was given to the order of the Good Shepherd. The house on Mott Street had been built by an old uncle in 1860. His name was Kerrigan and it was said he had defended old St. Patrick's Cathedral on Mott Street during the Know Nothing riots, standing on the steps with a gun in his hand.

At 115 Mott Street, there was a rear house which had been the original house, and had had a long yard in front; there also was the front house, twice as deep, four rooms on either side of a long narrow hall. The rear house had two rooms on either side with one toilet between them, open fireplaces, a sink and a washtub in each kitchen. In these primitive, unheated, bathless flats, made up of a kitchen and bedroom, the Irish first came to live and then the Italians. Katie, the vegetable woman on the corner, told me her mother had lived in the first floor of the rear building and that St. Francis Cabrini had visited her there. That two-room flat was dark and airless, surrounded as it was by five-story buildings on every side. The sun never reached the rear room whose long window looked out on another five-story building, one foot away. Yet when the priest came to read the prayers for the dying in that dark room, a ray of sunlight fell on his book so that the candle held by Katie herself was no longer needed!

This entire rear house was empty when I first saw it. Half of the apartments in the front building were also empty. Miss Burke offered us the use of the empty apartments provided we would collect the rents on the rest and be caretakers. It was so much worse a neighborhood than Fifteenth Street that I was appalled at the idea. I asked Rose Clafani, whom I met on the stairs, if she had lived there long and she said stormily, "I was born in this g——d——place!" And that was all I got out of her! I found afterward that she was afraid we were going to buy the building and evict them, and her heart was there. She loved her home.

I turned down the offer then but within a few years I regretted it. I felt it was wrong to take rent for such a place—that it had far better be torn down, or given rent free to the poor. I might easily have expressed myself along these lines, so imprudent am I, so hasty in speech.

When we had found the house on Charles Street too small for us, I telephoned Mary Lane and asked her to intercede for us with Miss Burke, to tell her that we had reconsidered and would be most grateful for the use of the rear house at 115 Mott Street. We would not, however, collect rents on the front building. There was one store empty at that time and we asked for that too. Miss Burke reminded us of the fact that we refused the house when we could have had it—we had not understood her previous offer in this way—and that now she had given the place to the House of Calvary. However, she would ask them if we could use it. The housing crisis was not on us at that time. So, finally we obtained the use of the house and moved in. The other store in front was a speakeasy, run as a dry-goods store. When the tenants moved out we took that as an office. As the apartments became vacant, we rented them for eighteen dollars each. We ended by having twelve rooms in the front house for women, another four for men, which with those in the rear house made twenty-four rooms for men. Four were used for laundry and storerooms. We did not use the basement because of rats and defective plumbing. The neighbors used one cellar of the rear building for winemaking, and hogsheads of wine were stored there. Once, one of our workers, a former seaman, went down in the cellar and in trying to obtain wine, let much of it escape. We had to pay for it. These apartments and stores, on this narrow, pushcart-lined street, were our home for fourteen years.

The people who worked for us! For the first six months that we published *The Catholic Worker*, we longed for an artist who could illustrate Peter's ideas. An answer to our prayers came in the form of a young girl just out of high school who signed her work, A. de Bethune. Her woodcuts were of worker-saints, St. Peter the fisherman, St. Paul writing in prisons, walking the roads and indoctrinating St. Timothy, St. Crispin the shoemaker, St. Conrad and a host of minor saints, if any saints could be called minor who gave their lives for the faith, whose hearts burned with so single-hearted a fire.

"A picture," Ade reminded us, "was worth ten thousand words." Through a misunderstanding as to her name, we signed her pictures Ade Bethune and so she was called by all of us. She was Belgian and it was only some years later that we knew her title, which her mother continued to use, Baronne de Bethune. The aristocrat and the peasant Peter got on famously. "Our word is tradition," he said happily, and wrote a little essay, "Shouting a Word."

Mrs. Bethune and her daughter illustrated for Peter many ideas besides *noblesse oblige*. He liked to illustrate his ideas by calling attention to people who exemplified them. The Bethune family performed all the works of mercy out of slender resources, earned by the labor of their hands. They had come to this country at the close of World War I. They exemplified voluntary poverty and manual labor and the love of neighbors to the highest degree.

When Ade built up her studio in Newport where the family moved soon after we met them, she took in apprentices, young girls from different parts of the country who could not have afforded to pay tuition or to support themselves. Two of her apprentices married and went to live on Catholic Worker farms, and are now mothers of large families. My own daughter went to her when she was sixteen and stayed a year, learning the household arts. For to Ade, as to Eric Gill and Peter Maurin, the holy man was the whole man, the man of integrity, who not only tried to change the world, but to live in it as it was.

Whenever I visited Ade I came away with a renewed zest for life. She has such a sense of the sacramentality of life, the goodness of things, a sense that is translated in all her works whether it was illustrating a missal, making stained-glass windows or sewing, cooking or gardening. To do things perfectly was always her aim. Another first principle she always taught was to aim high. "If you are going to put a cross bar on an H," she said, "you have to aim *higher* than your sense of sight tells you."

Dom Vitry, a Benedictine monk from Mared-sous, said this same thing in regard to music, "Aim higher than the note you wish to reach, and you will come down on it."

Ade came to learn from us as well as give us her woodcuts and we have learned from her. Peter taught her, and she translated his teachings into pictures which we used again and again in the paper.

Once I was attending a steelworker's open-air meeting in Pittsburgh, and when we had distributed the papers we brought, I was amused and delighted to see a huge Slovak or Hungarian worker pointing to the pictures of the working saints and laughing with the joy of discovery.

Ade not only drew for our paper—she allowed her work to be copied by papers all over the world, Catholic and non-Catholic. We saw reproductions of her woodcuts in Japanese papers, Portuguese papers, Indian papers, to mention but a few.

Before she was mid-twenty she had designed and with unemployed steelworkers helped build a church in the outskirts of Pittsburgh. She made the stained-glass windows in the Church of the Precious Blood in Brooklyn and recently finished mosaics in a church in the Philippines. In addition to her work of painting, carving, et cetera, she edits a Catholic art quarterly and is a trustee of St. Benedict's farm in Massachusetts, one of the Catholic Worker centers.

On that farm where four families live, one family is made up of seven boys, a father who must go out to work and a mother who has been hospitalized for some years. Ade and her mother have helped this family, as they have helped a number of others in many ways. Not only money and clothes but hard manual labor made up their contributions. Every week a bundle of clothes was sent—and this went on for years—to the Baronne de Bethune in Newport, and she washed, ironed and mended these clothes and sent them back.

It is wonderful to think of and to write of such good works. Hundreds of pairs of socks for men on our breadlines, funds collected—she was always the great lady with special projects into which she drew many others.

I like to speak of her nobility because in her case that is actually what the word connotes. We emphasize the "Prince" when referring to Kropotkin precisely because he gave up titles and estates to be with the poor. We can recognize too our own country's claim to greatness in that here titles are naturally discarded in an attempt to reach the highest principle of human brotherhood.

The de Bethune family lost much in World War I, but when they came here their philosophy of work was so vital that they made what Eric Gill called a cell of good living.

It is amazing how quickly one can gather together a family. Steve Hergenhan came to us from Union Square. He was a German carpenter, a skilled workman who after forty years of frugal living had bought himself a plot of ground near Suffern, New York, and had proceeded to build on it, using much of the natural rock in the neighborhood. He built his house on a hillside and used to ski down to the village to get groceries. He did not like cars and would not have one. He thought that cars were driving people to their ruin. Workers bought cars who should buy homes, he said, and they willingly sold themselves into slavery and indebtedness for the sake of the bright new shining cars that speeded along the super highways. Maybe he refused to pay taxes for the roads that accommodated the cars. Maybe he was unable to. At any rate, he lost his little house on the side of the hill and ended up in New York, on a park bench during the day, telling his grievances to all who would listen, and eating and sleeping in the Municipal Lodging House, which then maintained the largest dormitory in the world, seven hundred double-decker beds.

Peter loved the articulate, and after having one of his "round-table discussions" with Steve in Union Square, he invited him to come and stay with us. The technique of the Square then was for two people to have a discussion together with no one interrupting until he was given permission by one of the two speakers, who might cede "the floor" to another.

Both Peter and Steve were agreed on a philosophy of work and the evils of the machine—they followed the writings of the distributists of England and the Southern agrarians in this country. But Steve differed from Peter on works of mercy. He declaimed loudly with St. Paul, "He who does not work, neither let him eat." And no physical or mental disability won his pity. Men were either workers or shirkers. It was the conflict between the worker and scholar that Peter was always talking about. Steve considered himself both a worker and a scholar.

He did not attend church but he used to say scornfully, when he was living with us on our hilltop farm near Easton, Pennsylvania, "If I believed as you do, that Christ Himself is present there on the altar, nothing in this world would keep me from it." He heard just enough of the discussion about the sacrament of duty and the self-imposed obligation of daily Mass and communion to know which side to take. He was a carper and constant critic and sometimes his language was most immoderate. He aimed to goad, to irritate, and considered it the most effective agitation. Peter never irritated but if Hergenhan became too vituperative he would walk away.

When he came to us, Peter begged him to consent to be used as a foil. Steve was to present the position of the Fascist, the totalitarian, and Peter was to refute him. They discoursed at our nightly meetings, in Union Square and Columbus Circle, and in Harlem, where we had been given the use of another store for the winter. They were invited to speak by Father Scully at a Holy Name meeting, and a gathering of the Knights of Columbus. How they loved these audiences in the simplicity of their hearts. Steve the German, Peter the Frenchman, both with strong accents, with oratory, with facial gesture, with striking pose, put on a show, and when they evoked laughter, they laughed too, delighted at amusing their audience, hoping to arouse them. "I am trying to make the encyclicals click," Peter used to say joyfully, radiant always before an audience. They never felt that they were laughed at. They thought they were being laughed with. Or perhaps they pretended not to see. They were men of poverty, of hard work, of Europe and America; they were men of vision; and they were men, too, with the simplicity of children.

But Hergenhan had bitterness too. The articles he wrote for *The Catholic Worker* about life in the Municipal Lodging House and the quest for bread of the homeless were biting. After the first one appeared, one of the city officials drove up with some companions in a big car and with unctuous flattery praised the work we were doing and asked us why we did not come to them first rather than print such articles about the work of the city.

"I tried to tell you," Hergenhan said. "I tried to tell you of the graft, the poor food, the treatment we received, the contempt and kicking around we got. But you threatened me with the psychopathic ward. You treated me like a wild beast. You gave me the bum's rush."

Perhaps he looked to them like a dangerous radical, like a wild beast. In the helpless resentment of these men there was a fury which city authorities were afraid would gather into a flood of wrath, once they were gathered into a mob. So among every group in the public square, at the meetings of the unemployed, there were careful guardians of law and order watching, waiting to pounce on these gray men, the color of the lifeless trees and bushes and soil in the squares in winter, who had in them as yet none of the green of hope, the rising sap of faith.

Both Peter and Steve tried to arouse that hope. Both of them were personalists, both were workers. They did not want mass action, or violence. They were lambs in the simplicity of their program. They wanted to see the grass spring up between the cobbles of the city streets. They wanted to see the workers leave the cities with their wives and children and take to the fields, build themselves homes, where they would have room to breathe, to study, to pray, where there would be work for all.

"There is no unemployment on the land," Peter used to shout, and he would be met by jeers. "What about the migrants, the tenant farmers. They either work like slaves for the bosses, or they rot like the men in Tobacco Road."

"Fire the bosses," Peter used to say.

The trouble was that he never filled in the chasms, the valleys, in his leaping from crag to crag of noble thought.

He wanted men to think for themselves. Voluntary poverty, the doing without radios, cars, television sets, cigarettes, movies, cosmetics, all these luxuries, would enable men to buy the necessities. In a village community there would be work, even work in the gardens for the invalids, the children, the old, the crippled, the men and women who hung around the street corners and the market places, waiting for someone to hire them.

"Personalism and communitarianism," was Peter's cry.

Steve wanted to flog men into action. His impatience was ferocious.

We were put out of the store in Harlem by the owner, who did not agree with our pacifism. As a member of the National Guard, he thought we were subversive. But not before there had been a riot in Harlem which wrecked store fronts, and resulted in some casualties to man and property. During the long night of the rioting, the Negroes who made up the mobs passed us by. "Don't touch this place," Steve and Peter and the old professor who inhabited the store heard them say. "These folks are all right," and the windows smashed all around them and the roaring of the mobs passed down the avenue. It was a fearful night, the men said, and it but reinforced their conviction of the futility of violence.

To build a new society within the shell of the old! It was the old I.W.W. slogan.

Soon we rented a twelve-room house with a big attic, in Huguenot, Staten Island, right on the water, and there Steve planted a garden which was a model to all who came to participate in week-end conferences. Groups of young people came and speakers from Columbia University, from the Catholic University, from colleges in the Midwest, for these retreats and colloquiums. But as usual in groups working together, they went off on tangents and spent hours discussing rubrics and whether or not to say "compline" in English or Latin and there was discussion too of machines and the land, organization and organism, the corporative order and the corporative state and the rising tide of fascism and nazism.

They all talked, and Steve talked with the best of them, but they were young and he was past fifty; they were young students, second- or third-generation Italian, German, French, Irish, and Peter and Steve were first generation. They listened to Peter because he never turned on them. Steve hated their avoidance of work, and after a good deal of recrimination turned from them to cultivate his garden.

The young fellows picketed the German consulate in protest against nazism; they gave out literature at the docking of the *Bremen* and became involved in a riot when some Communists who called themselves Catholic workers tore down the swastika from the ship and were arrested. But Hergenhan just vented his scorn on youth in general and brought in great baskets of Swiss chard, tomatoes, beans and squash for us to admire and eat. It choked him to see the young people eat them. He wanted disciples who would listen to him and work with him.

The next year we received a letter from a Baltimore schoolteacher who wished to invest in community. She offered us a thousand dollars provided we would build her a house and deed her three acres of the farm near Easton, Pennsylvania to be purchased with her down payment. She would provide second-hand materials for the house.

We tried to dissuade her from coming to us, telling her of our dissensions, warning her she would be disappointed, but she insisted on contributing the money. She was disappointed of course, but when she sold her little house some ten years later, she got out of it a great deal more than she put into it. That didn't prevent her from writing to the Archbishop of Baltimore telling him that she had been lured to contribute to our farming commune by promises of community, which promises had proved false.

Steve always insisted that he had built her house singlehanded. But Peter, and John and Paul Cort helped clean secondhand brick, pull nails out of the secondhand lumber, cart water up the hill from the spring and cisterns and dig the cellar, and there were many others who contributed many man hours of labor. Of course much discussion went on with the building and digging. Hergenhan lived in a little shanty on the edge of the woods and came down to the farmhouse for his meals. He worked with great satisfaction on the house for two years. He was starting off the Catholic Workers with their first farming commune. He was showing them how to work, how to build, and he had great satisfaction in his toil. It was a spot of unutterable beauty looking down over the Delaware and the cultivated fields of New Jersey. Two and a half miles away at the foot of the hills were the twin cities of Easton and Philipsburg, one on either side of the river. Easton is a railroad center and a place of small factories, an old town with many historic buildings, and a college town, with Lafayette College perched upon a hill. There were Syrian, Lithuanian, German, Italian and Irish churches, and we had all these nationalities among us too.

Hergenhan built his house and then returned to the city to indoctrinate. He got tired of being considered the worker, and wanted to be a scholar for a time. But his bitterness had increased. In protest against our policies, specifically our works of mercy, he went to Camp La Guardia, a farm colony for homeless men run by the city. He wanted efficient and able-bodied workers building up village communities. We were clogged up with too much deadwood, with sluggish drones—it was the same old argument again, only this time it was a true worker and not just a young intellectual who was arguing the point.

He became ill and returned to us at Mott Street. We were his family after all. He was by then fifty-six. When he was examined the doctors discovered cancer, and after an operation he was taken to St. Rose's Cancer Hospital on the East Side, to die.

"Abandon hope all ye who enter here," he cried out when I came to visit him. He had not known of his cancer—they had talked of an intestinal obstruction at the hospital where the operation was performed— and when he was brought to St. Rose's he saw written over the door, HOME OF THE CANCEROUS POOR.

His was a little room on the first floor; all day one could look into the garden and past that to the river where tugs and tankers steamed up and down the tidal river and clouds floated over the low shore of Brooklyn. The world was beautiful and he did not want to die. There was so much work he wanted to do, so small a part he had been allowed to play.

Peter and I used to go to see him every day. By that time I had just made what came to be known as our retreat and was filled with enthusiasm and ready to talk to anyone who would listen on the implications of the Christian life—and Steve always loved to converse, provided one gave him a chance to get in his share of the conversation.

I went to St. Rose's each day with my notes, and read them to him. He gradually became happy and reconciled. He had said, "There is so much I wanted to do." And I told him how Father John Hugo had talked of work, "that physical work was hard, mental work harder, and spiritual work was the hardest of all." And I pointed out that he was now doing the spiritual work of his life, lying there suffering, enduring, sowing all his own desires, in order to reap them in heaven. He began to realize that he had to die in order to live, that the door would open, that there was a glorious vista before him, "that all things were his."

"All things are yours," St. Paul wrote, "whether it be Paul or Apollo or Cephas, or the world, or life, or death, or things present, or things to come. For all are yours. And you are Christ's. And Christ is God's."

I read Bede Jarrett's *No Abiding City* to him, and some of Father Faber's conferences on death, and he enjoyed them all. They offered him the richness of thought that he craved, and when the Sister who cared for him asked him if he did not want Baptism, he shouted wholeheartedly, "Yes!"

Peter and I were his sponsors, and to me it was a miracle of God's grace that the lack of dignity with which the Sacrament was conferred did not affront Steve, who was always hypercritical. He was baptized with speed and his confession listened to. He received Viaticum. I remember his anointing most vividly. Three other men were lined up on the bed at the same time, sitting there like gaunt old crows, their simple solemn faces lifted expectantly, childlike, watching every move of the priest, as he anointed their eyes, nose, mouth, ears, their clawlike hands stretched out to receive the holy oil, their feet with horny toes to which the priest bent with swift indifference.

He finished the job, he performed the outward signs, he recited the Latin prayers in a garbled monotone in the back of his throat, and despite the lack of grace in the human sense, Grace was there, souls were strengthened, hearts were lifted.

Ritual, how could we do without it! Though it may seem to be gibberish and irreverence, though the Mass is offered up in such haste that the sacred sentence, "hoc est corpus meus" was abbreviated into "hocus-pocus" by the bitter protestor and has come down into our language meaning trickery, nevertheless there is a sureness and a conviction there. And just as a husband may embrace his wife casually as he leaves for work in the morning, and kiss her absent-mindedly in his comings and goings, still that kiss on occasion turns to rapture, a burning fire of tenderness and love. And with this to stay her she demands the "ritual" of affection shown. The little altar boy kissing the cruet of water as he hands it to the priest is performing a rite. We have too little ritual in our lives.

Steve was baptized and anointed but he did not rally. Daily he became weaker and weaker and sometimes when I came I found him groaning with pain. Earlier at Roosevelt Hospital they had given him a brown-paper bag to blow into when he had an attack of pain. He would go through this ridiculous gesture as though he were going to break the bag explosively, as children do, but it was a desperate device like a woman's pulling on a roped sheet attached to the foot of the bed in the agonies of childbirth. Perhaps the intensity of pain and the intensity of pleasure are both somehow shameful because we so lose control, so lose ourselves, that we are no longer creatures of free will, but in the control of our blind flesh. "Who will deliver me from the body of this death?"

Steve died suddenly one morning, and there was no one with him. We found in his papers afterward notations which indicated his bitterness at not being more used, as writer, speaker, teacher. That has been the lament of so many who have died with us. Just as they are beginning to open their eyes to the glory and the potentialities of life their life is cut short as a weaver's thread. They were like the grass of the field. "The spaces of this life, set over against eternity, are most brief and poor," one of the desert fathers said. It is part of the long loneliness.

There was the French professor who could speak many languages, and who was inventing a universal language. He had been a drug addict and had been cured. Now he had begun to drink, but it was only occasionally. He loved to go on nature walks, up along the Palisades and through Bear Mountain Park, with others who came together by correspondence. This was a part of his life we knew little about. He liked to translate articles for us, not for publication, but for our information. He would write them out in notebooks in a small fine hand, but when he gave them in, it was always with the expectation of money for something to drink. Since we passed many a day with little or no money on hand, and often had to run up gigantic grocery bills (our bill has gone as high as $6,000) he did not often get the fifty cents or a dollar he was expecting. Fifty cents was enough to start him off because he could buy a pint of wine on the Bowery for thirty-five cents.

One of our readers in Burlington, Vermont, a woman doctor who admired Peter Maurin very much, once told him that he could charge books to her account at Brentano's. For a while Peter had a field day. He was buying books for all his friends, even ordering them from England and from France. The professor found a way to increase his pay by asking Peter for dictionaries, German, Italian, French, Latin, Greek, et cetera. The friend in Burlington probably thought we were becoming impossibly intellectual, but she did not protest until bills came in for three French dictionaries. She wrote to us then saying that she could understand the need for one, but not for three. The professor had been selling them all. After that Peter limited his book-buying to one volume a week, and that for himself. It was a luxury, but also a necessity. It was the one luxury he enjoyed, and he shared it with young students who could not afford books and with others whom he tried to induce to read.

But as one young man who shared a room with Peter said, "Peter is always asking you to read his list of essential books, but when you settle down for a long evening of reading, he finds that an opportunity to talk." He liked catching you alone, serious and ready to think. He thought the role of teacher more effective than that of author.

There were these friends of Peter, some of them writing for the paper from the depths of their own experience. There were Margaret and Charlie and Francis who also wrote for the paper—Margaret, the Lithuanian girl, and Charlie, the convert Jew who used to sell gardenias on street corners, and Francis, who had been in Sing Sing for robbery with a Brooklyn gang. We knew many youths who had been in jail for robbery. The Italians love to gamble and the stakes often reach into the thousands. Families have to mortgage homes, take up collections among themselves to pay off. If other payment fails the youths are given "jobs" to do, and they find themselves part of a gang. They have seen the penalty for nonpayment of gambling debts in the slums in many a gang killing. One time, John Cort coming home from Mass saw a man lying dead in the center of the street, while the car from which the shooting was done sped away. John took the number on the license plates, though it was as much as his life was worth, but nothing ever came of this that we knew of. Women rushing out from tenements all around feared for their own. On this occasion, the young girl who lived in our house said to me bitterly, "There isn't a house on this block that hasn't got a son in Sing Sing."

Many college students and graduates came to live with us and to help us. It was usually the war or marriages which caused them to leave, or other opportunities for interesting work. But they always left with what they called their positions, their basic principles, firmly fixed in their minds, their faith confirmed, their lives in a way integrated. They did not go away to make a material success. And certainly there were many happy marriages. At *The Catholic Worker* there is always work for people to do. Peter glorified manual labor and taught what he liked to call his philosophy of labor. Ed Marciniak, one of the Chicago *Catholic Worker* group, began a Labor weekly called *Work*. Ade Bethune wrote a pamphlet WORK, the size of a small book, which has run through many editions. Father Rembert Sorg, the Benedictine from St. Procopius Abbey in Chicago, had written a book called *Towards a Theology of Manual Labor* which has much in it from the early Fathers of the Church. This emphasis on the manual work of the world, which will go on no matter how many machines we may have to lighten labor, made students eager to help with hauling, cleaning, moving, cooking and washing, all the multitude of household tasks that come up about a hospice.

In the early days, every afternoon saw visitors engaged in the work of moving evicted families. Now there are only occasional apartments for rent and occasional movings, but Helen Adler, one of the girls working with us, spent a number of months hunting apartments for women and children who were in the Municipal Lodging House. Charles McCormick, another of our staff, not only moved them but collected furniture from all over Greater New York, to supplement our own old furniture and also to help furnish the homes of the poor. He is kept busy driving to pick up food at the Essex Market, fish at the Fulton Market, or transporting supplies and our home-baked bread from our Staten Island farm to the city.

Selling the paper in front of Macy's or St. Francis Church, or in Times Square or in front of Grand Central Station made one indeed look the fool. It was more natural to sell it along Fourteenth Street or Union Square where people were always selling or giving out literature. Once when we distributed along the water front to longshoremen, publicizing a meeting for longshoremen and seamen, one of them said, "They're always poking stuff at us, papers, posters, leaflets; first it's the Communists and then it's the Jehovah's Witnesses, and now it's the Catholics."

It was a difficult job, giving out literature, or selling the paper on the streets, but when one got used to it there was joy and freedom in it too, and the camaraderie of those who live on the streets and talk to each other freely. We learned their point of view. We were constantly confronted with the fact that on the one hand our daily papers, radio commentators and now television were shaping the minds of the people, and yet they were still responsive to basic and simple religious truths. They were attracted to the good; they were hard-working, struggling human beings living for the day, and afraid of the unknown.

Once that sense of fear of the unknown was overcome, brotherly love would evoke brother love, and mutual love would overcome fear and hatred.

The Communists recognized the power of the press, and also that the simple maxim "go to the people" meant literally going to them. The first time Trotsky was arrested it was for distributing literature at factory gates. When some of our friends were arrested in Chicago at stockyards during an organizational drive, we felt truly revolutionary and effective since organized industry, through the hands of the law which they controlled, had reached out to stop us.

It is easy enough to write and publish a paper and mail it out with the help of volunteers to the four corners of the earth. But it becomes an actual, living thing when you get out on the street corners with the word, as St. Paul did in the early days of Christianity.

MARGARET
BOURKE-WHITE

"Here were faces engraved with the very paralysis of despair . . ."

        Both Dorothy Day and Margaret Bourke-White experienced epiphanies during the thirties, but Bourke-White's was not religious. Before the Depression struck, few would have labeled Margaret Bourke-White a social activist. Instead she was famous as one of America's most daring and glamorous commercial photographers.

 Born in New York City in 1904, the daughter of an inventor of printing equipment, Bourke-White had, by the early twenties, established a national reputation for her striking architectural and industrial photographs. A successful woman in an almost exclusively male profession, she became one of the first photographers hired in 1929 by the newly established Fortune *magazine. Until the mid-thirties she divided her time between lucrative free-lance advertising work and assignments for* Fortune. *Her studio in New York's Chrysler building was the epitome of Art Deco elegance. She filled it with aluminum panels, frosted glass, and a live alligator in a tank.*

As Bourke-White recounts in these pages taken from her autobiography, Portrait of Myself, *an assignment from* Fortune *in 1935 to photograph the Dust Bowl changed her life. This woman, who had previously dressed herself in suits from Paris and moved easily among New York's business elite, was overwhelmed by the suffering she witnessed. She decided that she wanted to produce photographic documents that would spur social change. She wanted to photograph people, not things. In that same year she met the writer Erskine Caldwell, whom she would marry in 1939 and divorce in 1942. Between 1935 and 1937, Bourke-White and Caldwell collaborated on a famous documentary account of sharecropping life in the South,* You Have Seen Their Faces. *She took the photographs and he wrote the text.*

As she notes in this excerpt, she had decided to use the "magic eye of the camera" to document suffering and testify to the need for greater social justice. It was a course she continued for the rest of her life. She was a fearless war photographer who traveled to the Russian front and was one of the first to enter the Nazi death camps at the end of World War II, producing grimly classic images of Buchenwald. She traveled widely for Life *and other magazines, photographing people throughout the world until the ravages of Parkinson's Disease cut short her career in the mid-fifties. But* You Have Seen Their Faces *was to remain her most significant work.*

SOURCES: Margaret Bourke-White published five books of photojournalism in addition to her autobiography. They are *Eyes on Russia* (1931); *Dear Fatherland, Rest Quietly* (1946); *Halfway to Freedom* (1949); *Shooting the Russian War* (1942); and *They Called It "Purple Heart Valley"* (1944). Among several biographies of Bourke-White, the best is Vicki Goldberg's *Margaret Bourke-White: A Biography* (1986), which is based upon hundreds of oral interviews and the Bourke-White papers, housed at the George Arents Research Library at Syracuse University. Other works are Theodore Brown, *Margaret Bourke-White: Photojournalist* (1972) and Jonathan Silverman, *For the World to See: The Life of Margaret Bourke-White* (1983). William Stott's *Documentary Expression and Thirties America* (1973) includes an extensive analysis of Bourke-White's influence on photojournalism during the Depression. Also informative is Robert E. Snyder, "Margaret Bourke-White and the Communist Witch Hunt," *Journal of American Studies*, 19 (April 1985), 5–25, and Theodore M. Brown's essay in *Notable American Women*, 94–95.

O NE STORY WHICH *Fortune* SENT me out to cover was in a sphere quite new to me and left a very deep impression on me. This was the great drought of 1934. Word of its severity came so suddenly, and the reports we had were so scanty, that *Fortune* editors didn't know exactly where the chief areas of the drought were. Omaha, Nebraska, seemed as good a starting point as any, since it was in the middle of the corn belt. I left on three hours' notice and on arrival in Omaha found that the drought extended over a vastly greater area than we had known when I was in New York. It ran from the Dakotas in the North to the Texas panhandle. I was working against a five-day deadline, and it was such an extensive area to cover that I chartered a plane to use for the whole story.

My pilot was a barnstormer of the old school, who earned his livelihood by stunt flying at country fairs. His tiny two-seater was a plane of the old school, too—how old I fortunately did not know until the job was done, when I learned the Curtiss Robin was considered extinct long before the drought reached Nebraska. But luckily, unaware of this, I did not worry on the long hops except about such basic matters as choosing the right place and getting to it in time for the right photographic light, and keeping my film holders freshly loaded and ready for whatever we might meet. The unloading, boxing and reloading was an almost continuous process, which I had to do with my hands and films hidden from the light inside the big black changing bag I carried in my lap. Like woman's work it was never done, and I kept at it whenever we were aloft. The little Robin held up quite well. Crash it finally did, but very gently and only after sundown of my last day. By then I had my pictures and my disturbing memories.

I had never seen landscapes like those through which we flew. Blinding sun beating down on the withered land. Below us the ghostly patchwork of half-buried corn, and the rivers of sand which should have been free-running streams. Sinister spouts of sand wisping up, and then the sudden yellow gloom of curtains of fine-blown soil rising up and trembling in the air. Endless dun-colored acres, which should have been green with crops, carved into dry ripples by the aimless winds.

I had never seen people caught helpless like this in total tragedy. They had no defense. They had no plan. They were numbed like their own dumb animals, and many of these animals were choking and dying in drifting soil. I was deeply moved by the suffering I saw and touched particularly by the bewilderment of the farmers. I think this was the beginning of my awareness of people in a human, sympathetic sense as subjects for the camera and photographed against a wider canvas than I had perceived before. During the rapturous period when I was discovering the beauty of industrial shapes, people were only incidental to me, and in retrospect I believe I had not much feeling for them in my earlier work. But suddenly it was the people who counted. Here in the Dakotas with these farmers, I saw everything in a new light. How could I tell it all in pictures? Here were faces engraved with the very paralysis of despair. These were faces I could not pass by.

It was very hard, after working with the drought and with the people who must weather it through, to return to the advertising world again. . . .

For me this was the turning point. . . . I felt I could never again face a shiny automobile stuffed with vapid smiles. . . .

Then I had a dream. I still remember the mood of terror. Great unfriendly shapes were rushing toward me, threatening to crush me down. As they drew closer, I recognized them as the Buick cars I had been photographing. They were moving toward me in a menacing zigzag course, their giant hoods raised in jagged alarming shapes as though determined to swallow me. Run as fast as I could, I could not escape them. As they moved faster, I began to stumble, and as they towered over me, pushing me down, I woke up to find that I had fallen out of bed and was writhing on the floor with my back strained. I decided that if a mere dream could do this to me, the time had come to get out of this type of photography altogether. If I believed in piloting one's own life, then I should go ahead and pilot mine. Since photography was a craft I respected, let me treat it with respect. I made a resolution that from then on, for the rest of my life, I would undertake only those photographic assignments which I felt could be done in a creative and constructive way.

Later that day the phone rang, and appropriately enough it was one of the advertising agencies. A new job had come up—a series of five pictures to be taken in color. Despite my resolve, it was impossible not to feel some curiosity and I inquired about the fee. The fee was to be $1,000 a photograph. I had never received $1,000 a photograph. I had never received $1,000 for a single picture. I hesitated only a second. It all flooded back, the grotesque unreality, the grief. Why should I go through that again? I found it was not too hard to say, "No, thank you." I recommended another photographer who I thought could do the job well, and I hung up.

Good. I knew now what I would not do, and it was time to figure out what I should do. The drought had been a powerful eye-opener and had shown me that right here in my own country there were worlds about which I knew almost nothing. *Fortune* assignments had given me a magnificent introduction to all sorts of American people. But this time it was not the cross section of industry I wanted. Nor was it the sharp drama of agricultural crisis. It was less the magazine approach and more the book approach I was after. It was based on a great need to understand my fellow Americans better. I felt it should not be an assignment in the ordinary sense but should be as independent of any regular job as my steel mill pictures had been.

What should be the theme, the spine, the unity? I did not consider myself a writer. I felt this book had to be a collaboration between the written word and the image on the celluloid. I needed an author. Yet curiously enough I gave very little thought to what kind of author. I knew it must be someone who was really in earnest about understanding America. But a good writer or a merely competent writer? A novelist or a nonfiction man? A famous author or an obscure one?

To all these things I gave no thought. I simply hoped that I would find the right one.

It seemed a miracle that within a week or two I should hear of an author in search of a photographer. He had a book project in mind in which he wanted to collaborate with a photographer. I gathered he had paid little attention to the possibility that there might be mediocre or gifted photographers in the world. He just wanted to find the right one—someone with receptivity and an open mind, someone who would be as interested as he was in American people, everyday people.

He was a writer whose work had extraordinary vitality, an almost savage power. He was the author of an exceedingly controversial book which had been adapted into an equally controversial play. Among the thousands who had seen the play or read the book were many who considered the characters exaggerated, the situations overdrawn. The author wanted to do a book with pictures that would show the authenticity of the people and conditions about which he wrote. He wanted to take the camera to Tobacco Road. His name was Erskine Caldwell.

I could hardly believe this large shy man with the enormous wrestler's shoulders and quiet coloring could be the fiery Mr. Caldwell. His eyes were the soft rinsed blue of well-worn blue jeans. His hair was carrot—a subdued carrot. The backs of his hands were flecked with cinnamon freckles—cinnamon which had stood long on the kitchen shelf. His whole appearance suggested he was holding himself ready to step back at any moment and blend into the background, where he would remain, patient and invisible, until he had heard what he wanted to hear or experienced what he wanted to experience. Later I learned this was just what he had a special gift for doing. His voice matched his appearance. He spoke softly when he spoke at all.

His seeming mildness and gentleness came as a surprise against the turbulence of his writings. Hoping to ease the painful bashfulness I so strongly felt in him, I suggested it was cocktailtime. No, he seldom drank. This astonished me in the face of the Bacchanalian scenes in his books.

I was equally surprised that, humorist though Caldwell was known to be, his tight-locked face suggested a man who rarely laughs. I remember saying to myself, "This is going to be a colorless and completely impersonal type of man to work with." But I didn't care what he was like as long as we worked well together. I knew (and I knew I wasn't supposed to know) that he did not particularly like my photographs. Caldwell's literary agent thought I should hear the worst before I began, and he told me in secret. Well, that didn't bother me. There were a lot of my pictures I didn't like either—the grinning models, for example.

Another difficulty, and again I was informed in confidence, was that Mr. Caldwell did not like the idea of working with a woman. As a countermeasure he planned to hedge himself in with a second woman, a sort of literary secretary with whom he had worked in Hollywood. She would take shorthand notes of important conversations and keep identification data. (She was to go out of my life as abruptly as she came into it, and I no longer remember much about her except that we called her Sally.) If Erskine Caldwell had further misgivings about my pictures, or about my being a woman, which I could not change, he did not give voice to them. We set a date to start work on the book: June 11, 1936.

June eleventh was five and a half months away. As meticulously as though we were leaving next week, Erskine Caldwell set the details. We would meet in Augusta, Georgia, early in the morning in the lobby of Augusta's best hotel. We would look over the Tobacco Road country and then circle through all the cotton-growing states in the Deep South. Mr. Caldwell expressed the hope that the delay would not inconvenience me. He had several pieces of writing he wanted to finish before we started in on our book project.

I, too, had things to finish and was thankful for the extra time. First I had the trifling item of a penthouse to get rid of. Then, I wanted to make my exit from the advertising business as orderly as possible. Though I had come to dislike advertising, there were a lot of people in advertising whom I liked very much indeed. Especially certain very talented art directors who had taught me a great deal, men such as the many-faceted Gordon Aymar at J. Walter Thompson in the early '30s who had helped me over my earliest advertising hurdles. Then there was the imaginative, humorous and very knowing Chris Christensen of the Kudner Agency, with his tremendous experience in how to use photography. Chris had helped me out of many scrapes, even some occurring outside the work I did for him. Now that I had stepped out from under the perpetual crises in this turbulent world, I wanted to lay my advertising jobs to rest in seemly tranquility.

The chores of disengaging myself from my immediate past were moving so smoothly that I found I had time to slip away to South America, to take pictures for an educational project on coffee growing. I came back from this pleasant South American interlude refreshed and with my spirit restored.

I returned to spectacular news. We were going to have a new magazine. The idea had been germinating at *Time* and *Fortune* for some time, but now it was to be a reality. The new baby magazine had as yet no name, and its form was amorphous but the direction was clear. It would tell the news in pictures, but it would try to go much further than that by illuminating the background that made the news.

I remember the excitement with which Ralph Ingersoll took me to "21" and told me about it. Ingersoll had been appointed *Fortune*'s editor when Lloyd-Smith had left that post vacant by his suicide. In recent years, Ralph had become Harry Luce's chief assistant and this new magazine was his special charge. It was midafternoon, and "21" was almost empty and very quiet. We sat in a shadowy corner and both talked our heads off for the rest of the day.

As when *Fortune* was in the planning stage, now again with this new unnamed magazine waiting to be born, I could almost feel the horizon widening and the great rush of wind sweeping in. This was the kind of magazine that could be anything we chose to make it. It should help interpret human situations by showing the larger world into which people fitted. It should show our developing, exploding, contrary world and translate it into pictures through those little black boxes we photographers had been carrying around for so long. The new magazine would absorb everything we photographers had to give: all the understanding we were capable of, all the speed in working, the imagination, the good luck; everything we could bring to bear would be swallowed up in every piece of work we did. And then, under the stress of it all, we would go out and push back those horizons even farther and come back with something new. I know nothing more satisfying than the opportunity to lay a few small foundation pebbles when a new magazine is about to be born. Lucky me, to have had this rewarding experience twice in my lifetime.

This was a year unlike any year I have ever lived through. Perhaps the very fact of having made a definite choice in my own life had cleared the way so I could be receptive to the best of everything that came: the wonderful opportunity to work with Erskine Caldwell on the book and now this splendid advent of a new magazine which would set its stamp deep on photography, just as we photographers, to some extent, would set our stamp on the young, elastic publication. My cup was running over.

Publication date for the nameless magazine was still more than half a year away, but the office was a beehive. Experimental layouts were being drawn up all over the place, and all sorts of pictures were being swept into them. Pictures representing everything, in my case, even some photographs I had taken of the Olympic contenders including the great Jesse Owens and the equally great Glenn Cunningham under training as they prepared to go overseas for the Olympic games. I had taken them for a news agency, but this did not mean that I was trying to become a sports photographer. I remember Harry Luce's surprised expression.

"Why, Maggie, I see you are taking sports pictures now."

It was fun for me to see them going into a layout.

The budding magazine took over my darkroom equipment: the sinks, the enlargers, the sharp cutting knives, the tanks, the dryers. These became the nucleus of its first photo lab.

With me, in the great transfer, went four former members of my staff: Oscar Graubner, who for the first several years of the magazine was chief of the photo lab; Cornelius Wells, a youthful lab assistant; Thomas Styles, an excellent printer and enlarger; and, most important, my secretary, Peggy Smith Sargent, destined to rise high in the responsible and difficult job of film editor for *Life*. She had come from the Pacific coast, where she had worked for a Hollywood director, and was in New York looking for a job. I remember she came up to my studio dressed in a brilliant green suit. It was in the middle of one of our advertising crises, with phones ringing on all sides, and no one had time to answer them. Nor did anyone have time to interview her. Miss Smith, which then she was, sat down to answer the phones, and from then on, one could hardly remember a time when she hadn't been there. . . .

When it took over the photographic equipment and the staff members from my studio, there was one thing the new magazine definitely did not want to acquire, and that was my pair of alligators which had grown to be enormous and savage. The magazine promised to find homes for them, and in no time at all they had run down satisfactory housing arrangements in an experimental school.

There were also some assorted turtles. Peggy, who had a personal friendship with the turtles (they had lived under her desk and bumped into her legs and taken lettuce leaves from her noonday sandwiches), felt they were her responsibility. She investigated fountains and decided the one at the Loew's Lexington movie theater was the most suitable. She paced the grandiose lobby, waiting for a moment when all the people present seemed to be looking in another direction. The moment came, she hurried to the splendid fountain and slipped in her reptilian load. It was only later that she found out that all but one were land turtles.

Finally the anonymous stranger to whom we had all pledged our allegiance found a name. There had been a number of suggestions, each one more cumbersome and unwieldy than the last. The closest candidate was "The March of Time," a name that had been used for Time Inc.'s newsreel. Publication date was drawing closer, and nobody had the ghost of an idea what to christen the infant soon to be born. Then, at just the perfect moment in time and space, the venerable magazine of humor, *Life*, was about to declare itself out of business and was searching for a buyer. Harry Luce hesitated not one moment. He bought the magazine only for its name. The new magazine would be called *Life*. Of its staff only two were transferred to the new *Life*—Bernard Meurich, a C.P.A., and his sister, Madeline Auerbach, whom all of us find charming even though it is she through whom we channel our expense accounts.

In the midst of all this happy activity of preparation, one thing pleased me above all others, the fact that my new editors-to-be, Dan Longwell and John Billings, were much interested in the collaboration between Erskine Caldwell and myself and were enthusiastic about the possibility of running a spread of our book in the magazine.

As with any change of direction in one's life, there were a thousand insistent last-minute details. I wanted so much to come to the book project with all the mind and ideas and serenity that I was capable of. A few more days would wind up everything. After all, it was nearly half a year ago that we had set our starting date. Maybe Mr. Caldwell also had extra things to do; I could always ask.

Through his agent, I learned that Mr. Caldwell was already in Georgia, staying at his father's house in the tiny town of Wrens. I phoned Wrens and got Erskine Caldwell on the line. I explained about the new magazine starting and all the circumstances and said, if it was all the same to him, I would like to have one more week. Instead of the eleventh, could we begin, say, the eighteenth? The frozen wordlessness at the end of the line conveyed to me we might never begin at all. I could hardly believe it. Heavens, I had been planning toward this for all these months! Several long telephone conversations between the literary agent in New York and Mr. Caldwell in Georgia verified my fears. It was all off. At least, it was off until some mythical time when it would be "more convenient" for all parties. I was sure that meant off, period.

What had I done, what had I done! To me it seemed not unreasonable that a date made half a year ahead, with a trip to another hemisphere in between, could be just a little bit elastic. To wreck the entire plan because I had requested postponement for a few days! But reasonable or unreasonable, that was not the point. To have our idea die stillborn, that I could not bear. With Erskine Caldwell already down South and just around the corner from Tobacco Road, there was nowhere unobtrusively to corner him for a little heart-to-heart chat. It was plain that I had worn out my welcome on the telephone. All means of communication seemed to have failed me.

I did the only thing I could think of to do. It was a long chance, but I would try. First I must rule out of my mind every thought except of things I absolutely had to do before leaving New York. I went ahead just as I had planned. It took a tight-packed four days. I had kept clothes and cameras packed, and when my chores were done, I jumped on the plane at midnight.

The hot sun was rising as we landed at Augusta, Georgia. I checked into the shiny, newly varnished "best" hotel and found, on inquiry, that Wrens was six miles away. Over my breakfast I composed a letter as quiet in tone as I could make it. I had come in the hope we could reconsider. I so wanted to start our important work with the slate wiped clean so that I could give my entire attention to this project of ours. Everything was in order now. Summer would be without interruption. I hoped he would believe me and see that I was deeply sincere in wanting to do the book and do it as well as it could possibly be done. I added that I would be at the hotel in case he wanted to send me a message.

I tried unsuccessfully to get a Western Union messenger. The one mail delivery a day did not leave until afternoon, and I wanted Mr. Caldwell to get my note early in the day. I finally secured the personal services of a young lad who swept out the post office. The idea of going on his bicycle to deliver the letter in exchange for five dollars seemed fine to him, as it did to me, and I sat on the porch of the hotel watching him pedal furiously away until he disappeared in his own trailing plume of dust.

It was still not quite eight o'clock. The day dragged on. There were dull-looking movies, but I dared not leave the hotel to go to them. Normally I love walking down Main Street in a town where I have never been before, window-shopping and strolling around the drugstore. But today I dared not take my eyes off the telephone operator at the hotel desk. I thought I would never escape this day, which showed no sign of ending. At six o'clock in the evening, a large figure in a loose blue jacket came into the lobby. His face was flushed with sun and shyness. We went into the coffee shop, sat down at the counter and ordered hot coffee. While we waited to be served, Erskine Caldwell looked quietly down at his hands. We drank our coffee in wordless communication. When the last drop was drained, Erskine turned to me and smiled.

"That was a big argument, wasn't it?"

I nodded.

"When do you want to leave?"

"Now."

And so we did.

We drove until midnight and then checked in at a small hotel which we were lucky enough to find open. I remember my midnight impression—the wide porch of graying woodwork, square-cut wooden pillars a bit off plumb. Plainly the home of some departed family had been salvaged to make the little hotel. A soft damp breeze touching me everywhere like the moist palm of a warm hand made me sleepily and pleasurably aware I was in the Deep South. I was in a new land, a land that had a pace of its own. Its own special enchantment hung over it.

In the morning this film of mystery was dispelled, and the rather ramshackle building where we had spent the night was much like a hundred others which one sees throughout the South. Erskine drove his Ford to the front of the hotel and started loading up. The residents of the town from one end of the short main street to the other gathered to see the largest stack of assorted baggage the townspeople had ever known to be packed away in a single automobile. Sally, the literary secretary, refereed the operation efficiently. She supervised a small squad of bellhops out of uniform as they tucked valises, cameras, lighting equipment, sweaters, films and tripods into every inch of the car except the front seat and a kind of nook in the back seat amidst the precarious towers of luggage. Someone would have to sit there. Sally volunteered.

"I'm the hired help," she said. "Hired help sits at second table. I'll sit in the back seat."

I fear no one contradicted her, not even out of politeness.

Just before the takeoff, I leaped out of my front seat and ran back to the trunk compartment to check the position of two glass jars containing egg cases of the praying mantis. I was photographing the life cycle of the mantes, and since they were due to emerge soon— only the mantes knew when—I dared not leave them behind. While I was tucking them in so they would ride smoothly, the lid of the trunk came down on my head. Not hard enough to do any real damage, but hard enough to make me want to avoid trunk lids from then on.

Erskine gave a delighted chuckle. Why, he can laugh after all, I said to myself, and Erskine said, "I hope something funny happens every day like a trunk lid coming down on Margaret's head."

I could think of no suitable reply, but inwardly I thought, after all, I'd been ready to trade in almost anything for the opportunity to work on this book, and if getting whammed on the head with the rear end of a car was part of the price of admission, I guessed I could take that too.

For the next several days we took a meandering course off the beaten highways from Georgia to Arkansas. During this time I was groping to read the mind of this enigma of a man. I wished I could divine how he "saw" the broader outlines of the book. Certainly the material was very rich and to me quite fresh and new. And yet I like to have the feeling of architecture while I work—of shaping up a group of photographs so that they form a meaningful whole. I was sure Erskine had the same feeling, but he did not talk about it readily. Several times he asked me if I had suggestions. I wished I knew enough to make suggestions. I was just getting my bearings. But if I was not making suggestions, I was making a very careful study of my author-partner, trying to guess what was in his mind. In this field of trying to guess what's in the mind of a quiet man, I felt relatively competent, for this was an area in which my silent father had given me a lot of practice. I longed for the time, which I was sure was not far away, when my horizon would be widened by looking through the eyes of another, as people do who work in partnership. Meanwhile, I was happy to be moving in a sphere which seemed both so worthwhile and so promising.

We had been on the road for four days when we reached Little Rock, Arkansas. On the morning of the fifth day, Erskine came up to my room, as he always did, to help me down with my cameras. But this time he wanted to have a talk. I remember how we sat down on the wide windowsill of my second-floor room overlooking a street lined with shade trees. Erskine told me what was on his mind. He said he didn't think we were getting anything accomplished. He felt like a tourist guide just showing somebody around. He thought we should give the whole thing up.

I was thunderstruck. How could I have been so obtuse as not to even guess things were so far off the track? I tried desperately to tell him how much this meant to me, this opportunity to do something worthwhile, but I wasn't making much sense, because, of course, I was crying. Then suddenly something very unexpected happened. He fell in love with me. From then onward, everything worked out beautifully.

Something unexpected happened on the sixth day too. At the hotel desk, Erskine received the surprising information that "the other young lady" had checked out at three o'clock in the morning. There was a note.

Sally explained she was tired of sitting in the back seat. She could work with one temperamental writer, or one temperamental photographer, she wrote, but nobody could compel her to put up with two temperamental artists in the same automobile in the summertime in Arkansas.

From now on there were no more surprises, except personal and pleasant ones. The work was flowing along, a wide stream, with the deepening understanding between us.

Whether he was aware of it or not, Erskine Caldwell was introducing me to a whole new way of working. He had a very quiet, completely receptive approach. He was interested not only in the words a person spoke, but in the mood in which they were spoken. He would wait patiently until the subject had revealed his personality, rather than impose his own personality on the subject, which many of us have a way of doing. Many times I watched the process through which Erskine became acquainted with some farmer and the farmer's problems.

Erskine would be hanging over the back fence, and the farmer would be leaning on his rake, the two engaged in what I suppose could be called a conversation—that is, either Erskine or the farmer made one remark every fifteen minutes. Despite the frugal use of words, the process seemed productive of understanding on both sides. While this interchange went on, I lurked in the background with a small camera, not stealing pictures exactly, which I seldom do, but working on general scenes as unobtrusively as possible. Once Erskine and a farmer had reached a kind of rapport, I could close in quite freely for portraits, and perhaps we would be invited into the tiny one-room sharecropper's home, which gave me a chance to photograph an interior.

Erskine had a gift, over and above the Southern tongue with which he was born, for picking up the shade and degree of inflection characteristic of the state in which we were working. His proficiency surprised me because he was uninterested in music. But in this he had a musician's ear. This was a useful talent in an area in which you are considered an alien and treated with appropriate distrust if you come from only as far away as across the state line. The people we were seeking out for pictures were generally suspicious of strangers. They were afraid we were going to try to sell them something they didn't want and fearful we were taking their pictures only to ridicule them. Reassuring them was a very important part of our operations, and a reassuring voice in their own mode of speech eliminated many a barrier. Of course, no amount of doctoring could disguise my mode of speech. I was unmistakably a Yankee, "down South on her vacation," Erskine would say. I could be labeled only as a foreigner, and sometimes I am afraid I acted like one.

I remember one occasion when we went into a cabin to photograph a Negro woman who lived there. She had thick, glossy hair, and I had decided to take her picture as she combed it. She had a bureau made of a wooden box with a curtain tacked to it and lots of little homemade things. I rearranged everything. After we left, Erskine spoke to me about it. How neat her bureau had been. How she must have valued all her little possessions and how she had them tidily arranged *her* way, which was not my way. This was a new point of view to me. I felt I had done violence.

As we penetrated the more destitute regions of the South, I was struck by the frequent reminders I found of the advertising world I thought I had left behind. Here the people really used the ads. They plastered them directly on their houses to keep the wind out. Some sharecropper shacks were wrapped so snugly in huge billboard posters advertising magic pain-killers and Buttercup Snuff that the home itself disappeared from sight. The effect was bizarre.

And inside, the effect was equally unexpected. The walls from floor to ceiling were papered in old newspapers and colorful advertising pages torn from magazines. Very practical, Erskine explained to me. Good as insulation against either heat or chill, and it's clean and can be replaced for next to nothing. I had the uneasy feeling that if I explored around enough, I would find advertisements I had done myself.

I remember a little girl named Begonia, with whom I struck up a kind of friendship. When I asked how big her family was, she informed me she had a "heap" of brothers and sisters but hadn't ever counted them. Among the uncounted, I learned, was her twin sister. They went to school on alternate days so as to share their single nondescript coat and their one pair of shoes. And here, right behind Begonia's wistful little face as she told me this, was this spectacular and improbable background showing all the world's goods. Begonia and her sister could look their walls over and find a complete range of shoes, jackets and coats. But never would they find that real coat and real pair of shoes which would take the second twin to school.

The Buttercup Snuff advertised on the outside of their house—that they would have. In an impoverished Southern household, snuff is frequently bought ahead of food. It dulls the pain of aching teeth and empty stomachs as well.

As we drove off, I glanced back over my shoulder. The snuff-wrapped shack looked like an immense cocoon which I felt might at any moment hatch a giant bug that would walk away with the house.

Cocoons were on my mind. At my side in the front seat I carried the glass bottles I had cared for so tenderly, each with its twig bearing a praying-mantis egg case the size of a golf ball. Ever since my childhood days when raising insect pets had been my hobby, I had wanted to take pictures of the metamorphosis of insects, and now with the new magazine coming out, I was glad that I had elicited Mr. Billings's interest in photographs of the life cycle of this dramatic insect. I was especially anxious to catch this hatching, because of a small tragedy which took place just before I left New York, wiping out a whole generation of mantes. The massacre occurred when writers, researchers and layout men were just settling into *Life*'s new offices, and the place was a whirlwind of plaster and paint. The exterminator arrived, someone jerked a careless thumb, and by mistake he went into the office I was using to house my praying mantes. Five egg cases had hatched during the night, and I came in to find piles of the fragile miniature creatures, perhaps a thousand, lying on desks, chairs, bookshelves, the floor, each one perfectly formed but rigid as a wire hairpin.

So it was natural that I should look down at frequent intervals to check the precious cargo. Emerging insects wait for no man. Following a mysterious timetable which only praying mantes can read, some minute weather change may unlock the door of the tough cocoon case, and out they come. Fortunately, when the first baby mantis wrestled its way free, we were on a back country road with a split-log fence perfect for holding the egg cases in position. I began to photograph the pouring river of midget creatures. Slithering out of their protective sheaths, they began climbing with great effort on their new and tender legs, dragging themselves upward on the shoulders of their brothers till they reached the upper air with its space and light. There they rested, some two hundred of them, each smaller than your fingernail.

I, too, rested and, looking up, saw we were surrounded by a solemn ring of little children who had collected silently to watch and now began delightedly singing out, "Look at the little devil horses! Oh, look at the little devil horses!"

I was glad my insects had hatched out here so I could learn this charming name for them.

I received a new name too. I have been Peggy or Maggie to friends and colleagues, but Erskine, wanting his own name for me, called me Kit, because he said I had the contented expression of a kitten that has just swallowed a bowl of cream.

Finding a nickname for Erskine Caldwell was much harder. Nothing can be made out of "Erskine" but Skinny, and even though he was anything but skinny, he had been called that by everyone most of his life. I disliked the name and searched for another. We tried "Skeats" for a while, but it never seemed to belong to him. Skinny he was and Skinny he remains.

Skinny and I hoped to find a chain gang somewhere on the road. One could never get any precise information. There were just enough objectors to the idea of chaining men together like teams of oxen to make a sheriff think twice before helping a photographer find such a controversial subject. So when Erskine and I were exploring some back-country roads one day and rounded a curve, all but running down a chain gang in tattered stripes, we were lucky indeed. They were chained man to man, each with his soup spoon tucked in his iron ankle cuff. The sudden sight was almost too theatrical to believe. They looked as though they had strayed from an M-G-M group on location.

Our reception was just as theatrical. The very unpleasant captain of the gang demanded our permit to photograph chain gangs, and began waving his shotgun wildly at us and shouting threats. When he yelled that he would blow off our tires, Skinny and I left, and returned, driving past in a zigzag course. The captain fired several rounds toward the wheels of the car. Whether they missed by design or accident, we decided this was the time to try to get a permit. Erskine recalled that an acquaintance of his school days had become a political personage in a town not far away. The handy friend took us in to see the Commissioner, and when we left, we carried a document which was fine indeed with stamps and seals. As we drove back to our location, I decided I could risk my right arm by hanging it out of the window and waving our license like a flag of truce. The captain looked at the document with rage on his face and felt the seals with an exploring thumb.

"The Commissioner, what the hell," he hissed, "he knows I don't know how to read."

So it was up to us to read and reread the permit aloud with such dramatic expression there was nothing the captain could do except allow us to bring out cameras and take photographs.

Twenty years later, while working on *Life*'s segregation story in the South, I found the road gangs again. Little had changed except for one detail. I had never before heard of segregated chain gangs. But now there were black chain gangs and white chain gangs. A newly arrived prisoner could shoulder his pickax and take his place on the road with the comforting assurance that the convicts with whom he would be so intimately bound would match him in skin color.

Anyone who has driven through the Deep South is familiar with the religious signs which punctuate the highways. We wanted to take a look at the religion behind the road signs. With the Negro churches

Margaret Bourke-White

this was easy and pleasant. Visitors were always welcome, even a visitor who came loaded with cameras. There was sure to be good hymn-singing and a fire-eating preacher. When the fiery sermon whipped up the parishioners to fever pitch and left them thrashing about on the floor in a religious frenzy, it all seemed close to some tribal ritual, as though the worshipers still answered to the rhythm of the jungle.

There is a white counterpart which fewer people know, furtive, shamefaced and hidden. Visitors are unwelcome. The churches are hard to find. It was something of an achievement when Erskine and I discovered the Holiness Church with a small, all-white congregation in a stony South Carolina town. The church matched the town— bleak and built of splintery boards which had never been painted. We made our great find on a Sunday morning. Everyone was already in church. I tucked a small camera into my jacket, and Erskine filled his pockets with flashbulbs. Finding the church door locked from the inside, we leaped through the open window and started taking pictures at once, Erskine changing flashbulbs as though he had been assisting a photographer all his life.

It was a strange little scene. Women were careening about in their cotton print dresses, and several times they nearly threw me off my feet and all but knocked my camera out of my hands as they waved their Bibles and shrieked their "Praise Be's." The worshipers were running the whole gamut of religious frenzy from exaltation to torpor. Some were writhing on the floor in that state of religious ecstasy known as "coming through." The minister, having whipped up his flock to this peak of hysteria, was overcome with exhaustion and sank down on the platform of his pulpit, where he held his head in his hands. Both men and women began rolling about on the floor, chanting their "Amens" in voices fading from hoarseness. Finally, the hallelujahs began dying away, and each amen was fainter than the last. The minister was beginning to stir in his coma. Plainly the time had come to leave. We sailed out through the windows the way we had come in, and in a matter of minutes we were out of town. I was amazed that we had been able to bring it off successfully. There was one item of my photographic equipment which I believe helped us. Synchronized flashbulbs in 1936 were somewhat new to photographers and new enough to me so that I underexposed some of the pictures, and only Oscar, working in the darkroom, managed to salvage a few of them. Certainly a backwoods congregation had never seen flashbulbs. Under the sway of the sermon with its fearful warnings of hell and all who did not mend their sinful ways, these worshipers must have thought we were avenging angels come down in a blaze of light in direct response to their preacher's fiery words.

Long after the excitement of jumping through the church windows to get the pictures has mellowed down in memory, I find myself still thinking of that bleak and splintery church on its plot of stony ground. The pitiful masquerade of religion I witnessed there has left its vivid image deep in my mind. It is obvious this shoddy little ceremonial, re-enacted each week in the name of religion, was the very antithesis of religion, but to me it is full of meaning. It illuminates the spiritual poverty of people who have no other emotional release, no relaxation and laughter, no movies or books and, far worse, no educational or other inner equipment with which to change the course of their meaningless lives. Worshipers come to church, bowed down with problems, and are given the church floor on which to throw themselves and drown their troubles in religious ecstasy every Sunday morning. Seen in the context of this barren existence, the drab little church is an ironic symbol.

Many times in sharecropper country, my thoughts went back to the Dakotas, where the farmers were stricken with the drought. Their very desperation had jolted me into the realization that a man is more than a figure to put into the background of a photograph for scale. The drought-ridden farmers had contributed to my education in a human direction, and here with the sharecroppers, I was learning that to understand another human being you must gain some insight into the conditions which made him what he is. The people and the forces which shape them: each holds the key to the other. These are relationships that can be studied and photographed.

I began watching for the effect of events on human beings. I was awakening to the need of probing and learning, discovering and interpreting. I realized that any photographer who tries to portray human beings in a penetrating way must put more heart and mind into his preparation than will ever show in any photograph.

Back in New York, Erskine took me to the theater to see *Tobacco Road*. He made a practice of dropping in at widely spaced intervals, particularly when new actors replaced the old, which had to happen now and then because of the play's phenomenally long run. (One actor had actually died onstage.) When *Tobacco Road* reached the end of the road, it had chalked up more than 3,000 performances in New York City alone, and such odd mementos from the stage sets as a well, a shack, and a wagon wheel had gone to the Smithsonian Institution.

Between the acts we ran into a friend of mine from Atlanta who was a typical Southerner, if I ever saw one. I introduced him to Mr. Erskine Caldwell, but it was obvious as he talked that he did not realize he was speaking to the author. Sam explained he had heard so much about the play, he thought he ought to come and see for himself whether it was true or false. "Because I come from just that part of Georgia," said Sam, "I would know better than anybody."

"How do you find the play?" I asked.

"Oh, it's greatly overrated," said Sam. "It's not true to life at all, it's greatly exaggerated." And, muttering, "greatly overrated" to himself, Sam went happily back to pull the second act apart, all unknowing that he had been expressing his opinions to the man who started it all.

Erskine was pleased. It is very seldom, he told me, that you have the opportunity to hear critical or derogatory remarks face to face. In the early years of the play, he used to skulk around between acts hoping to overhear adverse reactions.

"You don't learn much from praise," he said. "You learn from adverse criticism. If people are aroused and angry and take the trouble to let you know about it, you know you've made a dent. If it doesn't evoke any reaction, what use is it? If a book or play evokes a strong reaction, that's one of the highest tributes your work can have."

We plunged into writing captions for the book, and ours was a real collaboration. We did not want the matter of whether the pictures "illustrated" the text, or the words explained the pictures, to have any importance. We wanted a result in which the pictures and words truly supplemented one another, merging into a unified whole. We had a kind of ritual about this. We would arrange eight pictures in the middle of the floor. We backed away and, sitting against the wall separately, wrote tentative captions and then put them side by side to see what we had. Many times the final caption was a combination of the two—the thought mine and the words Erskine's, or vice versa. Occasional captions were all mine, and I was proud indeed when either my thought or my way of expressing the subject stood up in the final test. But it made no difference who contributed what, because by now we were sure that the book had unity.

"This book has to have a title, you know," Skinny said one day.

I had been so deep in finishing the pictorial touches that actually I had never given any thought to the title. But Skinny had. In fact, the title came to his mind two years before he met me. I learned what it was only when we went to see Viking Press, the publishers. I still recall the little scene vividly: the rather severe vestibule of the office, the exhilaration of completing a big piece of work which was a milestone in my life.

"The title is *You Have Seen Their Faces*," said Skinny. "How do you like it?"

The name implied just what I had been searching for as I worked. Faces that would express what we wanted to tell. Not just the unusual or striking face, but *the* face that would speak out the message from the printed page.

Since Skinny valued brickbats above praise, I was glad for his sake that when the book came out, a fair number of them appeared in the book reviews. There was the editor of a South Carolina newspaper who called the book "a new slander on the South." There was the reviewer who advised Mr. Caldwell "to go back to his novelistic knitting." And the commentator who, choking on his own vituperative prose, ended up, "Fie on Mr. Caldwell!" And since we were rating brickbats so high, I was glad to get my share of them too. There were many variations of the question which all serious photographers are asked in many forms: Why take pictures of the bad things in life? Why not find something more pleasant to photograph?

The version I enjoyed most came from an interior-decoration

magazine which scolded me for taking pictures of sharecroppers' tumbledown shacks: Why didn't I choose some modern living room which would certainly be decorated in better taste and more typically American?

The most intriguing comment of all came in the form of a letter which started out: "Margaret Bourke-White is a Yankee and doesn't know any better, but Erskine Caldwell is a born Southerner and he *does* know better." It went on to accuse Mr. Caldwell of building a stage set of the church, hiring actors and bringing me South to photograph the performance.

The other side of the ledger was more crowded. I don't think either of us was prepared—certainly I wasn't—for the wide response the book received. The editorial page of the Philadelphia *Record* reminded its readers that "it was a book—Uncle Tom's Cabin—that roused the world to the menace of slavery." There is today another kind of slavery, the editorial pointed out, "and there is no better way to gain an understanding of it than by slowly turning the disquieting pages of this book."

It was high praise when Harry Hansen wrote in the *World-Telegram*, "The pictures have the quality of the very finest portraits. They depict man and the intention of his soul." I hoped to continue to earn it. In any case it was a clear and even inspiring statement of what I wanted my camera to do in the years to come.

Erskine and I were particularly happy when reviewers treated the book in terms of collaboration, as did Malcolm Cowley who wrote, "This book belongs to a new art, one that has to be judged by different standards," and the *Boston Transcript* which wrote, "This is the South seen through the magic bitterness of text and the magic eye of a camera." This was just what I had hoped—that through the fusion of words and pictures, we would create something new.

PART TWO

In the Government

FRANCES
PERKINS

"There was no special deference because I was a woman..."

Frances Perkins's term in office as the nation's first woman cabinet official did not begin well. Organized labor, never very welcoming to women, was faced with a female Secretary of Labor who had never joined a union, and its leaders were furious. William Green, president of the American Federation of Labor, declared that "labor can never become reconciled to the selection." It is a testament to Perkins's great skills as a politician, mediator, and negotiator that such a bumpy start did not lead to a quick resignation. In fact, of Franklin Roosevelt's original cabinet, only she and Secretary of the Interior Harold Ickes remained to serve FDR throughout his four terms, from 1933 until 1945.

Born in 1880, Perkins, the daughter of a Boston merchant, belonged to an

*influential first generation of highly educated middle-class women who helped
to shape a number of emerging new professions such as social work. By 1910,
armed with a master's degree in economics from Columbia University, she had
launched a career as an activist and social reformer which would lead to
decades of government service at state and national levels.*

*Hired in 1910 as Secretary of the New York Consumers League, Perkins
lobbied for health and hours legislation to improve conditions for factory
workers. Her marriage to another economist, Paul Wilson, in 1913, and the
birth of a daughter in 1916 led Perkins to retire from paid employment, but
she continued to put in long hours as a volunteer for reform groups and for the
Democratic party. Her assumption of the traditional path which society
assigned a married middle-class woman with a young child was, however, to
be brief. After only a few years of marriage, Paul Wilson began to suffer
increasingly severe bouts of depression. By the early 1920s his mental
instability prevented him from holding a full-time position. He was periodically institutionalized for long periods of time, and, until his death in 1952,
Frances Perkins was the family's breadwinner.*

*In 1922, New York Governor Alfred E. Smith, for whom Perkins had
campaigned, appointed her to the New York State Industrial Board, which
administered the state's workmen's compensation program. By 1928 Perkins
had become one of Smith's key labor advisers, rising to the position of
industrial commissioner of New York. Al Smith's successor, Franklin Roosevelt,
retained Perkins in that post during his two terms as governor from
1929–1933 and then, in 1933, brought her with him to Washington as his
controversial new Secretary of Labor.*

*It was as Secretary of Labor that Perkins achieved national prominence.
She used the position as a pulpit from which to preach for a social welfare
agenda that included increased government guarantees of the rights of unions
and government involvement in wage-and-hours standards, workmen's compensation, and unemployment insurance. She was a chief architect of such
important legislation as the Social Security Act.*

*Although Perkins served Harry Truman as a member of the U.S. Civil
Service Commission, she remained most closely identified with her years of
government service under Franklin Roosevelt. Publicly always extremely
self-effacing, she chose to write a memoir about him,* The Roosevelt I
Knew, *rather than a formal autobiography. Published in 1946, as Perkins
was easing out of government work and preparing to accept the Cornell*

University professorship she held until her death in 1965, The Roosevelt I Knew *reveals as much about its author as it does about its stated subject. In the excerpts presented below, Perkins discusses her appointment to the cabinet and her role as an agitator for the rights of workers in the establishment of the NRA Steel Codes. These codes of fair practices were authorized under Title I of the National Industrial Recovery Act of 1933 and administered by the National Recovery Administration. Section 7a of Title I presumably gave workers the right to organize and bargain collectively, but it was often evaded by employers. When the NRA was judged unconstitutional by the Supreme Court, labor's organizational and bargaining rights were established by the Wagner Labor Relations Act of 1935. The Fair Labor Standards Act (wages-and-hours law) of 1938 also reenacted a section of the NIRA as a separate measure. Two surges of labor action, encouraged by 7a and the Wagner Act, respectively, occurred in 1934 and 1937. The NRA codes that Perkins refers to are also mentioned in selections following by Mary Anderson, Lucy Randolph Mason, and Mary Heaton Vorse.*

Perkins's self-portrait reveals a bright, tough idealist, not the official whom the New York Times *once condemned as a "colorless woman who talked as if she swallowed a press release."*

SOURCES: The best biography of Frances Perkins is George Martin's *Madame Secretary: Frances Perkins* (1976). Other information about Perkins can be found in Charles Trout's essay on her in *Notable American Women*, 535–539. Roy Lubove discusses her crucial role in the passage of the Social Security Act in *The Struggle for Social Security* (1968). Susan Ware's *Beyond Suffrage: Women in the New Deal* (1981) sees her as an important figure in the era's "Women's Network." Perkins's papers are divided between the Schlesinger Library, Radcliffe College, and the Franklin Roosevelt Presidential Library, Hyde Park, New York. The Columbia University Archives also house a five-thousand-page transcript of extensive interviews conducted with Perkins before her death. Winifred D. Wandersee is at work on a biography of Frances Perkins.

ONE MORNING LATE IN FEB-
ruary 1933 Roosevelt's secretary phoned and asked me to call at the
East 65th Street house that evening. My appointment was for eight,
but I arrived early.

The place was a shambles. Ever since the nomination six months
before, a great many visitors, from cranks to persons destined to play
important roles in the Roosevelt administration, had converged on
the house for conferences or to seek favors from the President-elect.
The press had established a base of operations on the first floor.

The constant flow of visitors left the small staff of servants power-
less to retain any semblance of order. Furniture was broken. Rugs
were rolled up and piled in a corner. Overshoes and muddy rubbers
were in a heap near the door. The floor was littered with newspapers.
Trunks were jammed into one corner, and in another stood boxes
containing Roosevelt's papers which had just been sent down from
Albany and had to be sorted and filed for reshipment to Washington.

I made my way to the comfortable second floor where Roosevelt
had his study. I was greeted by a secretary, who asked me to have a
seat. A stocky blond man whom I did not know was sitting on a sofa.
Shortly he was invited into Mr. Roosevelt's study. Finally my turn came.

Roosevelt gave me a friendly greeting and, extending his hand
toward the stocky blond man, said, "Frances, don't you know Harold?"

"Shall I just call him Harold or do you want to tell me his last name?"

"It's Ickes," he laughed. "Harold L. Ickes."

That was my introduction to the only person other than myself who
was to serve in the Roosevelt cabinet from its first to its last days. Ickes

had been practicing law in the Middle West. A former leader of the Progressive party, he had done yeoman work for Roosevelt in the campaign. Now he agreed to serve as Secretary of the Interior.

After Ickes left, Roosevelt came right to the point. "I've been thinking things over and I've decided I want you to be Secretary of Labor."

His words came as no great surprise to me. The newspapers had been speculating on this for days. Moreover, I knew that he wanted to establish the precedent of appointing a woman to his cabinet. Since the call from his secretary, I had been going over arguments to convince him that he should not appoint me.

I led off with my chief argument, that I was not a bona fide labor person. I pointed out that labor had always had, and would expect to have, one of its own people as Secretary. Roosevelt's answer was that it was time to consider all working people, organized and unorganized.

I told him that it might be a good thing to have a woman in the cabinet if she were best for the job, but I thought a woman Secretary of Labor ought to be a labor woman. He replied he had considered that and was going on my record as Industrial Commissioner of New York. He said he thought we could accomplish for the nation the things we had done for the state.

Since I seemed to be making little headway, I tried a new approach. I said that if I accepted the position of Secretary of Labor I should want to do a great deal. I outlined a program of labor legislation and economic improvement. None of it was radical. It had all been tried in certain states and foreign countries. But I thought that Roosevelt might consider it too ambitious to be undertaken when the United States was deep in depression and unemployment.

In broad terms, I proposed immediate federal aid to the states for direct unemployment relief, an extensive program of public works, a study and an approach to the establishment by federal law of minimum wages, maximum hours, true unemployment and old-age insurance, abolition of child labor, and the creation of a federal employment service.

The program received Roosevelt's hearty endorsement, and he told me he wanted me to carry it out.

"But," I said, "have you considered that to launch such a program we must think out, frame, and develop labor and social legislation, which then might be considered unconstitutional?"

"Well, that's a problem," Mr. Roosevelt admitted, "but we can work out something when the time comes."

And so I agreed to become Secretary of Labor after a conversation that lasted but an hour.

On Sunday, March 5, Mr. Justice Cardozo of the Supreme Court administered the oath of office to the new cabinet, and we solemnly swore "to support and defend the Constitution of the United States."

I was apprehensive and on guard at the first official cabinet meeting. As the only woman member, I did not want my colleagues to get the impression that I was too talkative. I resolved not to speak unless asked to do so. We sat stiffly and solemnly; we were not yet entirely acquainted with one another and we had not acquired official poise.

The President asked questions around the table and commented on the replies. Finally, he turned to me. "Frances, don't you want to say something?"

I didn't want to, but I knew I had to. There was silence. My colleagues looked at me with tense curiosity. I think some weren't sure I could speak.

I said what I had to say, quickly and briefly. I announced that I had called a conference of labor leaders and experts to draft recommendations for relief of unemployment. I said a program of public works should be one of the first steps.

The details do not matter here. As far as Roosevelt was concerned, I was one of the team. The men in the cabinet, from the beginning, treated me as a colleague and an equal. There was no special deference, beyond the ordinary daily amenities, because I was a woman. Nor was there any suggestion of a patronizing note. I recall that once Claude Swanson, the Secretary of the Navy, wondered whether he should tell a certain story since there was "a lady present."

"Go on, Claude," said the President, "she's dying to hear it."

Those early meetings were full of excitement, and always there was an easy give and take. Roosevelt wanted to have his advisers' reactions. He did not expect yes-men around him. He wanted a free expression of opinion, and it took place, under his leadership, in a stimulating atmosphere. . . .

*

There were eight or ten employees in the Department in this period who did little but serve on code committees, recommending wages, hours, and other working conditions based on Departmental and Bureau research and judgment. The advice of the Labor Advisory Board was good and, on the whole, sound, because of the experience of its members. However, one could not escape the fact that representation of working people through their own organizations was pathetically limited.

Consider the case of the steel code, one of the first proposed under the NRA. The way it was handled was typical of the problems of the day.

The depression had dried up the demand for steel, and it is doubtful whether any steel company was making money. Some were losing badly. United States Steel, for example, was in a difficult situation. It had relied largely on structural and heavy steel and had not been driven to put in new rolling mills and blast furnaces or equip itself to produce the small items which, in the depth of the depression, had almost the only market. United States Steel was pressing for a steel code, and Bethlehem and the other large companies were also willing, though doubtful on some points.

It is possible, as has often been charged, that the great industrialists of the steel corporations were mostly concerned with reaching agreements, with the blessing of the NRA, which would be legal under the anti-trust act—agreements on pricing, marketing practices, and other matters. Certainly, however, those who voted for the NRA, and, to a large extent, steel employers themselves, had learned from the depression that prosperity was a two-faced goddess and that no one would be prosperous unless the workers had a modest prosperity. Their wages must enable them to be a continuous market for consumer goods, and in turn the makers and distributors of consumer goods would be a continuous market for steel and durable goods.

The co-operation of the steel industry, basic in America to so many other activities, was essential to the success of the NRA. General Johnson, working through his friendship with Bernard Baruch and others in the group of industrialists whom the President had persuaded to agree to this experiment in planned recovery, made consistent efforts to get early agreements from the steel industry to enter into a code.

Consulting with General Johnson, I agreed that the Department of Labor would represent the steel workers in the preparation and development of this code. Since the workers in steel were almost totally unorganized and no one on the Labor Advisory Committee had any authority to speak in their interests, it was agreed that at the public hearing, the Secretary of Labor should present the steel workers' case. It was the best we could do under the circumstances.

I talked to the President, pointing out that it was unorthodox for a government official to submit a case for a partisan position.

"It is no more unorthodox than the NRA itself," he said. "After all, we are trying to do something. It is like a war. We are dealing with unusual factors. The codes have to be adopted. Otherwise we can't get recovery and purchasing power. Neither can we get the support of all the people unless they know that the real interests of labor have been considered.

"I think," he added, "the Secretary of Labor ought to be the Secretary *for* labor. Go ahead. Do the best you can. And," he went on with his big, hearty laugh, "if anybody says that's unorthodox, lay it onto me. They already have me tagged. But it's doing the country good."

The economic material and the arguments I presented were carefully prepared with the co-operation of my colleagues in the Department of Labor and particularly of Alexander Sachs, who contributed enormous economic knowledge to all NRA problems. To the steel workers hidden away in remote communities, with access to the news only through local newspapers controlled largely by their employers, we wanted to make clear the true interest of the government in them and their problems. We wanted to make this clear to the public and to the employers. We wanted it plain that there would not be a complacent agreement between the government and the employers, but that the workers' interests would be realistically and vigorously considered. To promote this I decided to visit some steel-producing areas. I wanted to seek out the workers themselves, asking their views and complaints.

I telephoned the President. "Ostensibly, I am going to get some information for my appearance in the public hearing on the steel code," I told him. "Actually we probably know right now the best level of wages, hours, and general working conditions to recommend.

But I want you to know that I am going, among other places, to Homestead, Pennsylvania, which has such a bad historical record, and to other towns in that valley, and down by Sparrow's Point where Bethlehem has its newest and, theoretically, most efficient plant. All the old-fashioned steel companies are afraid of it. I don't know the labor situation there."

"That's a good idea," he said, and chuckled. "But don't get yourself arrested."

I took Father Francis Haas with me. I chose him because he was a friend of labor, because the cloth of his profession, I felt, would give us standing, and because I needed at least one other individual to go along as aide and observer and helper. I did not want to go "in state" with a battery of economic advisers, publicity men, minor public officials, and obsequious secretaries.

Later, when I told the President that I had been rebuked for not taking an entourage, he said, "You and I have the instinct for freedom of association. Unfortunately, I can't practice it any more. What with the Secret Service and the politicians, I never get the opportunity to get close to anybody." He spoke with a touch of sadness. "But keep it up as long as you can, don't let them get you down. The common people don't care about all that style, Frances, and, after all, you and I are engaged in trying to bring them into things.

"You know, that is one of the great things about Eleanor," (Mrs. Roosevelt) he added, "she has already thrown off the Secret Service. They can't keep up with her. The result is that she goes where she wants to, talks to everybody, and does she learn something!"

Before going on this trip I telephoned Myron Taylor, president of United States Steel, and Eugene Grace, president of Bethlehem Steel. I asked for their co-operation and told them that I wanted, above all, to talk with the workmen privately. Both gentlemen politely agreed, whether reluctantly or not I shall never know. The result was that plant managers were informed by the top officers that I was to have complete co-operation.

It was in one of these towns, I think McKeesport, that I met William Irwin, who later became president of United States Steel. He had concluded in his own mind that I should be given assistance.

He was courteous, frank, and vigorous in his co-operation. I felt that he had a better appreciation of the steel workers and their problems than anyone I met in the steel industry. I felt there was a human exchange between him and them. They were not as sour and secretive about him as they were about other officers of the local mills.

I visited several big steel plants, and every courtesy was shown me by the superintendents. I talked with a good many steel workers on the job. Perhaps they did not speak freely because they were on the premises of their employer. I even visited some of their homes. I also escorted reporters from Pittsburgh newspapers and the wire services inside steel mills they had never been allowed to enter before.

The workers and their wives were quite uncritical. The idea that the government wanted to put a floor under wages was "wonderful." Everything we said was "just fine."

"You tell the President," many told me, "we are with him. Tell him we thank him."

My trip to the steel areas was made dramatically successful by the bad judgment of the Burgess of Homestead. Otherwise it would hardly have been noticed by anyone except the workers with whom I had conversations.

The Burgess, as the local executive officer is called somewhat archaically in these Pennsylvania communities, had consented to let me hold a meeting in the Hall of Burgesses.

The Burgess and all his officers were in the hall when the meeting started, which was proper and added a touch of official courtesy. The local newspaper editors were there, and many workingmen from the mills. These men were not too articulate, but they asked questions and stated points of view on what was the matter with the steel industry—usually specialized local complaints.

At the end of the meeting, as I was saying good-by to the Burgess, there was a disturbance downstairs. A newspaperman whispered that a lot of men were in the lower hall and on the sidewalk because the Burgess had not allowed them to come in. With naïve simplicity, because I believed that the Burgess was a public officer to whom all citizens of his community were equally important, I told him I was sorry these men had not been able to attend. Could we not have the hall for a few moments more?

The Burgess, red in the face, puffed and stormed. "No, no, you've had enough. These men are not any good. They're undesirable Reds. I know them well. They just want to make trouble."

Perhaps they did want to make trouble, but if I didn't hear them they would make more trouble. Perhaps they might have something constructive to suggest about the code. If I did not hear these people the public reaction would be bad—"steel workers have no voice, steel trust controls the code." I could imagine the words and the headlines! Nor did I think it would be good for the steel industry. I had met good men in it, and not all of them were determined to "suppress their workers." At any rate I had been brought up in the tradition of free speech. I took it for granted that it was the "duty of public officers," as Plato says, "to listen patiently to all citizens."

I said good-by to the Burgess and went downstairs. I found a couple of hundred people, many of them angry. They had been pushed out of the building onto the sidewalk by the local police. I tried to be as pleasant and polite as possible. The last thing I wanted was a difference with the local authorities. I stood on the steps of the Burgesses' Hall and started to make a little speech.

"My friends, I am so sorry that you were not able to get into the hall," I began. "It was very crowded, but perhaps we can hear what you have to say right here."

By this time the Burgess, two secretaries, and the police appeared, shouting, "You can't talk here! You are not permitted to make a speech here—there is a rule against making a speech here."

The men on the sidewalk were tense with interest, wondering what I would do next.

There was a park across the way. "All right—I am sorry. We will go over to the public park."

Immediately the red-faced Burgess and his police were at my side. "You can't do that, there is an ordinance against holding meetings in a public park."

I protested, "This is just a hearing, not a meeting; it won't be long, only a few minutes."

The Burgess kept reiterating that they were "undesirable Reds," although they looked like everybody else to me.

As I hesitated, my eye caught sight of the American flag flying over a building on the opposite side of the square. Ah, I thought, that must be the post office, and I remembered that federal buildings in any locality are under the jurisdiction of the federal government. I did not know the politics of the postmaster, but I was an officer of the federal government and I must have some rights there.

To the crowd I said, "We will go to the post office, there is the American flag."

It was almost closing time. I have never forgotten that postmaster and his assistance. I had only a moment to explain matters to him. Nothing very dramatic happened. The people filed in, and the employees hung around to enjoy the meeting. We stood in the long corridor lined with postal cages. Somebody got me a chair, and I stood on it and made a brief speech about the steel code. I asked if anybody wanted to speak. Twenty or thirty men did. They said they were greatly pleased with the idea. They said they wished the government would free them from the domination of the steel trust. One man spoke about philosophic and economic principles. A few denounced the community. I invited the most vocal and obstreperous of the speakers to come to Washington and promised that he would have an opportunity to appear at the public hearing. We ended the meeting with handshaking and expressions of rejoicing that the New Deal wasn't afraid of the steel trust.

That evening in Homestead, McKeesport, and in one or two other communities we held meetings in the parish hall of local churches. Father Haas had been busy arranging for these during the day, and the local pastors had sent word to steel-worker parishioners. One pastor in particular I remember—a Polish priest who spoke almost no English. His parishioners came scrubbed within an inch of their lives, with hair slicked down and with clean overalls or coats on. They understood no English either. The priest brought along an interpreter. First, under the pastor's direction, we said a few prayers, including a prayer for the President, which the people recited in unison and with great feeling. I was handed a translation; they were asking the blessing of Almighty God upon the President. I spoke, and many of them spoke briefly, and with confidence in this protected place. I learned as much about the hopes and needs of the steel workers through those half-dozen meetings in the parish halls as from the economic studies which the learned people in the Labor Department had prepared.

My own lamentable lack of instinct for publicity prevented me from making effective use of that visit. But a smart local newspaperman wired the story of the Burgess of Homestead turning me out of the hall and of the meeting we held in the federal building. On my return to Washington the press was at my door wanting to know what had happened. When one reporter asked me why the Burgess had acted like that, I replied, "Why, he seemed a little nervous."

The President read about the "nervous Burgess of Homestead" and telephoned me, laughing and saying, "You did just the right thing and you gave the post office free advertising. That's priceless." And he began expounding one of his favorite themes. "You know, the post office in every community ought to be the people's contact with the government. We ought to make more of it. The post office is a natural for co-operation between the people and the Federal Government." . . .

MARY
ANDERSON

"Many things we had to leave undone..."

Mary Anderson and Frances Perkins were colleagues in the U.S. Department of Labor for more than a decade, but the striking differences in their backgrounds, temperaments, and approaches to policy issues meant that these two officials often found themselves battling each other. Frances Perkins was a Boston blue-blood, with several degrees from elite universities. Mary Anderson was a Swedish immigrant without even a high school diploma.

Anderson, who came to the United States in 1889 as a sixteen-year-old steerage passenger, worked as a dishwasher and housemaid before finally obtaining employment as a shoe-stitcher in a Chicago factory. It was as a shoe worker that she first encountered trade unionism. In 1899 she helped to *organize her shop for the International Boot and Shoe Workers. By 1900 she had become a delegate to the Chicago Federation of Labor, by 1906 a member of the union's national executive board. While retaining her leadership position in the Boot and Shoe Workers, Anderson also became deeply involved in the efforts of the Women's Trade Union League to improve conditions for women workers in many trades. In 1911 she became a full-time organizer for the League, an alliance of middle-class female reformers and trade union women like Anderson which, from the early twentieth century until its demise in the 1950s, acted as an important organizational spokesman for working women.*

Anderson's connections within the labor movement brought her into federal government service during World War I. Recommended for a position as assistant director of the wartime Women in Industry Service, she stayed on after 1920 when Congress approved the creation of a permanent Women's Bureau within the Department of Labor to "investigate and improve" conditions for working women. From 1920 until her retirement in 1944, she directed that bureau. She never married and had few, if any, outside interests; her life-long cause—in fact, her life—was the advocacy of the interests of working women.

By the time the Depression struck, Anderson was near sixty and a seasoned federal bureaucrat with more than fifteen years of service. Unlike Frances Perkins, who perceived herself as a representative of working people generally, Anderson saw herself more narrowly as a champion of working women. As these passages from her 1951 autobiography, Woman at Work, *reveal, these differences in self-definition led to conflicts between the Secretary of Labor and her director of the Women's Bureau.*

SOURCES: In addition to Anderson's autobiography, information about her life is available in Sister John Marie Daly's unpublished dissertation, "Mary Anderson, Pioneer Labor Leader" (Georgetown University, 1968), and Edward T. James, "Mary Anderson," in *Notable American Women*, 23–25. For extensive treatment of Anderson's career as director of the Women's Bureau, see Judith Sealander, *As Minority Becomes Majority: Federal Reaction to the Phenomenon of Women in the Work Force, 1920–1963* (1983). Richard E. Neustadt and Ernest R. May, *Thinking in Time: The Uses of History for Decision-Makers* (1986), 171–179, discusses the relationship between Anderson and Perkins as a case study showing "the full potential for misunderstanding between strangers." Anderson's papers are housed in the Schlesinger Library, Radcliffe College.

MARY ANDERSON

WHEN FRANCES PERKINS CAME
in as secretary of labor, we were all jubilant, because we thought that
at last we would have someone who really understood our problems
and what we were up against and would fight for us. I felt that I had
a friend to whom I could go freely and confidently, but it did not
turn out to be that way. During the first months when she was
secretary, I was truly sorry for her. She had so many difficult
problems on her hands, because of the depression and the split in the
labor movement. The terrible publicity she was subjected to because
she was the first woman Cabinet officer was a great handicap. I
wanted to do anything I could to help and with my contacts in the
labor movement I hoped I could be of some use, but there never
seemed to be anything I could do. It was especially discouraging to
me to find that the Women's Bureau was not of great interest to her,
though I understood that she was preoccupied with other things and
did not want to be thought of as a woman who was too closely
identified with women's problems.

In April 1933, just a few months after she had been made
secretary, I got a real shock which seriously hampered me in my
relationship with her during the years to come. Like every new
secretary, when she first took office she did not know a great deal
about government routine, appropriations, and so on, and, because
she had great plans for the department, she wanted more freedom in
handling the department appropriations that had been granted by
Congress. She suggested to me that the appropriation for the Wom-
en's Bureau be turned over to her to be allocated in the way she felt

would be most useful. I was appalled at this suggestion, because I felt it would establish a precedent that might eventually threaten the existence of the bureau. It had taken many years of effort on the part of women and women's organizations to establish a statutory bureau in the Labor Department to deal with women's problems. Miss Perkins assured me that the work of the bureau would not suffer under this arrangement and I am sure she meant it. But, if this arrangement was made, the bureau was in danger of losing its statutory position and its program would be entirely dependent on the good will of future secretaries of labor who might, or might not, be sympathetic to our work. I pointed out to Miss Perkins the danger of establishing such a precedent and the outcry that it would cause among the many groups who had worked for so long to establish the bureau. I also offered to allocate such funds as she might need for other purposes and to put the members of my staff at her disposal, but I strongly protested against any arrangement that would take from the bureau's control the appropriations that Congress had passed specifically for our program. Fortunately, nothing more came of this suggestion, but I must confess the memory of it made things difficult for me from then on.

There were many new people brought into the department who had very close contacts with the secretary and I gradually found that I did not have the entree to her that I had hoped to have. When our appropriations were discussed with the Bureau of the Budget and the Appropriations committees in Congress, we had very little help from the secretary's office. I understood the reason for this and realized that there were many more important projects to be considered and pressed for. But as the years went on I became more and more discouraged at the lack of backing I received. I felt that I was fighting a losing battle among all the politics and strife that went on in the department. Eventually I decided that there was nothing I could do about it and I would just go along doing the best I could and stop worrying. That is what I did, and although the bureau did not get the appropriations I had hoped for and there were many things we had to leave undone, we kept on the job and I think we did useful work that will be of lasting value. . . .

*

137
Mary Anderson

The years from 1933 on were very busy ones. It was the beginning of the New Deal. We had first the problems of the National Recovery Administration, then all the relief work and the terrible unemployment, the beginning of the social security program, and the split in the labor movement.

I had known John Lewis for many years and I felt very enthusiastic in the early days of the [Congress of Industrial Organizations]. I think the CIO started out as a real crusade and many unorganized workers felt that at last they were going to get help. But there were very bitter and tragic feelings among many of the old-line trade unionists who were faced with the decision of whether to stick with their old union if it decided not to go over to the CIO, or to switch to the new group. I have seen some trade unionists actually cry when they had to give up their cards, which they had held almost all their lives, and become members of the new union. In my own case, the International Boot and Shoe Workers Union never affiliated with the CIO, but I really believed in this new method of organization. Women had not had much chance or attention under the American Federation of Labor and I thought that a new day was dawning for them. Although I was a member of the AF of L, I never had any feeling of animosity toward my friends who were members of the CIO. We were all trade unionists still and I always felt that if we were going to accomplish anything, we would have to stop making bitter charges against each other. We had to learn to give and take and work together....

During these years the Women's Bureau had so many irons in the fire it is difficult to sort them all out. One of the problems I always wanted to do something about was the employment conditions of domestic workers.

I had been a domestic worker myself and I was not a success at it, yet it did give me a living until I was able to get started in something else. I have always felt from my own experience that with training and proper standards, domestic work could be made into a respected occupation and not occupy the debased position it does at present. Much more thought must be given to training and standards of employment if we are to get out of the present chaos in domestic employment. I think in a way the employers are getting their training now, when they cannot get people to work for them and have to do the work themselves. In that way they are learning how much there is to do and how long it takes to do it. At the same time, the workers need training too. I think proper training would give dignity to the job instead of putting a domestic worker into a position of servitude. Really, it should be the most dignified occupation we have, because in many cases family life is so dependent on it, but so far no adequate training programs and standards have been set up.

I always felt that we should give more attention to this in the Women's Bureau and that we should collect the facts about this kind of employment, but we never did because we were always prevented from making a study. It was a "hot potato."

One day, when I sat next to Mrs. Roosevelt at lunch, she said, "Mary, you will have to do something about domestic service." I agreed, but I had just talked to Secretary Perkins about it and she had been opposed to our doing anything. While Mrs. Roosevelt was talking I decided that I was not going to take the responsibility for this decision myself, so I asked her to speak to the secretary about it. She agreed and eventually we got the Bureau of the Budget to approve a special appropriation of twenty-five thousand dollars for a study of domestic workers by the Women's Bureau. But when it came up to the Appropriation Committee, the members who were from the South just would not hear of it. It was one of the worst hearings we have ever had. The whole subject got mixed up with the race question, because in Washington and the South most of the domestic workers are Negroes. The southerners did not want to appropriate money for an investigation that might improve conditions of domestic employment because, they said, the colored people were all right as they were.

A few days after I appeared before the committee, the secretary talked to them, but they refused to budge and she told me, "Don't ever bring that up again." So we gave up trying to get a special appropriation. Instead, whenever we could, we did bits of research and gathered what information we could. We worked with other organizations too and tried to help them, but we never accomplished much.

While we were struggling with the problems of the domestic worker, we also had the question of the Negro woman industrial worker to deal with and this was even more serious. The Women's Bureau made several studies of the conditions under which Negro women were employed and our findings were really appalling. One of the most serious results of the low standards for Negro women was a general scaling down of wages. Just as white women got paid less than white men, Negro women got many jobs because they would work for less than white women, and as a result they did not get enough money to live decently.

I remember once in Birmingham talking to one of the employers who said he could not pay as much as twenty-five cents an hour to Negroes because if he did they would not come to work after they had been paid. He said he and other employers were then paying one dollar for a ten-hour day. I asked, "When do you pay them?" The reply was, "Every night we have to pay them one dollar." I said, "Of course they couldn't live if they weren't paid every day. If they only get one dollar a day they have to spend it all." He said they would not come back if they were paid for a whole week at a time, that they would stay out until the money was gone. I thought they would come back soon and said, "You know, it has always been said of the workers that if they got more money they wouldn't work. That's been said for the last century at least, but that has not been the way it has happened. The minute there was a way to keep a family in decency, the minute they had food and decent homes, the workers always responded and became real citizens of the country." But he stuck to his opinion, saying, "Those awful niggers wouldn't work." I asked, "Then why do you hire them?" His reply was, "Because we get them for so little." That was just the trouble. It is a vicious circle and it is one that must be broken if the South is to become prosperous.

On the whole I think the South has made tremendous progress during the past ten or fifteen years. This is partly due to the forward-looking program of the federal government during the thirties and the passage of such legislation as the Wage and Hour Law. But it is due also to the gradual development of liberal opinion in the South itself. The First Conference for Human Welfare, which took place in Birmingham, Alabama, in 1938, was the beginning of a very important movement all over the South. It was organized by prominent southerners such as Judge Louise Charlton of Alabama and Frank Graham of North Carolina. Leading southerners in all fields of interest were members of the conference. Its purpose was to focus attention on the problems of the South and to awaken the people there to a sense of responsibility for improving the conditions of the workers.

I was chairman of the section of women in industry at that conference and the Women's Bureau prepared special exhibits showing the part played by women in southern industries and their wages and working conditions. Mrs. Roosevelt came to the conference for one day and made a magnificent speech that night.

When the conference opened we had quite a bit of trouble on account of the Negro issue. The first day went along very well. There were many Negro representatives and they sat with the whites. The meetings had to be held where Negroes were allowed, but there was no segregation.

That evening, Judge Charlton, who was chairman of the conference, and others were called to the mayor's office and told that there had to be segregation at the meetings. The committee protested that it had been a long time since Birmingham had enforced segregation at meetings in the city, although there was a local ordinance to that effect. But the mayor was firm and said the ordinance must be enforced for this meeting because certain citizens had called upon him and insisted on it. In order to hold the meetings at all, therefore, we had to obey the ordinance. Resentment ran high and the delegates, as a whole, did not want to do it. Judge Charlton knew, however, that if there was defiance the meetings would be broken up, and in order not to destroy the unity of the meeting for the purpose it was called for, she begged the delegates to comply. They agreed, but the feeling of resentment was great that evening and the next day.

We were all afraid that when Mrs. Roosevelt arrived she would refuse to speak before a segregated audience. She had never done this before, but when the situation was explained to her, she agreed to make no change in her program. The evening that she was to speak, we were told we should get up there early since by six o'clock a crowd had already begun to assemble outside the hall. It was a huge hall, seating about five thousand people.

Some of us were to sit on the stage with Mrs. Roosevelt and we had a difficult time pushing our way through the crowd. There were thousands left on the outside and before she made her regular speech to the conference, she made a speech to those outside. Inside, all the Negroes were on one side of the hall and all the whites on the other side. It was really a sight from the platform.

Mrs. Roosevelt made a very fine speech, as she usually does—full of everyday common sense, and the crowd went wild about her.

After the conference was over the papers played up the controversy about segregation, but they did not tell of the good things that came out of the conference: the understanding, at least by some, of the special problems in the South that had to be attended to and the minimum standards that should be set up for the working people. In fact, the conference was a focus for the liberal movement in the South, and through the conferences of the same group that have followed from time to time, I think much has been done to educate the people in the South on the need for more progressive action and higher standards of employment for the workers.

One of the leading spirits in the liberal movement of the South has been Mollie Dowd, who is a member of the executive board of the National Women's Trade Union League. She started out as a retail clerk. Known throughout Alabama as "Miss Mollie," she is one of the real characters of the South. She is also one of the most insistent fighters for human liberty and human welfare that I know, never sparing herself in the least and never losing her sense of humor. She always has plenty of stories to tell, but they always have a point that is very refreshing.

One time when the National Women's Trade Union League was holding its convention in Washington, Mrs. Roosevelt invited a number of the delegates to stay with her at the White House. Many of the girls selected for this honor came from the South and Mollie was one of them. They drove up in an old jalopy, to save the cost of railway fare, and when they got to the White House they were much embarrassed because they did not know what to do with their old wreck of a car. Finally one of the White House aides took it away and parked it for them.

While they were at the White House, Mrs. Roosevelt had breakfast with them every morning except once when she was away and the President himself played host. Mollie Dowd with her wonderful stories was a great entertainer on that occasion.

Another problem that we worked very hard on, with more success than we had with standards for domestic workers, was the regulation or abolition of industrial homework. Everyone had known for years of the shocking conditions under which homework was done. The factories sent out work to be done in homes where the sanitary conditions were very bad and where women and children worked terribly long hours for a few cents an hour. The excuse for this was always that the people needed the work, they could not put in a full day's work at the factory, and that by taking work home they were able to get a little extra money. But those of us who knew of the actual conditions were horrified and shocked at this kind of exploitation and we knew, too, that the system was dangerous to public health as well.

The Consumers League was one of the organizations that campaigned against this evil, and some of the unions took it up too, but nothing much was accomplished on a national scale until the days of the National Recovery Administration, when a special committee on homework was set up. The Women's Bureau made a study of conditions under which homework was done and we circulated our findings all over the country. The homework committee of the NRA held any number of hearings and I think they were successful in abolishing homework in some industries. I remember that for the sweater trade in Philadelphia, the committee issued a statement saying that the work should be done in the factory and that if the work was sent into the homes the same wage should be paid as for the work done in the factory. After that, most of the home workers went to the factory to work and when one factory sent out work the women picketed it until the practice was stopped.

Actually there is no effective way to regulate industrial homework. It is impossible to have enough inspectors to see that standards are enforced. That would require one inspector for every home. The only thing to do about homework is to abolish it and to arrange for higher wages for the breadwinner in a family so that his wife and children do not have to supplement the family income by doing homework, or, if there is no regular breadwinner, to provide pensions or relief.

Of course, when the custom of industrial homework is well established in a place, there is nothing to do except try to regulate it. One thing that we advocated and that was tried with fair success was the establishment of workrooms to which the home workers could come for as many hours a day or a week as they could. In these central workrooms the conditions and pay could be regulated. We recommended this for the home industries of Puerto Rico. We sent an agent to study the situation in Puerto Rico and found the most deplorable conditions and ill health among the home workers. A typical case was found in a hut up in the mountains that could be reached only on horseback or on foot. Two sisters were living there. One was in bed with tuberculosis and the other was a cripple. They were trying to keep alive by doing embroidery on the fine handker-chiefs and baby clothes that sold for such high prices in New York. The employers came to Washington to testify before the National Recovery Administration that such people must have that work or they could not live. The trouble was that there was no feeling of civic responsibility for these workers; they were left alone to shift for themselves.

I think that one of the things that helped most in getting better wage standards for the home workers in Puerto Rico was Mrs. Roosevelt's interest. She went down there and rode all over the island seeing what the conditions were. Although homework in Puerto Rico was not abolished, under the National Recovery Administration and later under the federal Wage and Hour Law the rate of pay has been much increased over the two or three cents an hour that was customary.

In the United States, at least in twenty states, homework has been either prohibited by law or regulated to such a degree that it is no longer of great advantage to an employer to use it, because starvation pay is not permitted. . . .

Perhaps the most familiar and exasperating problem of any work-ing woman is the famous (or should I say infamous?) "pin money" theory. This theory, which has been advanced as long as women have been working, is that women only work for "pin money" and have no family responsibilities. Of course it is not true, but it has been so widely circulated and accepted that I think it is the chief cause of the low wages of women in comparison with men. It is an infuriating theory to anyone who knows anything about women workers. . . .

Next to getting the facts about women's employment and trying to lay to rest the ghost of the pin money theory, I think one of the most important issues that the Women's Bureau worked on was equal pay for women and men. From the very beginning of the Woman in Industry Service we said that wages should be based on the job content and not on the sex of the worker. We said this in the first standards issued and we have been saying it ever since. I think we have made some progress in getting this principle accepted but it has been slow, hard work and is not nearly finished yet.

In the early days, when we first issued the standards, we put in a statement on wages that said, "Wages shall be established on the basis of occupation and not on the basis of sex or race." But although this standard had the force of an official recommendation by the federal government, there was not much chance of its being adopted. A good many people endorsed it who did not really agree with it.

We always tried to push equal pay, but we ran into a great deal of opposition from employers, labor unions, and labor in general. I think the men always felt that they were inferior if they did not get more than the women and they did not realize that if they permitted lower wage rates for women the next thing that would happen would be that women would replace men because they were cheaper. Even if an employer theoretically accepted the policy of "equal pay for equal work" it did not do much good because he might then say that what the women were doing was not exactly the same as what the men were doing, so the women were paid less. In many factories there is a well-defined rule as to what is men's work and what is women's work. Even when the workers are all on piecework the rates are much lower for the women than for the men. This inequality applies to white-collar workers as well as to workers in industry. It is a matter of prejudice that is very hard to overcome. The women themselves present a problem. They do not have very strong bargaining

Mary Anderson

power. Most of them are not organized. When they are organized they do not have much influence in most of their unions. They have to get a job and they are not in a position to stand out for "equal pay." They must take what they can get.

One of our great problems has been how to formulate a statement on equal pay that would be really enforceable. The simple slogan "Equal pay for equal work" we found did not mean much when we came to apply it in a practical way. There are too many possibilities of evasion. It really requires a job analysis of each operation in a plant to show that women are or are not doing the same work as men. The unions are not equipped to do this and it is not likely that employers will do it either. If there is to be any law or union agreement on this matter, it must be carefully phrased so that a job analysis is not necessary.

Our first real advance on the equal pay front came in the days of the National Recovery Administration, which was set up during the depression to secure the cooperation of employers and workers in raising standards of wages and hours and working conditions. To this end code authorities were established for each industry and after prolonged hearings and negotiations with workers and employers specific codes were adopted. Industries that followed these codes were entitled to display the emblem of the National Recovery Administration, a blue eagle. It was through these hearings and discussions that the people in general began to understand that women are a part of the industrial setup and should not be used to depress wage standards. I think the labor men got a great deal of enlightenment from the National Recovery Administration, and learned a lot about other industries as well as their own.

When the National Recovery Administration was first being put into effect I got in touch with members of the committees working on standards for each industry, particularly in the women-employing industries, William Green, John L. Lewis, and others. Lewis was then head of the CIO. It was very interesting to see him when he found the low wages and the poor conditions in certain of the industries, particularly where women were employed. He was very perturbed. He had worked closely with the miners and knew their problems but had not had much time for other industries. By organizing the CIO he found out what was going on in other industries and he began a real crusade to raise the standards of work. He always helped us.

We had plenty of friends in the National Recovery Administration. Leo Wolman was appointed by the secretary of labor as the executive secretary of the Labor Division and Rose Schneiderman was also in the division. But most of the labor men and women could not give full time to the work of the NRA; they could only be present for meetings and they had so much to do with the industrial committees that they had little control over the general policies.

I had one of the people from our office go every morning to the National Recovery Administration to find out what hearings were coming up and to ask if we could be heard. Then, when she came back, we would write a statement that one of us would present to the committee holding a hearing. The purpose of these hearings was to help employers and employees to set up minimum standards, acceptable to both, on hours, wages, and certain conditions of employment. One of the problems taken up by the committees was the theory that competition of women with men lowered the men's wages. The Women's Bureau was the only place where there was much information on that score.

After the hearings were completed and a code adopted for the industry the National Recovery Administration put out the blue eagles to be given to the employers to show that they had set certain standards of employment and were trying to live up to them. Before they set the standards for the blue eagles in the industries where mostly women were employed, I was asked to agree to them.

I remember that once the laundry committee wanted me to accept five or six dollars a week as a wage for women. I would not agree, saying that I could never accept a standard of that kind. I could not understand how the government could set such a standard. They called and called me by telephone, but I would not change my mind. Then the next thing I heard was that Leo Wolman had signed the agreement. I went to the secretary of labor to ask her to protest. She was not in, but her secretary, Miss Jay, called Wolman, who said that he did not know much about it. His secretary had signed it and he had not looked into it at all. It was an "automatic" signing.

Miss Jay said, "Miss Anderson does not agree. She is here now. Would you like to speak to her?" He replied, "No, I'll withdraw that signature."

There were many crosscurrents of that kind, particularly where women were concerned, and we had to be constantly on the alert. One day one of the labor men from the heavy industries came to me and said, "You and Miss Christman object to women getting less wages than men. Our hearings on that are tomorrow morning and I expect you to be over to put up a real fight."

We went and made our objections. There were ten thousand women in the heavy industries and the suggestion was that the minimum wage should be set at forty cents an hour for the men and thirty-five cents an hour for the women, although the women were doing almost the same work. We protested against that.

The man who presided over the meeting turned to me and said, "Now I am in a dilemma. What would you do? I can get forty cents an hour for men and thirty-five cents an hour for women and there are women in this industry who are only getting eighteen cents an hour. Isn't that a pretty good raise? Shall I let the men go down to thirty-five cents an hour, or take forty cents for the men and thirty-five cents for the women?"

I said, "That is a hard question, when you put it that way, but I am afraid that is not all there is to it. There ought to be the same wage. I think it would be better for industry as well as the workers if they were all paid the same."

They finally permitted forty cents for the men and thirty-five cents for the women. The labor man was with them. He let us have our say but he did not back us up a bit. Nevertheless, we were able, because of our consistent nagging, to get the same minimum for women in about seventy-five per cent of the codes and in the others we were able to get the differential decreased.

This work took almost all our time because we were constantly making investigations to find what the differentials were and many times we had to send out an agent to get spot information for the hearings on the codes. In the bureau, almost our whole Division of Research worked on this question.

The women workers themselves were not at all prepared to argue their case and the National Women's Trade Union League did a great deal to help. Elisabeth Christman worked on certain code authorities herself, especially the glove workers' code authority, and she worked and helped in general, speaking before industrial committees and often using our information. She and the bureau both helped the women prepare cases, notified them of the hearings, and assisted wherever we could. Many of the women's organizations too, especially the YWCA and the League of Women Voters, did a great deal, speaking before the authorities and keeping very close to the general staff to see what was going on and giving what information they had.

After the National Recovery Administration came the Walsh-Healy Act, which gave us another opportunity to raise pay rates for women. This act, passed in 1936, was really the entering wedge for the federal Wage and Hour Law that followed in 1938. The Walsh-Healy Act gave to the Department of Labor the power to set up standards of employment in the production of materials produced under contract with the federal government. I think this act had a tremendous effect on women's employment. The Women's Bureau made a number of surveys, particularly in the garment industry, for the Contract Division of the department and our findings were used by the industry committee called by the Contract Division to set minimum wages. The employers would attack us but our facts always stood up. It was a different kind of work from what we had been doing and it was not easy for our investigators, but I was sure they were very happy to see that our investigations were being so useful and that the bureau was getting more recognition.

Then came the federal Wage and Hour Law in which we really made some progress. This act set standards of minimum wages and maximum hours for workers employed in the manufacture of goods used in interstate commerce. I think I had a good deal to do with getting into that law the statement in connection with fixing wage orders that "No classification shall be made under this section on the basis of age or sex." It was an anxious time for me while the hearings on the bill were going on. The secretary of labor was going to appear and the solicitor of the department, Gerard Reilly, was working up her testimony. I talked to him and said, "Well, Gerry, I think we had better put in something for her to say about the same minimum for men and women."

He put in a bit, about two lines. When I went to the committee hearing the day she was going to testify the women of the press came up to me and asked what she was going to say about the same minimum for men and women. I answered, "Well, I know it is in her testimony and she will speak about it but you will have to wait and hear what it is." Unfortunately, when she came to that part she left out the two lines and went on to the next paragraph.

When the hearing was over, I nearly died because not a word had been said about the same minimum for men and women. The newspaperwomen all rushed up to me and asked why she had left that out. I answered, "God knows! Go up and ask her." But before they got a chance to, Senator Robert La Follette asked if she did not think that women should have the same minimum as men. She said, "Yes," and I heaved a sigh of relief. As she went out she said to me, "I fixed that all right, didn't I? It was such a long statement that I couldn't read it all." It was all right in the end, but I could not help feeling discouraged that she had picked those two lines to leave out.

All through the time she was secretary of labor, I think Miss Perkins rather minimized the importance of women's problems because she knew that a good many of the representatives of organized labor did not like her very well, partly because she was a woman and partly because they thought of her as a social worker and not a real labor person. So every time there was a chance to single out women, she leaned over backward not to do it. I understood her difficulties and sympathized with her, but just the same it was discouraging not to have more enthusiastic backing.

The result of the inclusion of the clause on the same minimum for men and women in the Wage and Hour Law was that later on when committees met to set higher minimums than were in the act itself, there was never any question of a differential for women, because it was in the law that there should not be any.

HALLIE
FLANAGAN

"Did I consider the theatre a weapon? . . ."

Hallie Flanagan, director of the Federal Theatre Project, typified women government workers during the Depression: like most women who achieved influence as New Deal administrators, she worked for a new rather than an established agency; and, like many of her female cohorts, she sought to expand the federal government's role in American life.

As in the case of Frances Perkins, a tragic marriage altered Flanagan's life and, in the end, spurred her career. Born in 1890, the eldest daughter of a prosperous businessman in a small South Dakota town, Hallie Flanagan gave no early indication that her life would be in any way exceptional. Married in 1912 to Murray Flanagan, an insurance salesman, she soon had two sons and embarked on the comfortable life of a happy middle-class housewife and mother. Between 1912 and 1922, however, she found herself forced to cope with the total disruption of the plans she and her husband had made for their lives. Murray Flanagan contracted tuberculosis and, after years of suffering and hospitalization in a series of sanitariums, died in 1919. Jack Flanagan, the couple's elder son, died in 1922 of spinal meningitis. Hallie Flanagan was a young widow with a son to support.

Taking insurance money left her by her husband, Flanagan, who had written plays and taught English during her years of nursing sick family members, went east to obtain a master's degree from Radcliffe College. Within three years this tiny woman with "fiery" red hair and a fierce disposition had obtained not only the degree but also a position as a theater teacher and playwright in residence at Vassar College. During the next decade she emerged as an influential voice in American theater. The Vassar Experimental Theater, which she founded in 1925, the year she began at Vassar, acquired a reputation for staging gritty, realistic dramas, some from Flanagan's own scripts.

She was a logical choice, then, when Harry Hopkins sought a director for the Works Progress Administration's proposed Federal Theatre Project. Between 1935 and 1939 Flanagan created a new kind of American public theater. What had originally been conceived as a relief measure for out-of-work theater people became instead a national theater network. Twelve thousand Federal Theatre employees put on more than fourteen hundred plays, entertaining twenty-five million Americans, many of whom saw live drama for the first time.

These plays and programs spanned a wide spectrum, from dog acts to musicals to Shakespeare, but the Federal Theatre also spotlighted contemporary social problems, hired talented leftist playwrights, and often allowed racially integrated casts during a time of national segregation. Hundreds of plays about hunger, loss of farms, the right to unionize, and other controversial subjects brought Flanagan's agency unwanted attention from congressmen concerned about funding radical causes. In 1938, as the following excerpt from Flanagan's autobiography, Arena, *details, Congressman Martin Dies of Texas held hearings to determine whether the Federal Theatre Project was "un-American." Although, as Flanagan relates, some of her WPA colleagues simply laughed at the Dies Committee's visions of communists under every bed, she knew the committee's attacks were "not funny." In 1939 Congress canceled the Federal Theatre, and Flanagan returned to academic life as a professor in theater departments, first at Vassar, then at Smith College from 1942 until her retirement in 1955. As an educator she continued to advocate making drama accessible to all the people, but never again did she have the chance to reach millions with "free, adult, uncensored" entertainment.*

SOURCES: In addition to *Arena*, Flanagan also wrote *Dynamo: The Story of a College Theater* (1943) about the Vassar theater experiments. The full-length biography is Joanne Bentley, *Hallie Flanagan: A Life in the American Theatre* (1988). Jane DeHart Mathews, *The Federal Theater 1935–39: Plays, Relief and Politics* (1967) includes biographical information about Flanagan, as does John O'Connor and Lorraine Brown's *Free, Adult, Uncensored: The Living History of the Federal Theater Project* (1978). See also Helen Chinoy's essay on Flanagan in *Notable American Women*, 237–239. Hallie Flanagan's papers are housed in the Billy Rose Theater Collection at the New York City Public Library.

HALLIE FLANAGAN

AS AN AMERICAN WHO BELIEVES it the center and core of our democratic way of life that decisions rest not with any one man or group but with the people through their elected representatives, I can feel no resentment that Congress had, co-equal and co-existent with its power to create a government-sponsored theatre, the power to end it.

Congress, in the case of Federal Theatre, however, was misinformed by witnesses before two committees, by members of those committees, and by other Congressmen: first, by witnesses before the House Committee to Investigate Un-American Activities (Chairman Martin Dies) during the period from August to December, 1938; later by witnesses before the sub-committee of the House Committee on Appropriations (Chairman Clifton A. Woodrum), set up for investigation and study of the Works Progress Administration, in the spring of 1939; and finally by Congressman John Taber (Republican, New York), Congressman Everett M. Dirksen (Republican, Illinois), on the floor of the House of Representatives; and by Senator Robert Reynolds (Democrat, North Carolina), and Senator Rush D. Holt (Democrat, West Virginia) on the floor of the United States Senate.

In July, 1938, when I first read a statement in a New York paper that Federal Theatre was dominated by Communists and that you had to belong to the Workers' Alliance in order to get on the project I released an immediate and unequivocal denial. This was an infraction of the rule that only the W.P.A. information division in Washington answered press stories and I was told by W.P.A. officials that on no account was I to reply to these charges. It was the fashion at that time, in the W.P.A. and out, to laugh at the Dies Committee; but it never seemed funny to me. As days went on and the papers gave more and more space to the testimony of a few unqualified witnesses, it seemed to me increasingly incredible that the congressional committee called no officials of the project and no theatre experts from outside the project.

On August 5, 1938, when the W.P.A. was still ignoring the whole matter and still refusing to allow me to issue statements to the press, I wrote to Representative Dies asking him to hear me and six regional directors who constituted the National Policy Board; I told him that regional and state offices were waiting to give co-operation to the Committee, but that as yet no use had been made of available information, while in the meantime a half-dozen witnesses, no one of whom was in any position to know the broad sweep of project operation or administration, were making statements which, as the Committee could easily ascertain, were biased, prejudiced, and often completely false.

To this letter I received no answer.

The W.P.A. still refused to take the continued attacks seriously. Many people believe that this was because that organization had already decided that the Federal Theatre was a political liability and wanted to end it before 1940. I do not think, however, that the appeasement policy, in the air in Washington in the spring and summer of 1939, started as early as this. I incline rather to the belief that W.P.A. was following government tradition that attacks on people in government service are not answered by anyone except heads of departments. Any agency like the W.P.A. which depends for its continued existence upon periodic appropriations wants to keep out of the papers. It goes on the supposition that if you do not answer an attack, the attack will cease.

These attacks did not cease. Again I wrote Chairman Dies, saying that the jobs of thousands of people were being jeopardized and that I wished to put the record of their work before the Committee. Again no answer. In the meantime the allegations left their mark on the public mind and the project morale.

Emmet Lavery, who had charge of the final clearance of play contracts, in August wrote a vigorous letter to Chairman Dies saying that he was a Catholic and that he had never authorized a communistic play for the project and that he demanded to be heard. The letter was not answered. On September 1 Congressman J. Parnell Thomas (Republican, New Jersey) declared in the *New York Herald Tribune* that "practically every play was clear unadulterated propaganda." Mr. Lavery immediately challenged Representative Thomas to debate the production record of the project on the radio, play by play. That challenge, like all others, went unanswered.

I have often been asked why we did not demand to attend the hearings of the Committee, insist that project officials or professional theatre people be called, see that the project record of the witnesses be examined by the Committee; and above all why we did not bring libel suits against some of the Congressmen, including Representative Dirksen who called our productions "salacious tripe."

The answer is that citizens are not able to insist on the same measure of due process of law in Congress that they receive in the courts. A congressional committee may hold its hearings in public or private as it sees fit, may or may not hear witnesses as it pleases, may cite for contempt witnesses who do not respond to its subpoena but on the other hand may not be compelled to hear people who demand to testify. At the bar of a trial court an accused person may demand through his lawyer that accusing witnesses be cross-examined, that evidence be relevant and legally probative; the accused has the advice of counsel and may summon expert witnesses for the appraisal of technical points. These are rights granted at the bar of our courts; but congressional committees operate as quasi-judicial bodies which are a law unto themselves; and a Congressman is immune from libel suits for statements he makes while engaged in the conduct of his official duties.*

Thus it came about that during the year from June, 1938, to its end on June 30, 1939, a project, in which 90 per cent came from relief rolls, the vast majority of which showed membership in theatrical unions (American Federation of Labor affiliates), was accused of being made up largely of non-relief amateurs; a project which had brought in cash to the government approximating $2,000,000,** a record which so far as I know has never been equaled by any W.P.A. project, was accused of being inefficient; and a project which from first to last had stood on American principles of freedom, justice, and truth, was accused of being through its plays, its audiences, and its personnel, subversive, communistic, and indecent.

By November the W.P.A. could no longer ignore the attack of the Dies Committee and arranged to have me go before the Committee to submit the brief in which Emmet Lavery and Theodore Mauntz, director of information on the New York City project, with assistance from the legal division of W.P.A., had answered, with affidavits, every charge made by every witness. On the three major allegations that audiences, plays, and personnel were communistic, the brief presented:

1. A list of New York organizations and groups which, through theatre parties, made up a large part of Federal Theatre audiences. This included organizations: social, 263; welfare and civic, 264; educational, 271; religious, 95; business and industry, 21; trade unions, 66; professional unions, 82; consumers' unions, 17; fraternal organizations, 29; political organizations, 15, including every party.

2. A list of plays... with specific analysis of every play criticized.

3. A statement that no person chosen for any policy-making post on Federal Theatre was a Communist; that the politics of relief

---

*Section 6, Article 1, United States Constitution, provides that "for any speech or debate in either House they (Senators and Representatives) shall not be questioned in any other place." The decision in the case of Kilbourn *vs.* Thompson, 103 U.S. Reports 168, indicates that the protection provided is not necessarily limited to statements made on the floor of either house.

**Figure given by the Division of Statistics of the W.P.A. through March 31, 1939, was $1,925,919. This did not include final figures on *The Swing Mikado, Run, Little Chillun*, and other outstanding box-office successes of the spring of 1939.

persons were not legally subject to our scrutiny; that we had no way of knowing whether the Workers' Alliance was, as the Committee alleged, a Communist Front organization; but that in any case the large majority of Federal Theatre workers did not belong to the Workers' Alliance because they were under the jurisdiction of theatrical organizations which forbade other union affiliations.

Since witnesses before the Dies Committee had called into question my political faith, the brief gave my own statement that I am not and never have been a Communist; that I am a registered Democrat; that I have never engaged in any communistic activities, or belonged to any communistic organizations; it further stated that I had planned and directed Federal Theatre from the first as an American enterprise. The many articles I had written on this point for *Theatre Arts Monthly*, the *New York Times*, and the *Magazine of Art* were cited.

To prepare the brief was a comparatively simple matter; to get to present it was more arduous. Emmet Lavery, Theodore Mauntz, and I, together with Henry Alsberg, whose project was also under attack, were called to a meeting in Mrs. Woodward's office on December 4 and told by Mr. Niles that the decision was we were not to present our briefs; that Mrs. Woodward would speak for us. Henry Alsberg and I pointed out with a good deal of heat that we had been silenced for months, while our projects were being subjected to attack, always on the promise of a day in court. We felt that Mrs. Woodward, with the best intentions in the world, would not be able to answer technical questions. However, when we could not change Mr. Niles' decision we went over our briefs with Mrs. Woodward. On December 5* she made a gallant attempt to defend the projects, but she was in no position to give answers to specific questions in the technical field. Courageously she called the Committee's method of handling the case "un-American" and this produced an outburst from Representative Starnes. When, in proving her point, she made an attempt to find out whether the committee members had ever read the plays criticized, she was compelled by Congressman Starnes to apologize to the Committee. "You are not here to ask the Committee questions," said Congressman Starnes. "You are here to answer

*Hearings on H. Res. 282, Investigation of Un-American Propaganda Activities in the United States; Vol. 4 (Government Printing Office: 1939).

questions. You and every other witness are here to answer questions; not to ask them. . . . I must insist that you be respectful to this Committee. . . . We were appointed to ask questions and to investigate, not to be investigated."

On December 6, when Mrs. Woodward retired from the witness stand because the Committee wanted more specific information than she could give, I was called to testify. It was indeed much later than the W.P.A. thought. Could a few hours offset the months in which allegations had gone unanswered, and charges had been magnified by the press?

Before me stretched two long tables in the form of a huge T. At the foot was the witness chair, at the head the members of the Committee. At long tables on either side of the T were reporters, stenographers, cameramen. The room itself, a high-walled chamber with great chandeliers, was lined with exhibits of material from the Federal Theatre and the Writers' Project; but all I could see for a moment were the faces of thousands of Federal Theatre people; clowns in the circus . . . telephone girls at the switchboards . . . actors in grubby rehearsal rooms . . . acrobats limbering up their routines . . . costume women busy making cheap stuff look expensive . . . musicians composing scores to bring out the best in our often oddly assembled orchestras . . . playwrights working on scripts with the skills of our actors in mind . . . carpenters, prop men, ushers. These were the people on trial that morning.

I was sworn in as a witness by Chairman Dies, rangy Texan with a cowboy drawl and a big black cigar. I wanted to talk about Federal Theatre, but the Committee apparently did not. Who had appointed me? Harry Hopkins. Was that his own idea or did somebody put him up to it? I said I had no knowledge of any recommendations made in my behalf; I said that while the Committee had recently been investigating un-American activity, I had been engaged for four years in combating un-American inactivity. The distinction was lost on the Committee. I sketched the project's concern for the human values, the return of over 2,000* of our people to jobs in private industry, but the Committee was not interested in any discussion of the

*When I spoke before the Sirovich Committee the number returned to private industry totaled 1,500. At the time the project ended the figure was 2,660.

project. Wasn't it true I taught at Vassar? Yes. Went to Russia? Yes. Wrote a book about it? Yes. Praised the Russian theatre? In 1926 I had been appointed as a fellow of the Guggenheim Foundation to study the theatre in twelve European countries over a period of fourteen months; Russia was one of the countries in which I carried on such observations. What was it I found so exciting in the Russian theatre? It was at that time an interesting theatre about which little was known. It was my job at that time to study it. That, I pointed out, was twelve years ago. It was part of the background of my profession—the American theatre. The Committee was giving more time to the discussion of the Russian theatre than Federal Theatre had in the four years of its existence.

Mr. Starnes was curious about my visits to Russia. Had I gone there in 1931 as well as in 1926? Yes, for three weeks. Was I a delegate to anything? No, I had gone, as had many American theatre producers, to see the Russian theatre festival. Did I meet at the festival there any of the people later employed in the Federal Theatre? Certainly not.

Hadn't I written plays in Russian and produced them in Russia? I had not (I remembered my struggles to learn to order a meal or buy galoshes in Russian).

Then back to the project. Had communistic propaganda been circulated on the project? Not to my knowledge. Were there orders on my part against such activity? Yes, stringent orders which appear in the brief. Mr. Starnes took a different tack: Did I consider the theatre a weapon? I said the theatre could be all things to all men. "Do you see this?" Congressman Starnes suddenly shouted, waving a yellow magazine aloft. "Ever see it before?" I said it seemed to be an old *Theatre Arts Monthly*. This described a meeting of workers' theaters in New York in 1931. Hadn't I been active in setting them up? No. I had never been connected in any way with workers' theatres. I wrote a report on such theatres for *Theatre Arts Monthly* under the title "A Theatre Is Born." This theatre, however, was not born through me; I was simply a reporter.

How about these plays that had been criticized by witnesses before the Committee? Were they propaganda? For communism? "To the best of my knowledge," I told the Committee, "we have never done a play which was propaganda for communism; but we have done plays which were propaganda for democracy, for better housing. . . ."

How many people had we played to so far? Twenty-five million people, a fifth of the population. Where did our audience come from? Was it true that we "couldn't get any audiences for anything except communist plays"? No. The list submitted would show our wide audience support. Back to the article, "A Theatre Is Born," and the phrase where I had described the enthusiasm of these theatres as having "a certain Marlowesque madness."

"You are quoting from this Marlowe," observed Mr. Starnes. "Is he a Communist?"

The room rocked with laughter, but I did not laugh. Eight thousand people might lose their jobs because a Congressional Committee had so pre-judged us that even the classics were "communistic." I said, "I was quoting from Christopher Marlowe."

"Tell us who Marlowe is, so we can get the proper references, because that is all we want to do."

"Put in the record that he was the greatest dramatist in the period of Shakespeare, immediately preceding Shakespeare."

Mr. Starnes subsided; Mr. Thomas of New Jersey took over. How about this play, *The Revolt of the Beavers?* Didn't Brooks Atkinson of the *New York Times* disapprove of the play? Yes, he did. But Mr. Hearst's *New York American* thought it a "pleasing fantasy for children," and an audience survey by trained psychologists brought only favorable reactions from children such as "teaches us never to be selfish"—"it is better to be good than bad"—"how the children would want the whole world to be nine years old and happy."

Was it true that we had been rehearsing *Sing for Your Supper*, the musical in New York, for thirteen months? It was true and the delays were not of our choosing. We kept losing our best skits and our best actors to private industry. Was that, I asked, un-American? Mr. Mosier brought us back to the question of propaganda. Had we ever produced any anti-fascist plays? Some people claimed that Shaw's *On the Rocks* was anti-fascist and others thought it was anti-communist; Shakespeare's *Coriolanus* caused the same discussion.

"We never do a play because it holds any political bias," I declared.

"We do a play because we believe it is a good play, a strong play, properly handled, with native material."

Was it true that Earl Browder appeared as a character in *Triple-A Plowed Under?* Yes. Did he expound his theory of communism? He did not; he appeared as a shadow on a screen along with Al Smith, Senator Hastings, and Thomas Jefferson. Had we ever produced plays that were anti-religious? On the contrary, we had produced more religious plays than any other theatre organization in the history of the country. Was I in sympathy with communistic doctrines? I said:

"I am an American and I believe in American democracy. I believe the Works Progress Administration is one great bulwark of that democracy. I believe the Federal Theatre, which is one small part of that large pattern, is honestly trying in every possible way to interpret the best interests of the people of this democracy. I am not in sympathy with any other form of government."

What percentage of the 4,000 employees on the New York project were members of the Workers' Alliance, Mr. Thomas wanted to know. We had no way of knowing. Was it a very large percentage? No, we knew it could not be large because the vast majority belonged to the standard theatrical organizations like Actors' Equity and the various stage unions, and these unions did not permit their members to join the Workers' Alliance.

Chairman Dies asked if we were out to entertain our audiences or to instruct them. I said that the primary purpose of a play is to entertain but that it can also teach.

"Do you think the theatre should be used for the purpose of conveying ideas along social and economic lines?"

"I think that is one justifiable reason for the existence of a theatre."

"Do you think that the Federal Theatre should be used for the purpose of conveying ideas along social, economic, or political lines?"

"I would hesitate on the political."

"Eliminate political, upon social and economic lines?"

"I think it is one logical, reasonable, and I might say imperative thing for our theatre to do."

Could I give the Committee one play, dealing with social questions, where "organized labor does not have the best of the other fellows"?

Certainly. I mentioned *Spirochete*, the living newspaper on the history of syphilis, endorsed by the Surgeon General of the United States Public Health Service. I mentioned the living newspapers being prepared on flood control (*Bonneville Dam*); the history of vaudeville (*Clown's Progress*); the history of California real estate (*Spanish Grant*). The Chairman waved these examples aside. Didn't *Power* imply that public ownership of utilities is a good thing? Is it proper for a government theatre to champion one side of a controversy? We do not choose plays by picking sides in a controversy.

On this matter of the writing of plays it was apparent that the Committee confused the Theatre and the Federal Writers' Project. Chairman Dies insisted that he had received admissions from Federal Theatre workers who were Communists, Communists who had placed their signatures openly in a book. I said this had not happened on our project.

"Well," declared the Chairman triumphantly, "Mr. De Solo said he was a Communist."

"But he is not on the Federal Theatre Project."

"He is on the Writers' Project."

"Yes, but not our project."

Suddenly Mr. Starnes remarked that it was a quarter past one, the Chairman announced an adjournment for an hour and said that Mr. Alsberg would be heard when they resumed.

"Just a minute, gentlemen," I interrupted. "Do I understand that this concludes my testimony?"

"We will see about it after lunch," the Chairman promised.

"I would like to make a final statement, if I may."

"We will see about it after lunch," the Chairman repeated and the gavel fell. We never saw about it after lunch.

As the hearing broke up I thought suddenly of how much it all looked like a badly staged courtroom scene; it wasn't imposing enough for a congressional hearing on which the future of several thousand human beings depended. For any case on which the life and reputation of a single human being depended, even that of an accused murderer, we had an American system which demanded a judge trained in law, a defense lawyer, a carefully chosen jury, and above all the necessity of hearing all the evidence on both sides of the case.

Yet here was a Committee which for months had been actually trying a case against Federal Theatre, trying it behind closed doors, and giving one side only to the press. Out of a project employing thousands of people from coast to coast, the Committee had chosen arbitrarily to hear ten witnesses, all from New York City, and had refused arbitrarily to hear literally hundreds of others, on and off the project, who had asked to testify.

Representative Dempsey, who throughout the hearing had been just and courteous, came up and told me that he felt my testimony had been "completely satisfactory." Congressman Thomas was jovial.

"You don't look like a Communist," he declared. "You look like a Republican!"

"If your Committee isn't convinced that neither I nor the Federal Theatre Project is communistic I want to come back this afternoon," I told him.

"We don't want you back," he laughed. "You're a tough witness and we're all worn out."

Mrs. Woodward and I weren't satisfied. We told the secretary of the Committee that I had not finished my testimony. He said, "In any case your brief will be printed." He accepted the brief for inclusion in the transcript. It was not included.

After the testimony, one thing stood out in my mind: the brief must be made public. Mr. Niles, when approached on the point, said that my apprehension was groundless. "They'll have to include the brief. They can't suppress evidence. However, I'll tell you what to do. You send five hundred of those mimeographed briefs to my office and if the Committee does not print it I will then see that copies are distributed to every Senator and to a number of Members of the lower House." We sent the briefs to Mr. Niles' office. They were never distributed to Members of Congress.

We made one more attempt to give the Committee a realistic view of the project. On December 19 I extended an invitation to each member of the Committee to come to New York for the opening production of *Pinocchio* at the Ritz Theatre on December 23, or for any of the holiday performances.

"You might be especially interested in this production," I wrote Congressman Dies, "not only because it represents one of our major

Hallie Flanagan

efforts in the field of children's theatre, but because it is a visualization of what we have been able to do in rehabilitating professional theatre people and retraining them in new techniques. In *Pinocchio* we use fifty vaudeville people who were at one time headliners in their profession and who, through no fault of their own, suddenly found themselves without a market. Now they are artists in a new field and I feel certain you will find that this re-creation of theatre personalities is no less exciting than the presentation of the play itself."

The Committee, however, proceeded to its final deliberations with its theatre-going record intact: officially it never saw a production of the project under examination.

The Dies Committee Report, filed with the House of Representatives January 3, 1939, may in the future be of as much interest to students of jurisprudence and government as of theatre. A great amount of space was given over to condemnation of the Federal Writers' Project; but on the case of the Federal Theatre six months of sensational charges tapered down to one short paragraph:

We are convinced that a rather large number of the employees on the Federal Theatre Project are either members of the Communist Party or are sympathetic with the Communist Party. It is also clear that certain employees felt under compulsion to join the Workers' Alliance in order to retain their jobs.

It will be noted that the report did not say a word in criticism of three of the major points dwelt upon by witnesses and about which I had been questioned: type of plays; type of audience; type of leadership. Just what constituted "a rather large number," what amounted to "sympathy" or how many "certain employees" ever felt any "compulsion" was left to the imagination.

ANZIA

YEZIERSKA

"Tossed together in a strange fellowship of necessity..."

Like Hallie Flanagan, Anzia Yezierska *was a creative artist employed by the Works Progress Administration. Unlike Flanagan, Yezierska was not an influential New Deal official. She was but one of many hundreds of writers employed on the WPA Federal Writers' Project, earning much-needed money researching background for a guidebook on New York City.*

Yezierska, in her fifties when the Depression hit, had already lived a kind of fairy-tale life, although one without a happy ending. Few records remain to document Yezierska's life. She probably arrived in America in 1890 at about age ten in the company of her large Russian Jewish family, whom immigration officials at New York's Castle Garden renamed Mayer. As Hattie Mayer, the young girl went to work with her three teen-aged sisters sewing dresses in Lower East Side sweatshops. She also began to quarrel with her strictly Orthodox father.

By the time she was seventeen or eighteen, Hattie Mayer had reclaimed her own name, fled home and her father's demands for obedience, and enrolled in Columbia Teachers' College, supporting herself by working nights. In spare moments she also wrote short stories, then novels, largely about women like herself, ambitious immigrants eager to break out of a ghetto world and find love and a better life. By 1920 she had married, given birth to a daughter, left her husband and child, conducted a passionate and improbable six-month affair with the famous educator John Dewey, and published her first collection of short stories, Hungry Hearts. *A novel,* Salome of the Tenements, *and a collection of short stories,* Children of Loneliness, *appeared in 1923. Her next three novels were* Bread Giver *(1925),* Arrogant Beggar *(1927), and* All I Could Never Be *(1932).*

By the mid-twenties she was famous, her photograph splashed everywhere. Her love affairs and other exploits appeared in the tabloids. Hollywood beckoned, and she journeyed west to rewrite several of her stories and novels into screenplays. Americans seemingly could not get enough of the immigrant seamstress become rich and notorious novelist. Then, with the Depression, the years of fur coats, fine automobiles, and interviews in national magazines ended abruptly. Sales of Anzia Yezierska's sixth book, published in 1932, were meager. The craze for her work was over. She was suddenly just another broke writer, looking for work, lucky to get hired by the WPA to write guidebooks.

Yezierska did not publish a book again until 1950, when her autobiography, Red Ribbon on a White Horse, *appeared. In the following excerpts from that book, she describes her time as a government worker. It is important to note that Yezierska rarely made clear distinctions between fiction and autobiography. Each included elements of the other when she wrote. Her daughter Louise Levitas Henriksen, who has edited Yezierska's letters, has noted, for instance, that a few of the characters she describes as co-workers in the Writers' Project were semi-fictional composites.*

After the Depression, no great novels remained in Yezierska either. She regained none of her earlier fame or fortune but eked out a perpetually precarious living as a magazine writer and book reviewer. Only after her death in 1970 did scholars begin to rediscover her work.

SOURCES: Anzia Yezierska's autobiography was republished in 1981. See also Babbette Inglehart, "Daughters of Loneliness: Anzia Yezierska and the Immigrant Woman Writer," *Studies in American Jewish Literature*, 1 (Winter 1975), 1–10; Carol B. Schoen, *Anzia Yezierska* (1982); Charlotte Goodman, "Anzia Yezierska," in Daniel Walden, ed., *Twentieth-Century American-Jewish Fiction Writers, Dictionary of Literary Biography*, Vol. 28 (1984), 332–335; Sally A. Drucker, "Anzia Yezierska: An Immigrant Cinderella," doctoral dissertation, State University of New York, Buffalo (1988); *Contemporary Authors*, New Revision Series, 126 (1989), 470–472; and Jules Chemetzsky, "Anzia Yezierska," in *Notable American Women*, 753–754. Yezierska's daughter, Louise Levitas Henriksen, has edited a heavily annotated collection of letters, *Anzia Yezierska: A Writer's Life* (1988). Yezierska's papers are housed in the Special Collections Library at Boston University.

ANZIA YEZIERSKA

Working for the Government

THE AMAZING RESILIENCE OF people! How they cling to life, even on the edge of an abyss!

In the smoky half-light of the waiting room, faces rushed to me in a whirl of color and sound. I had seen these people at the relief station, waiting for the investigating machine to legalize them as paupers. Now they had work cards in their hands. Their waiting was no longer the hopeless stupor of applicants for mass relief; they were employees of the government. They had risen from the scrap heap of the unemployed, from the loneliness of the unwanted, dreaming of regeneration, together. The new job look lighted the most ravaged faces. . . .

My name was called and I jumped up. . . .

John Barnes, the director, drew up a chair for me at his desk. He was a tall, very thin man with a long face and a sad mouth. His well-tailored clothes, and something scholarly in his manner, at first

167
Anzia Yezierska

reminded me of the men I had met in the days when I went to literary teas.

"Anzia Yezierska." He shook hands. I smelled the liquor on his breath and saw the unguarded gleam of his eyes. "What brings you here?"

"The same thing that has brought thousands of others to W.P.A."

A pause. A long silence.

"You know, I used to review your books in the old days," he said.

"That immigrant stuff was so long ago, in a past existence. When I stopped turning it out, I saw my own funeral procession go by."

He smiled so understandingly that I stopped talking. His eyes seemed to see at a glance all I had been through, and they made anything I might say in defense of myself superfluous. How amazing, I thought, that after all the deaths I had died I could still be so alive to a little bit of friendliness, and I heard myself talk again.

"What a story Dostoevski could write of the poor people here!"

"Dostoevski's dead," he said, offering me a cigarette. "You write it."

I waved the cigarette aside. "There's a man out there in the waiting room," I said. "A skeleton in rags with a brief case. He looks like the Ancient Mariner with the dead albatross on his neck. If any one here knew enough to write his story, he'd know what God and man is."

Barnes looked at me in silence. With fumbling fingers, he relit his cigarette. After a pause he said, "Why don't you write it, or better still, have you thought of writing your own story?"

The telephone rang. Barnes picked up the receiver, and after a pause snorted, "Well, Somervell! What do you want me to do? Stand over them and watch them do their work? I'm not a timekeeper."

He raised his voice to a querulous shout. "Boondoggling—hell! What can you expect of people who haven't worked so long they've forgotten how? Remember, they were hired because they were on relief. I can't park on their tails every minute."

He slammed down the receiver. "Christ! I give up! An army man in charge of the Writers' Project! But of course it's not a Writers' Project—it's a landmark in nonsense. All the misfits and maniacs on relief have been dumped here."

His eyes shone with the brilliance of exhaustion, lit up with the aid of drink.

"Can you imagine what it is to keep six hundred bums busy with the pretense of writing?"

Liquor was getting him to the point of tears. "The phoniness, the stupidity that I have to put up with," he wailed. "I was a poet. Now I'm a glorified office boy."

He checked himself. "I'm an awful lush. But you've got an idea. See what you can make out of it. Even an army man wouldn't mind having a good autobiography come out of W.P.A.!" . . .

The New Society
of Arts and Letters

On the first payday everybody went to Tony's Bar to cash his check. I followed, swept along by the wild elation. While the bartender was on the way to the bank we sat around the bar nibbling free pretzels. When the money arrived we treated one another to beer with the magnanimity of new millionaires. Then we crowded into the smoke-filled banquet hall at the rear of the bar, ordered a feast—a thirty-five-cent table-d'hôte dinner—and tossed nickel tips to the waiter. We were as hilarious as slum children around a Christmas tree. Pockets jingled with money. Men who hadn't had a job in years fondled five- and ten-dollar bills with the tenderness of farmers rejoicing over new crops of grain.

"Friends! Quiet, please!" Barnes stood up, and with a wave of his hand, brought silence. "I'd like to say a few words. But for heaven's sake, don't consider me a 'boss.' I've been unemployed just like the rest of you. We've all been kicked around. Suddenly we're handed an opportunity to really become human beings again. We have to live up to the responsibility of this trust. Who knows, among us even now may be a new Gorky, a new Dostoevski."

One after another rose to give his testimonial of faith.

"Folks!" Richard Wright said jubilantly. "Where I come from, they're all singing:

"Roosevelt! You're my man!
When the time come
I ain't got a cent

169
Anzia Yezierska

You buy my groceries
And pay my rent.
Mr. Roosevelt, you're my man!

"But now we've been given more than a bellyful of grub. The President has given us Negroes a chance at last, and I tell you I mean to make the most of it. I've had all kinds of jobs. I've shined shoes, washed dishes, I've been a Pullman porter, I've scrubbed floors, cleaned toilets. Those are nigger jobs. Some folks think that's all we're fit for—art is only for white folks. This is the greatest day of my life. I'm just rarin' to go. . . ."

I turned to Barnes as Wright sat down. "We are lucky to have a man like you for our director. You're a poet, not a boss, and that's what we need. I feel like a bit of withered moss that has been suddenly put into water, growing green again. Give people a ray of hope and they rise out of their ashes and begin to dream and live again."

Bill Adams, a dark sallow-faced youth with sad old eyes, burst into mirthless laughter. "To hear you people talk, one would think the millennium had come. A rotten tree can only bear rotten fruit. All they're after is to prime their voting machine to keep their busted capitalistic system going. . . ."

"Lay off, stinker!"

"Dry up!"

Voices of disapproval were heard from every corner of the room; even the Marxists of the group were too joyous at that moment to tolerate their gloomy ideologist. Bill Adams went on, unheeding.

"Mass bribery, that's what W.P.A. is. Government blackmail. We'd fight, we'd stage riots and revolutions if they didn't hush us up. We're all taking hush money. But if we were smart, we'd take the money and keep hollering."

He flicked the ash from his cigarette. "The Mellons and the Morgans and the holy crusaders of the Liberty League must laugh when they think how cheaply they silenced the voice of an entire class and averted a revolution with a few billions of the people's money."

A diabolical grin distorted his face. "They're going to kill us off soon enough in the next war. This sop to hunger, the W.P.A., is our prewar bonus. Folks, that's a hot one! Instead of calling it Works Progress Administration, we ought to call it Victims for Future Wars!" ...

Every day new events fired our enthusiasm. A week later, there was a crowd at the bulletin board reading the announcement of lectures to be held at the Writers' Union: Theodore Dreiser on the novel, Stephen Vincent Benét on poetry, and Sherwood Anderson on the short story.

"How is this for a literary workshop?" Paul Yellin addressed the crowd. "Those famous authors are coming down to talk to you man to man—writer to writers. We're bringing you the master-craftsmen of America. You've got the blocks, and those big guys are going to show you how to put your blocks together."

He paused to look at their shining faces.

"And now we've got some business to attend to," he went on. "We still have to fight to keep our jobs. That takes dough, fellers. We need money for leaflets, for picket signs, for delegations to Washington. I expect every one of you to cough up your two bits today. Free riders and chiselers will see their names on the bulletin board." ...

Fellowship of Necessity

Each morning I walked to the Project as lighthearted as if I were going to a party. The huge, barrackslike Writers' Hall roared with the laughter and greetings of hundreds of voices. As we signed in, we stopped to smoke, make dates for lunch and exchange gossip. Our grapevine buzzed with budding love affairs, tales of salary raises, whispers of favoritism, the political maneuvers of the big shots, and the way Barnes told off Somervell over the phone. There was a hectic camaraderie among us, although we were as ill-assorted as a crowd on a subway express—spinster poetesses, pulp specialists, youngsters with school-magazine experience, veteran newspaper men, art-for-art's-sake literati, and the clerks and typists who worked with us—people of all ages, all nationalities, all degrees of education, tossed together in a strange fellowship of necessity.

There was old Jeremiah Kintzler, urging everybody to write to the President to abolish the Army and Navy and set up a "permanent

Society of Arts and Letters of America," and young Richard Wright, as yet unpublished and unknown, but always the center of the serious aspirants to literature.

There was also Edwin Peck, a former professor of English, an authority on *Beowulf* and Chaucer, who stood aloof from the social caldron. His eyes were sunk so deep in their sockets that you could see no color, no light in them. The reverses that drew others together separated him and carved on his gray face the loneliness of his pride.

Another figure of proud isolation was Priscilla Howard, a thin, white-haired New England spinster. Each day when she stood in line to sign in with the loud, pushing mob, she felt an alien in her own country. Her shoulders shrank in fastidious protest at this horde of foreigners who neither knew nor cared that her ancestors had landed in 1620. She always wore earrings, a brooch and a ring of flowered mosaic, heirlooms of her English ancestors, and her fingers, with their swollen knuckles, would hold onto her brooch in fierce protectiveness. She was born a Howard, and she would always bear herself like a Howard.

It was hard for Miss Howard to talk to any of us, and after a few rebuffs we left her alone. But Pat Ryan and Paul Yellin, the gregarious leaders of the Writers' Union, had a mission. Every one on the Project was to them a brother- or a sister-worker to be won over to the union.

That this Irishman and Jew should consider themselves relatives of hers and should want her to join their union so outraged Miss Howard that she told them who she was and why she would have nothing to do with them. But automatically she was handed the same literature we all got, union leaflets, political tracts, and even *Red Pen*, which she conspicuously tore up and threw into the wastebasket. Ryan and Yellin ignored this minor rebellion.

No two men on the Project were more unlike in background and personality than our union leaders. Blond Pat Ryan had been a world traveler and lecturer; Paul Yellin was a dark young Jew from the gutters of the ghetto, who had worked without pay on a Left Wing magazine. Ryan's big-boned athletic body exuded the ease of a man who enjoyed every moment of life. Yellin was short, stocky, grim-faced, with a stubborn intensity born of poverty. But the two had one thing in common—their passion for the union. No doubts, no confusion, no introspective questioning wasted them. They had nothing but the relief tickets that entitled them to their jobs on W.P.A., but they carried themselves with an assurance that millionaires might envy. They had nothing, and because they had nothing, they believed themselves destined by historic forces to change the world.

Yellin was the only supervisor who still wore his old work clothes, the only untamed peasant among the white-collared gentility who sat on swivel chairs behind desks marked "Supervisor." The desks were new. The men at their new jobs wore brand-new suits; you could almost see the price tags dangling from their crisp new ties. But Yellin wasn't in their class. Every cent saved from bare necessities and every free moment went to the union.

Yellin and Ryan were brave men, for not even Finley, the guard, could intimidate them. At first they tried to win him over to a realization that he was a worker and should favor the workers. But Finley, swaggering in his new uniform with brass buttons, was born to keep discipline for the bosses. He loved to bellow, "Keep in line there! Where's your card? No card? Then stay out!" He snorted with satisfaction whenever he had a chance to vent his authority and push people back into place.

The only person he never pushed around was red-haired Jean Williams. Finley melted when she smiled at him. Jean was young and beautiful and as free as thistledown from the cares that weighed on others. She wore a soft black jersey that showed every curve of her body—she had nothing to hide. Men's eyes followed her, and she accepted their admiration as naturally as their free dinners. She was so friendly she could even make women forget their jealousy.

The first time I saw her was at Tony's, where we cashed our checks. She was sitting at the bar as we came in, and she pushed aside an empty glass, opened her compact and outlined her mouth with lipstick. Bill Adams stared in fascination.

"Are you on the Project?" he asked. "I haven't seen you before."

She looked at him with newly reddened lips. "I wish I were." Her husky voice had a vibrant eagerness. "You writers are having such a swell time. You get paid every week. I never know where my dinner's coming from."

He ordered her a drink. "Why don't you get on too?"

"For one thing, I'm not a writer." She laughed. "I'm an artist's model. But I've always wanted to write—"

"The story of your life?"

"How did you guess?"

"It's in your eyes." He patted her knee. "I'll make a writer of you. Just get on relief."

She widened her eyes at him. "Wouldn't that be an awful thing to go through? I don't want any of those reliefers prying into my affairs."

"But it's very simple. I know an investigator who'll do anything for you, if you're nice to him."

Jean threw back her head and laughed. "Lead me to him."

"Baby! You stick with me. I'll do the writing for you, too."

Arm in arm, they walked out. One of the men at the bar set down his glass and shook his head in mock bitterness. "Why can't a man sleep his way into a job like those luscious babes?"

"Brother," a woman writer retorted, "bitching from bed to bed is specialized work."

Two weeks later, with a relief card in her hand, Jean was on her way to the personnel head of the Project. She quickly got to know everybody.

I was lucky to be on the Creative Project. Those who worked on the *Guide* had to sign in each morning at nine, get their assignments from their editors, and sign out at four. I did my writing at home and had to report once a week to Barnes.

After he had read a rough draft of my day-to-day story of W.P.A., he said, "You're still too close to it to get the meaning that will come later on. Perhaps you're trying to say too many things at the same time."

"Well, there's so much to write. I'm so anxious to show something for my time."

"Don't be too anxious," Barnes said. "Writing that amounts to anything takes a lot of time. The Creative Project was meant to give writers a chance to work in peace and confidence."

He picked up a publicity release. "This is what I have to submit to the Colonel. 'The total production of six hundred writers for the past week was 1,200,000 words, an average of two thousand words per writer.'" He flung the page aside. "These millions of words will never see the light of day. In the end we'll have to hire professional journalists to do the guidebooks." . . .

Even the leaders of the union thought Barnes a good fellow. Once a week when the union delegation had their meeting with Barnes in his office to present their grievances and new demands, it was done with great formality.

Pat Ryan, the president of the union, and Paul Yellin, the executive secretary, maintained that to keep what we had, we had to stay on the offensive and persistently make demands for better working conditions and more pay.

And then one day the weekly union delegation meeting with Barnes coincided with one of his daytime binges. He was bleary-eyed and met the delegation with a frown. Pat Ryan ignored Barnes's mood and proceeded with the business of the meeting. He demanded that our pay checks be increased from twenty-three to thirty dollars. "We're doing skilled work," Pat Ryan boomed in his challenging voice. "The minimum wage scale for journalists is a dollar an hour. Why should we work for less?"

Barnes glared at the union leaders with bloodshot eyes. He struck the desk with his fist. "You know what you can do with your demands!" he yelled. "More pay? For what? Misfits, bitches, bums calling themselves writers, just because the government is giving them a handout." He swept the papers off his desk, then slumped back into his chair.

With grim dignity, Pat Ryan and Paul Yellin opened the door. The others filed out after them. I stayed to pick up the papers and straighten the desk.

"Boondoggling bums!" Barnes passed his hand wearily over his forehead. "Christ! I might have been a poet, but instead I wind up director of a madhouse."

He started to get up and knocked over an ash tray. He waved his arms at the mess on the floor and began to ramble. "In my novel, death will be the hero—death—" With the voice and gestures of a John Barrymore, he declaimed:

"Life, like a dome of many-colored glass,
Stains the white radiance of Eternity,
Until Death tramples it to fragments.—Die,
If thou wouldst be with that which thou dost seek!
Follow where all is fled! . . ."

"Follow—where all is fled!" He lurched into his chair. "Listen. We're like the ghosts in *Outward Bound*. A ship of dead souls drifting in the dead of night. I know we're dead, but we keep on getting drunk, making love, and talking politics."

His eyes closed, and the crescents of dark skin below them stood out sharply. I looked from the overturned ash tray to Barnes sprawled in sodden sleep. I saw the beginning of the end.

Selling New York to the World

A few days after our disastrous meeting with Barnes, I opened the morning paper and saw on the front page the glaring headlines:

WPA OFFICIAL AND RED-HAIRED WRITER
IN HOTEL FIRE
WRITERS' PROJECT DIRECTOR AND GIRL IN HOSPITAL

The tabloid story of a "drunken illicit tryst" was such a shock that I couldn't eat breakfast. W.P.A. was again under fire, lampooned as "counterfeit work, supported with taxpayers' good money." Impatient to find out what had happened, I hurried to the office.

The noise of the Writers' Hall rushed at me as I opened the door. A crowd was already there, piecing together the details. The scandal had blasted us all out of our ruts and made us realize the precariousness of our jobs.

Perched on his desk, Paul Yellin read to the avid listeners:

". . . John Barnes and Jean Williams admitted they had a few drinks in his apartment. . . . A bellboy, investigating the smell of smoke, discovered their bed in flames. . . ."

"Well, the fire cooked their goose," Paul said. He went on reading:

"... The Project, which has been a source of trouble and embarrassment to the Administration, will be reorganized. It is reported that Colonel Somervell is determined to choose a director who will see that the *Guidebook*, upon which 600 writers have been employed for over a year, is promptly completed. The Colonel stated that the new director he will appoint will put less emphasis on sensationalism and more on efficiency and production. . . ."

We looked at one another in panic. The military threat of efficiency frightened us. Those of us whom Barnes had befriended knew we'd never get another director with his creative understanding.

Work was at a standstill. All over the huge hall there were knots of people, talking through clouds of smoke. The hum of speculation never ceased until the afternoon Somervell announced that Barnes had resigned and that Nathan Tashman was appointed acting director.

We waited for Tashman the next day, sitting at our desks like children awaiting the arrival of their new teacher. We already knew something about him. Our grapevine provided a complete *Who's Who*. We knew that he had published a mediocre novel years ago and that he had been a reader for movie companies and a writer of detective pulp.

Our first sight of him as he stepped out of the elevator filled us with alarm. His face resolute with purpose, he looked the picture of Somervell's idea of an executive. He was dressed in an Oxford-gray suit, white shirt, and maroon-striped tie. Our eyes followed his triumphant progress through the hall to his office.

All that day and for days after, the acting director was busy with reorganization. From his office issued memos, pink, yellow, blue, and white. People rushed back and forth with fear in their faces. Tashman's "new standard of production" drove us all into a panic of hurry and confusion. One by one, we were called before him. Although I was prepared for anything, I trembled as I walked in with my manuscript.

"There's no record here of any work you have done," he began.

"I am working on a novel. I have part of it here...."

"Oh, yes, I know—the great American novel." The frown of authority hid the uncertain expression of his eyes. "I'm putting a stop to boondoggling."

"Mr. Barnes assigned me to the Creative Project...."

"Mr. Barnes is no longer with us. I'm sorry, but we're cutting the Creative Project. The great urgency is to complete the *Guide*."

"But I'm not a journalist."

"You're free to write your novels after hours. No one is stopping you. But all of us on government pay must work for the government." He toyed with a new rubber stamp: "Acting Director." It was a powerful little stamp. I could feel his fingers itched to use it. "You haven't produced anything in years."

"Have you?"

"I'm a busy man." He arranged the papers on his desk. "I'd like to write novels, too, but I have a job. Washington has set a deadline for the *Guide*. We can only use writers who can turn in copy."

"I'd be glad to have you read my manuscript." I offered it to him but he waved it aside.

"My dear lady! This isn't helping the *Guide*." He looked at the clock with an expression of dismissal. "Report to Bailey hereafter." ...

Bailey, our newly appointed supervisor, called us to attention.

"I want you to know what's expected of you. Our job is to sell New York to the world. Our *Guide* is the biggest thing ever undertaken in this country. We have the biggest staff of journalists ever assembled under one roof."

Bailey went on like a Coney Island barker. "You must describe the great skyscrapers, theaters, office buildings, and churches that make New York the wonder city of America. You must play up the colorful sights, Greenwich Village, Harlem, the markets, the slums. Crowds of tourists from farms, mines, and logging camps will flock here to see the sights. The *Guide* will earn the thanks of hotels, department stores, and the movies for bringing crowds to their doors."

He picked up a paper and read the names of those who had failed to bring in the required wordage. "There's going to be a change," he threatened. "Those who can't produce will be fired and new ones hired. You artists think the government owes you a living. Well, it doesn't. Whether you live or not doesn't matter unless you give value for value received. Hereafter, the minimum for each and every one of you is two thousand words a day. Surely a paltry wordage of two thousand isn't much to do for your government in return for all you're getting."

"Wordage, poundage, yardage—" Jeremiah fumed. "Barnes was drunk only with liquor, but this faker is drunk with his own bilge." The old man tightened his hold on his brief case. "How could such a fool become a supervisor of writers?"

Bill Adams laughed. "He must have belonged to the right political clubs."

Wordage Machine

My new assignment was to catalogue the trees in Central Park. Most of us took the slips of paper that Bailey handed out like some bitter medicine we had to swallow. . . .

I waited half an hour outside an office of the Park Department and got a list of the 253 varieties of trees in Central Park. The rest of the day I walked around the park and thought that doing wordage for Bailey wasn't so terrible after all. But the next day I was assigned to the library to look up the story of Hofmeister in Smith's *History of New York, 1779.*

The circulating department of the Forty-second Street library was a book traffic center as bewildering to me as a foreign country. S, Smith—I opened the first drawer of the catalogue, and then another. Smiths peopled the world. They crowded about me. Smiths who built colonies, wrote on finance and invented patent washing machines. Down through endless rows of Smiths, my eyes blurred—nowhere a Smith who had written *History of New York, 1779.*

I took my place in line at the information desk.

"Where can I find Smith's *History of New York, 1779?*" I asked the librarian.

"Look in the catalogue," came the voice of trained efficiency, immersed in records.

"But I've looked under all the Smiths."

"Try New York."

I began hunting through the cards once more. Hundreds, thousands of cards with cryptic numbers and abbreviated descriptions. One of them must conceal the information I sought. I began to feel a personal enmity against these oblong slips of cardboard, a nervous irritation born of fatigue. This second search was as futile as the first.

"I've looked through the entire catalogue," I told the librarian. "I can't find Smith's *History of New York, 1779*."

"Go to the Reference Room," she said. "Room 300."

Desperation did it. I found the card. I filled out a slip. I handed it to the man. At last the book was in my hand. Now for the story of Hofmeister.

But there was no index. I looked through the whole book, page by page. There was no Hofmeister.

It was getting late. Lamps were being turned on at every table and my assignment was still undone. The whole day's work at those files gone to waste. I staggered over to the central desk.

"I've looked all day for Hofmeister who lived in 1779."

The pretty face of a young librarian smiled up at me. "Let's see." She turned to the catalogue. Inanimate index cards came alive at her touch. She was like a trained musician opening his piano. In a moment one book after another, records, encyclopedias, yearbooks, were gotten from the shelves and consulted.

"You must have the wrong name," she said. "We have a record of William Havemeyer, but no Hofmeister."

The wrong name! It was almost evening and still no words for the wordage machine.

I was not putting the cards behind me. They would be waiting for me tomorrow and tomorrow.

The next morning when I signed the time sheet, Bailey demanded, "Where's your assignment?"

"I spent the day on a fool's errand. You told me to look for Hofmeister and there isn't any Hofmeister, only Havemeyer."

"Well, for Christ's sake! Why didn't you bring in the facts on Havemeyer?"

"But you asked for Hofmeister. How should I know that you don't know what you want?"

"After all, we expect you to use a little common sense." Bailey's voice was full of long-suffering patience. "I'm sorry, but we have a quota to maintain. Double wordage tomorrow.". . .

Richard Wright . . . stopped for a moment on his way from the library. "Look! Did you see this?" He showed us the announcement of *Story Magazine* offering a prize of five hundred dollars for the best story by any writer on W.P.A.

"I've got plenty of stuff to send them," he said with refreshing eagerness.

"When do you find time to write?"

"At night. I'm going home now to work."

I watched him stride through the crowd—young, strong, immune to weariness. Whatever hardship he had known he had transformed into his creative drive. . . .

"Wake up and live! I've solved the W.P.A. problem: how to get by with the least possible work."

Bill [Adams] said he had been assigned to catalogue the city museums. So he went to the tourist information service and there, in a couple of folders, he found all the dope he needed. He copied in an hour what was supposed to have taken a whole week to do.

"They've got all the stuff you need stacked up there in folders," Bill said. "So why waste time? The assignments we bring in go into the wastebasket anyway.". . .

Typewriters clicked memos in answer to memos, orders to change orders that had already been changed; copying paragraphs that had been copied from pages that had been copied from dust-covered books. Words dug up from dust to make more dust. Words to be filed away and buried in dusty cabinets till doomsday. . . .

Payday

Friday morning the six hundred of us stood in line, holding our identification cards, our names, and our numbers in our hands, waiting for our weekly checks.

The thought of our checks always charged payday with the excite-

Anzia Yezierska

ment of a holiday. Those of us who had cigarettes gave away drags, those lucky enough to have any change left lent nickels for coffee.

We were a restless, pushing crowd, constantly breaking up into knots of shrill debate, but Mike Finley, the guard, was determined to keep us in a straight line.

"For Christ's sake! Let's have order here! Don't block the aisles!" He had caught some one edging up front. "All right, wise guy!" His eyes gleamed. "You people would get away with murder if I weren't around."

Payday was Mike's day of glory. He strode about, a uniform on short, thick legs, collecting our identification cards. But the anticipation of our money made us magnanimous; we could even laugh at Mike's roughneck tyranny.

"Don't push me!" Bill Adams scoffed, "I'm an American citizen!"

"I'll push anybody who blocks the passage." Mike jerked up his bullet head.

"Take it easy, Mike!" Pat Ryan gave the guard a friendly little shove. "You're not herding cattle."

"Jesus! Cattle would be easier to handle!" Mike wiped the sweat from his beefy face. "It's my job to keep this howling mob in order. Hell'd break loose if I didn't watch you every minute."

He moved on, and as soon as his back was turned, the line sprawled out into friendly groups. Flirtations started, dates were made while propagandists expounded political views and union leaders attended to business.

A crowd had gathered at the bulletin board, reading an announcement of a special union meeting.

FIREWORKS!
YOU CAN'T AFFORD TO MISS THE BIGGEST SHOWDOWN OF THE YEAR.
COME TO THE LOCAL.
HEAR THE GRIEVANCE COMMITTEE REPORT
ON VACATIONS WITH PAY ON WPA.

"Do you really think they'll give us vacations?" I asked.

"They will if we fight for it," Pat Ryan said militantly. "We have the same right to our vacations as other government employees." And he handed me a petition to sign.

One after another signed until it reached Miss Howard. She pushed away the petition. "I'll sign nothing of the kind."

We stared at the pale, white-haired lady, withered by the years into a straight line. And yet she stood against us all so erect, so conscious of her dignity, that she commanded attention.

Paul Yellin put his hand over her arm with the patience of a grownup reasoning with a child. "Haven't you worked hard all year? Couldn't you use a vacation in this sweltering heat?"

Miss Howard pulled her arm away. "I don't feel overworked."

Every one turned to look at her. It was the first time we had heard her speak with such open hostility.

"Some of us here—thank heaven—have a sense of duty. But you people, instead of being grateful for what the government is doing for you—"

"Grateful?" Yellin's mouth twisted into a wry smile. "Lady! They didn't hand us our jobs on a platter. We went out and shouted and fought for them. We made enough noise until they heard us in Washington."

"All this agitation is un-American."

"If we hadn't agitated, *you* would still be on relief."

"The trouble with you foreigners, you've been given privileges you haven't earned."

"Foreigners?" Pat Ryan laughed. "I was born here. Besides, this country belongs to those who inhabit it—not to those who inherit it."

We gathered around him, caught up in the energy that poured out of him as he talked. But Miss Howard stood there with her gaze fixed over our heads.

"My people have been here three hundred years. And you foreigners, who come here with nothing, do nothing but agitate."

Angry voices rose from every corner of the room.

"Your people were foreigners, three hundred years ago."

Bill Adams jumped upon the desk, clapped his hands for silence.

"Hear ye! Hear ye! Fellow-paupers!" he shouted, waving his hat up and down like a town crier's bell. "The question before us is not whether we came here with the Pilgrims on the *Mayflower*, or just got off the last boat, but how long will we continue to be here, without our checks? It's very simple. Are we going to starve or not? If I have to wait on this line much longer, you can carry me out on a stretcher."

Everybody laughed, except Miss Howard and Joe Lane, a wiry little man from Vermont who was standing beside her. With tightened lips she turned to him.

"Where are the real Americans? The decent, loyal, God-fearing Americans?"

Richard Wright closed the book he was reading and shoved Ryan aside. "Why waste time with her? One signature more or less—what difference does it make?"

Everybody was so tense that Wright's common sense stood out like the strength in his young face. I marveled at the way he took part in everything happening on the Project and yet never became involved in the endless talk.

I asked him if he had any news of the story he had submitted to the *Story Magazine* contest.

"Oh, there are hundreds of manuscripts," he said, casually. "Nearly everybody on the Project is competing." But his words belied the anxiety in his eyes. He had the self-absorption of a great ambition.

The noon whistle sounded. It was time for lunch and we were hungry. A whoop of protest bellowed down the line.

"Damn it! Are they printing those checks? Where the hell is the paymaster?"

With the recklessness of a hungry mob, we forced our way into the director's office.

For the first time we saw the director afraid of us as we had often been afraid of him.

"I've been on the phone all morning, trying to locate the paymaster," he said. "I just found out he'll be held up till late this afternoon. There's nothing more I can do. You'll simply have to wait."

A groan went up the line and burst into a rebellious clamor.

"It's a conspiracy to humiliate us."

"The old tricks of reactionaries to wear us out waiting."

"Let's have a protest meeting right now," Paul Yellin called out. "Nominations for chairman!"

Everybody began to shout.

"Yellin!"

"Ryan!"...

A door opened in the far end of the hall and the gray figure of the paymaster stalked in with the pay roll under his arm. Jubilant shouts greeted him. Immediately there was a stampede toward his desk.

With an expressionless face, he spread the yellow sheets of the pay roll, unlocking the black box containing the checks, and began calling our names.

Each person signed, and snatched his check with wolfish greed. One man lifted it to his lips. "Come to papa, darling," he crooned, and tucked it into his vest pocket.

"Don't spend it all on a Rolls Royce," the man next to him grinned.

"Nope! I'm keeping a dame in the Bronx with this."

"Me for hamburger and onions," said one of the clerks, making her way to the door....

Wright's Prize

... "Hello! Hello, there!"

I looked up as from another world and realized I was in the noisy, crowded, smoke-filled cafeteria. Richard Wright was smiling down at me. I had never seen him so radiant.

"Great day!" he laughed, and drew up a chair beside me.

"There's a new shine in your eyes. Have you fallen in love?"

"In love with the whole world. I got me a riding tag clear across the Jordan."

He handed me a copy of *Story Magazine*. On the first page was his picture, with the announcement that the first prize of the W.P.A. Writers' Contest was awarded to Richard Wright.

"*Story Magazine* is proud that such a new and vigorous talent as that of Richard Wright should have won the contest. It is a tribute to the entire Federal Writers' Project that its assistance to the writers of this country should have enabled a talent such as Wright's to emerge into full growth."

"Five hundred bucks!" He held up the check for me to see. "And they're going to publish my book!"

In his eyes I saw my own elation thirty years ago when my first story was published.

"Congratulations! You had it coming to you!"

I shook his hand. "Believe me. I know better than any one what this means to you. And if you're not too flushed with success to listen to an old lady—"

"Don't tell me nothing. Not now. You know, when I was a kid, they said I'd wind up on the gallows. I was no good, everybody said. My mother went to work and I ran wild, cutting school, stealing, lying, fighting everything in my way. I ran away from home and starved. I swept streets, dug ditches, but no matter what I did, or where I was, I always wanted to write. And, by God, I did it!"

It was in his face, the look of a man driving straight toward what he wanted. I knew the double-edged thrill of his triumph. It was not only recognition for his talent, but balm for all he had suffered as a Negro.

I thought of Hollywood when I had been as intoxicated with the triumph over my handicaps as Wright was now, wresting first prize from a white world. But he had the intelligence to take what he could get wherever he went and build with it. He would know how to take success for what it was worth and not become rattled by it as I had been.

He was smiling, blissfully aware of his achievement. And then a shadow of doubt effaced his smile.

"You want to know something? I'm scared to death. They asked to see my next manuscript. How do I know I'll be able to write anything as good as this?"

"That's just stage fright," I told him. "Don't try to do the next story until you've had a rest."

"But I don't want to rest, I can't afford to rest."

I looked at him and knew what he was in for. He had made his first step into the treadmill from which there's no respite. I knew his fear and haste to keep on producing—fear and haste more terrible than that of the day laborer who either starves or works himself to death. . . .

We walked out together. At the corner we parted. I watched him cross the street with his free, long-legged stride, head up, shoulders square. It was a walk of triumph, youth confident of power.

Did he know the source and substance of his power, the people who made him? He had climbed over their backs to reach the one opening of escape. Would his sudden opportunity only go to swell his ego? Or would he remember those he left behind? Would he use his chance to plead their cause? Or would he shake the dust of his past and succumb to ambition, the plague of those who rise from the poor?

His radiant face shamed my doubts. Time would catch up with him soon enough.

ELLEN

TARRY

"We had to close our eyes and minds to so much..."

Ellen Tarry and Anzia Yezierska were both writers employed by the Federal Writers' Project and assigned to work in New York City. Beyond that bond, however, they had almost nothing in common. Ellen Tarry was a member of a very tiny minority: black women professionals in government service. The number of women in top and middle-management federal jobs increased significantly during the thirties, but virtually none were black. The one major exception, Mary McLeod Bethune, head of the Office of Minority Affairs in the National Youth Administration, was seen and, publicly at least, saw herself as a representative of blacks, not women.

It is a telling commentary on the terrible problems educated blacks faced in the segregated world of America during the Depression that Ellen Tarry was, to all physical appearances, white. As she herself notes in her autobiography, her family could very easily have "passed" had she grown up in a city like New York or Philadelphia. Her father had one white parent. Her mother's black inheritance was contributed by one black great-grandparent. Like her mother, Ellen Tarry had red hair, pale, grey eyes, and fair skin. But in early twentieth-century Birmingham, Alabama, she was black.

The daughter of a prosperous Birmingham barber, Tarry early rebelled against her family and white expectations. In the face of the outrage of her Methodist parents, she converted to Catholicism and won a scholarship to a convent school, escaping the traditional educational path open to Southern blacks of industrial or vocational training.

During the 1920s Tarry taught at segregated schools in Alabama and wrote a column for a black-owned newspaper, the Birmingham Truth. *In 1929, with dreams of earning a journalism degree from Columbia University, she boarded a train for New York, just in time to join thousands of other unemployed writers and artists searching for work. Eking out a living as a waitress and an elevator operator, Tarry finally had the good fortune to land an assignment with the Federal Writers' Project, working on an essay about the history of blacks in New York. The following selection from her autobiography,* The Third Door, *describes her years as a WPA employee and a member of the New York City black intelligentsia.*

SOURCES: The world of black female professionals during the thirties has been neglected by scholars. Bethune, the best known, unfortunately did not publish an autobiography. Tarry's autobiography, however, provides fascinating glimpses. Because she wrote seven children's books between 1940 and 1967, while engaged in journalism and social work, very brief notes on Tarry appear in a number of reference works about authors. More comprehensive notes appear in Ann Commire, *Something About the Author*, 16 (1979), 250–256. The combination of Tarry's religion and writing accounts for her inclusion in Mary Anthony Scally, *Negro Catholic Writers* (1945), 108–110. Tarry wrote of her conversion to Catholicism in "I Found Peace," *Missionary*, 56 (July 1942), 299–305.

ELLEN TARRY

AN ALABAMA SUN WAS BLAZING
and heat waves were dancing on the pavements the day Little Sister
and I went shopping. Our last stop was a five-and-ten. We were
tired and the moment I saw the lunch counter I knew I was hungry and
thirsty, too. I plopped down in one of the "white" swivel chairs.
When I turned to ask my sister what she wanted I saw a strange
white woman sitting next to me. At the extreme end of the counter,
her eyes flashing danger signals, my sister was beckoning.

"What happened to you?" I asked. "I thought you were behind me."

"Come on out of here," she snapped, "before you get us all in
trouble." She walked hurriedly toward the door.

"What have I done now?" I asked after we were outside.

"Oh, you *know* they don't serve Negroes in there," she said.
"Anybody would think you had lived in New York all your life."

"But I'm hungry and thirsty," I insisted. "And I think they would
serve Negroes if any of them asked to be served. The waitress had
already offered to take my order."

My sister gave me a knowing look which reminded me that I might
have been ignored or forcibly ejected if the waitress had been sure I
was a Negro.

"There has to be someplace we can stop and eat or get a cold drink
of water," I said. "Even animals deserve that."

"You don't have to be so dramatic about it," my sister laughed.
"You won't starve before we get to the drugstore in the Masonic
Temple."

That summer I knew many days when no such incident marred

our goings and comings. It was a deceitful kind of existence, though, because we had to close our eyes and minds to so much before we could act like normal human beings. It seemed to me that the interests of my friends covered such a narrow range. I often thought it was as if the mountains around us were encircled by wire fences with posted signs: "BEWARE! DO NOT TRESPASS UNDER PENALTY OF ARREST!"

In the Negro business section there were sides of certain streets on which my friends would not walk. "Nobody that we know goes over there," they explained. In spite of what they said, I saw familiar faces. And when I was alone, I walked on the side of Fourth Avenue between Seventeenth and Eighteenth Streets that Octavus Roy Cohen had made famous. The same poolrooms, barbecue joints, cafés, and barbershops that he wrote about in his *Saturday Evening Post* stories were still there, with a dozen or more jukeboxes added. The streets were lined with Negro men who seemed to have nothing more inspiring to do or nowhere else to go. More often than not, one of them separated himself from the crowd and reminded me that we had gone to Slater together or that I had taught him. It was plain to see that most of them were long since defeated, but more alarming was the bitterness and rebellion in their voices and their eyes. At the slightest provocation, it tumbled off their lips. At night I would wonder what would happen if a stray spark ignited their smoldering emotions before one of their own alerted the white community. Though these encounters usually left me frightened and unhappy, one of them left me ashamed, as well.

I was passing one of the Fourth Avenue poolrooms when someone called my name. A man wearing a leather jacket and a cap came out and I saw he was a boy who had gone through Slater with me.

"I heard you were in town," he said as we shook hands, "but I didn't think I would get to see you."

"Why didn't you call or come out to the house?" I asked.

"You know how it is." He shrugged his shoulders. "You just bum around and before you know it you don't see the people you used to know any more. Things go wrong, you start drinking and hanging out in these joints and before long nobody you know wants to see you anyway."

"You always had so much talent in art," I said, and reminded him of all the opportunities given him to use that talent in school. "What are you doing now?"

"I pick up a few odd jobs," he admitted, "but there's no market for art work here—not for a colored man."

"Why don't you leave? I did."

"But you're different. Always were."

"We went to the same school, knew the same boys and girls, played the same games. How can you say I was always different?" I asked. "I didn't feel there was a market in Birmingham for what I wanted to do and I went to New York to find a market. Why can't you do the same?"

"You wouldn't understand," he laughed and took his cap off, then turned it around with the bill to the back the way he wore it when he was in short pants and, along with the other boys, chased the girls at the circus with whips. "It's easier for the women. But you'll always do things and I'll always be proud of you."

I thought of all I had *not* done during the years I wasted going to parties and night clubs and speak-easies and walked away.

A few days later I heard a younger version of the same story from a boy who had been a member of the second class I taught at Slater. He was the pupil who had helped me design and decorate the first bulletin board I had used for my children's stories about successful Negroes. "I guess you think I didn't try to go away to art school." He avoided my gaze as he talked. "But you're up there in New York and you don't know how it is down here. What can you do when you don't have any money and never make any more than you have to have each day?"

I thought of all the times I had asked myself the same questions as I walked down New York's street. Then I gave the youngster the only answer I knew: "Don't give up. Keep trying and one day you'll get a break."

After the boy left I sat on the porch for hours looking down on the twinkling lights of a busy city. The sky above the foundry lighted up with the glow from molten lead, and I thought that in the midst of so many natural resources, there was so much human waste; that flight and defeat cheated a community which should enjoy abundance and progress. And what could I do?

A kind fate balanced the scales at this point by throwing in a touch of romance. Arthur, one of four eligible young men from New Orleans who came to Birmingham for a weekend visit, was a fast worker. A few moments after we met he knew all about me and exactly where I had been all his life. The rest of my visit to Birmingham was overflowing with letters and long-distance calls from New Orleans that did or did not come when I expected them. The letter that made me happiest was the one which extended an invitation to my sister and me to visit the Creole City. Little Sister reminded me that convincing Mama of the propriety of our trip would not be an easy task. Even after I arranged to have a girl friend who lived in New Orleans invite us to be her guests, Mama had her doubts. But we left Birmingham in high spirits. Little Sister was looking forward to a round of social activities, as she was not particularly interested in Arthur's pal, who had invited her. I was looking forward only to being in Arthur's company.

The Old World atmosphere of New Orleans fascinated me. Whether we were uptown, downtown, or "back-o'-town," our surroundings were pleasant as long as we were in New Orleans. It was not until the night we were leaving for home that I had any indication that the arrogant, assured air I had admired in Arthur was but a defense for the brooding bitterness which lies curled up in the breasts of most of the Negro men I have known. It was what came between us from the first.

It was after we reached the station for our return trip that I remembered Jim Crow. I had not had an opportunity to see him in New Orleans but they told me he was in the coach behind the engine and we all walked down the track to meet him. The only other occupants of the car reserved for Negroes were a group of preachers who had been to a convention in New Orleans and were on their way home. It was obvious that they wanted to be friendly, and when the train pulled out Arthur was pointing in their direction and shaking his head. He need not have feared because I turned my face to the window and cried until the train stopped at Bay St. Louis, Mississippi.

A telegram from the friend who had made me a business offer was waiting when I arrived in Birmingham. Within a few days I was bound once more for New York and no tears were shed when I left Birmingham in 1936. I had found myself again.

Washington had become my Mason-Dixon Line and I felt freer with each mile the train traveled in the direction of New York. . . .

The Negro Writers' Guild, a group of journalists and creative writers, gathered periodically in a Republican club house on West 136th Street. It was at one of these meetings that I first met Claude McKay, the Negro poet-novelist who had just returned to America after living in Africa and Europe for a number of years. I had heard that Claude was a man of extreme moods, but he was at his best the night I met him. He was so attentive to me I felt guilty about the editorial I wrote in the *Truth* criticizing his *Home to Harlem* when it was published in 1928. The first few times I was in Claude's presence I remembered how I had accused him of selling his birthright for a mess of pottage and labeled the book a "gross and debased exaggeration of life in a Negro community." Then I forgot about the article.

Claude saw something I had written and asked if I had more samples. I was flattered to receive this attention from so famous an author and before long I was a pupil at his feet. He kept asking to see my scrapbook but it was in the bottom of an old trunk and I did not find it until one day when we had an appointment. I knew better than to keep Claude waiting and thought I would look through the book after I got to his house, but he was in one of his bad moods and snatched the book out of my hands soon after I was inside his door.

"You've got a good fist," he muttered as he thumbed through the clippings. "But I'm not sure it's strong enough yet."

I watched Claude as he read. His skin looked like polished mahogany and I wondered why his hair appeared kinky in most of the pictures I had seen of him. It was so pretty and wavy when he bothered to brush it. The little laugh wrinkles around his eyes belied the cynical lines at the corners of his mouth, which a silky mustache almost hid. Claude's expression did not change until he was almost at the end of the book.

"Now you've tightened your fist!" he cried, as he started pacing the floor. "That other stuff was just do-good business. Once you double your fist it's good and strong, but I think you have to get angry to do it. You need a lot of experience, but this"—he thumped the book with his forefinger—"is good stuff, even if you don't know what you are talking about!"

"I don't know what you are talking about, either," I smiled. "May I see. . . ."

"Here." He pushed the book at me, his thumb marking the place.

"SELLS BIRTHRIGHT FOR MESS OF POTTAGE" was all I saw and I knew I had forgotten to remove the article about *Home to Harlem* from the scrapbook. Claude's eyes were like two augers boring in a hard surface. I grabbed the book and left as fast as I could. I heard him chuckling as I ran down the steps.

That was the first of many occasions when I saw Claude McKay set the stage, then pull the strings to see how his friends would react to a given situation. I was an excellent puppet for Claude and he never hesitated to use me. I often suspected that he set his observations down in a little black book each time he cleared the stage. In return for the uneasy moments he caused me, Claude gave me my first orchid and also introduced me to James Weldon Johnson, Countee Cullen, Langston Hughes, Harold Jackman, Roberta Bosley, and many other important people in the literary world of that time.

Claude was credited with being the leader of the revolt in Negro literature, but he was also a lyric poet of rare ability. He was born in Clarendon, on the island of Jamaica, near the end of the last century. He lived in various parts of the United States, but his happiest years were spent in France and Morocco. As early as 1912 his *Songs of Jamaica* had been a medal-winner and the book I had criticized, *Home to Harlem*, had won the Harmon Gold Award. Like Carl Van Vechten's *Nigger Heaven*, the book had created a sensation, particularly among Negroes like myself who knew nothing of the life Van Vechten or McKay wrote about. Claude is best remembered by many for his *If We Must Die*, which is said to be "the most quoted and reprinted poem of this generation."

Every now and then someone said he had heard that Claude had once been married, but he seemed bitter whenever any discussion of love or courtship arose and there was nobody who dared to ask about his past.

In self-defense I had to acquaint myself with Claude's likes and dislikes of people and things. High up on the list of his many peeves were: "yellow Negroes," "people who spout religiosity," and "the Reds." He could say "you Catholics" with so much contempt it was useless to do anything but utter a silent prayer for him. That all of these prayers were answered is part of a later story. Despite my color and my religion, Claude opened closed windows for me and taught me the meaning of craftsmanship. I was grateful but he forbade me to say so. He always said, "Gratitude! I *hate* the word."

James Weldon Johnson, the poet, author, and diplomat who was also the first Negro professor to lecture in white universities, was occupying the Spence Chair of Creative Literature at Fisk University in Nashville, Tennessee, when I met Claude. All my life I had heard of Mr. Johnson, for he had attended Atlanta University at the same time that several of Mama's friends were there. With his brother, J. Rosamond, he had been a part of the first Negro song-writing team on Broadway. The Johnson brothers had written "Lift Every Voice and Sing," sometimes called the "Negro national anthem," for a Lincoln's Birthday celebration before they left their native Jacksonville, Florida, and had also collected a book of Negro spirituals. I was familiar with James Weldon Johnson's *Saint Peter Relates an Incident*, *God's Trombones*, *The Autobiography of an Ex-Colored Man*, and *Along This Way*.

I had heard that during the Negro Renaissance the home of James Weldon Johnson and his attractive wife, Grace Nail, had been one of the first gathering places in Harlem of the great literary minds of that time—colored and white. Through mutual friends I learned that Mr. Johnson had also been a sort of father-confessor to Claude and had straightened out many of the controversies with people in literary circles which Claude was said to have instigated.

I felt highly honored when Claude McKay invited me to accompany him to a meeting where James Weldon Johnson was to be the speaker. I especially enjoyed the warm human quality of Mr. Johnson's talk and detected a humor I had not discovered in his writings. After the meeting was over, Claude asked me to join them for refreshments and we went to a little place which was owned by one of Claude's West Indian friends. Mr. Johnson had been a guest in my Aunt

Annie Hutchinson's home when he went to Birmingham to lecture for the Periclean Club, and I told him how much pleasure Mama Ida had gotten from reading the autographed copy of *Along This Way* which he had given her. Then we spoke for a while of people he knew in Birmingham. Claude was pouting. When I could ignore his sullen glances no longer, I asked him if anything was wrong.

"Just look at you," he blurted. "You're sitting up here as white as alabaster. Why don't you buy yourself some brown powder?"

Though I was familiar with Claude's hostility toward light people, this unwarranted attack in front of Mr. Johnson left me spluttering.

Mr. Johnson raised a restraining hand and shook his head as his deep-set eyes twinkled. "Claude," he said, "don't you think it's a little too late for Miss Tarry to do anything about her color?"

Claude was contrite, but the night had been spoiled. To make up for it, he promised to have a party the next time Mr. Johnson was in town—if he had any royalty money. "And you will be the only woman I'll invite," he laughed.

Soon after this incident another member of the Negro Writers' Guild who had known Claude in Jamaica told me how the young poet acquired his dislike for fair complexions. According to his friend, Claude had once been a policeman. His immediate superior, a stern, uncompromising, sometimes unreasonable task-master, was a mulatto. The indignities—real and imaginary—which Claude suffered at this man's hands left their mark. I can also imagine that Claude, dressed up in a policeman's uniform, was not an obedient subordinate.

When Claude's friends heard that he had been offered a chair at one of the Negro universities they were delighted. He was writing a new book and working on the Federal Writers' Project, but we felt the new offer was more in keeping with the living standards of a man of his achievements. I was shocked when a mutual friend told me that Claude was going to refuse the offer.

"Why?" I asked. "Does he dislike teaching?"

"No. He says there are too many strings attached to the job," the friend told me. "He claims the board informed him that living quarters would be furnished for his family and that they have taken it for granted that he is married."

"If he feels that marriage is one of the qualifications necessary for this job, why doesn't he marry?" I asked.

"He can't decide between you and————." My friend said the name of a well-known woman once rumored to have had a torrid love affair with Claude. "He says you are *too* white and *too* ambitious, and she is too promiscuous."

"If he'd ask me," I laughed, "I could tell him a few more reasons why he can't marry me. Reason number one is: I'm not ready to go to jail for killing a distinguished Negro poet!"

It was impossible to stay angry with Claude. Soon afterward he sent for me. He wanted me to talk with one of the supervisors on his job. Negro writers were gathering material for a book about New York which was to be published by the WPA. Once before Claude and Ted had insisted that I come down to the Federal Writers' Project, which was housed in the American Express Building on 42nd Street across from the *Daily News*. By the time I had applied for the job, a relief status was necessary. Although I was eligible, I had discarded most of my rent receipts when I moved from Sugar Hill. The broken sequence of the receipts, plus my thick southern accent, made it difficult for me to prove I had been in New York for the required time.

Claude banged his fist on a desk. "If you were a member of the Party, you'd be working. But I'll show them a thing or two. They can't beat me. I'll get you on."

"What party?" I asked.

"The Reds!" He spat out the words. "They've gotten control. But I'm going to get them out somehow. And I'm going to get you a job, too."

"Claude, I don't know anything about the Reds," I told him. "Where I come from it's the whites we have to fear. However, I don't think they had anything to do with me not getting a relief status. I hate questioning. I've never been good at filling out applications and usually hide receipts and records so well that nobody can find them."

"You Southerners," he laughed, "are so naïve. I know these dirty Communists."

Later, I learned that Claude had a very good reason for hating "the Reds," but I thought there were times when he carried this hatred to an excess.

I was not on familiar terms with anyone in any of the social work agencies and the priest I had talked with had little or no conception of the problems of our community. Through a social contact I met the minister of the local Congregational Church and told him about some of the problems I was encountering. The kind old preacher agreed that it would be easier for me to study if I was engaged in work which was related to my field. When I told him about my experience with WPA, he offered to take me to an Emergency Relief Bureau office and intercede.

The preacher kept his promise and I found that he was highly respected by the workers at that district office. However, when he proceeded to deliver a sermon concerning certain workers who yielded to pressure from Communist groups, a crowd gathered and I was so embarrassed I forgot most of the answers I should have given when I was questioned about the length of my residence in New York City. The encounter left me so discouraged I would have gone back to waiting on tables if Claude and Ted had not kept prodding me. . . .

Internal friction broke out in the Negro Writers' Guild. Many of the older and more solvent writers complained that there were too many unknowns in the Guild. In answer to their charges, Claude started planning to build a prestige organization around James Weldon Johnson. Sometimes we suspected that Claude had not bothered to share all of his plans with Mr. Johnson, but we hoped it would all work out. Everybody knew that Claude was not a good organizer, but those who were qualified were afraid he would get angry if they offered their services. The preliminaries dragged on for months, but we had an excuse to get together almost every week.

Claude had quarters in the home of Augusta Savage, the sculptress who lived in a private house on West 136th Street near St. Nicholas Avenue, which was said to have belonged to the late actress, Florence Mills. Augusta's paying guests were either writers or artists who studied in her little art colony. Claude's place was furnished with rugs, stools, statues, tapestries, and paintings he had brought back from Morocco. It was here that we held our meetings and I was sitting on one of the tapestry-covered divans discussing the advantages of a writers' guild with one of the group when I heard Claude yell: "I'm Claude McKay, I don't want to write any *little* stories! Let Miss Tarry have it."

"What are you going to give Miss Tarry now?" I had learned to meet Claude's storms with calmness. "All she wants is a job."

"I'm going to get that, too," he said. "Jimmie has promised to straighten that out. But now he's telling me about some scholarship for a writer who wants to do stories for children. You go and take it. I write novels!"

"All right. I'll take it. Just tell me where to go. From here on, I'm not turning down anything."

"Good," he grinned and shooed his friend, whom he called Jimmie, in my direction. "You tell *her* about it," Claude said, "and leave me alone so I can get this writers' business on paper."

Jimmie told me that the Bureau of Educational Experiments was setting up a Writers' Laboratory under the distinguished educator and writer, Lucy Sprague Mitchell. The Bureau was making an effort to have as many ethnic groups as possible represented. A scholarship was being offered to a Negro who was a writer and had teaching experience or vice versa. He instructed me to write Mrs. Mitchell at the Bank Street headquarters and asked me about the job difficulties Claude had mentioned to him.

"Several people have suggested that I see a James Baker, who heads the ERB office in this district," I told Jimmie. "But I can never get past the reception desk. Do you know him?"

"Very well," he said.

"What kind of person is he?" I asked. "He's certainly hard enough to get to."

"We're very much alike," he laughed, "because *I* am James Baker. Claude has told me about your case already."

After Jimmie patiently explained how I must establish the fact that I had been a resident of New York City for a number of consecutive years, it was easier for me to take the grilling I went through before I acquired the status which enabled me to get a job as a writer-researcher on the Federal Writers' Project.

Claude and Ted Yates were happy that I was working with them, though Claude insisted that "the Reds" had tried to keep me off the project because I was his friend and a Catholic. Once he made up his mind, he would never admit he was wrong. The day when he would was still to come.

Mama was delighted when I wrote and told her I had a research job and was in line for a scholarship. Mabel was less impressed than I had expected, but she had seen so many of my dazzling ventures fail I could not blame her. . . .

Work on the Federal Writers' Project, where we gathered material for a book on the history of the Negro in New York, opened many new avenues of research to me. If I learned nothing else, I learned to make intelligent use of available library resources. My assignment was the Underground Railroad and I spent long hours in the labyrinthine stone building at 42nd Street and uptown in the Schomburg Collection, which was housed in the 135th Street branch. As I waded through documents which recorded the deeds of my favorite heroine, Harriet Tubman, my old interest in the life of the Underground Railroad's most daring conductor was revived. Lives of men like Frederick Douglass, David Ruggles, Isaac T. Hopper, Elijah Lovejoy, and the other brave abolitionists, writers, and statesmen who cried out against the evils of slavery and risked their lives to cheat the heartless men who trafficked in human flesh, became my daily fare.

Most of the talk about politics which I heard on my job flowed around or above my thought levels. We were told that the American Writers' Union protected our jobs but Claude told me never to attend any of the meetings and I didn't until the night when Emil Ludwig spoke. I had read the famous biographer's book on Napoleon and I enjoyed the speech. But the trend of the meeting before and after he spoke seemed focused on raising funds to send aid to Loyalist Spain. Though I recognized the need to broaden my horizons I clung to Mama's saying about charity beginning at home.

"What about Alabama?" I asked a woman who attempted to appoint me to a committee. "The crackers are still killing my people down there and nobody is raising a finger or lifting a voice to stop them. The only thing I know about what's happening in Spain is what I read. But I *know* what's happening in Alabama. When you get ready to raise money to fight Jim Crow, call on me."

LOUISE

ARMSTRONG

"I knew that I was in it to the end . . ."

Like Ellen Tarry and Anzia Yezierska,
Louise Armstrong was a government worker in a middle tier of professional
women, subordinates of such women as Perkins, Anderson, and Flanagan who
actually made policy. As the historian Susan Ware has noted, scholars have
only in the past decade begun to recognize the importance of the few dozen elite
women in top decision-making government positions. The work done by a
second echelon of women holding professional appointments in New Deal
agencies, women like Yezierska, Tarry, and Armstrong, still awaits scrutiny.
*   Louise Armstrong's autobiography,* We Too Are the People, *provides*
insights into this still largely untold story. One of the avenues of employment
in social work, in the thirties still a relatively new profession overwhelmingly

dominated by women, was the federal government. Louise Armstrong's history may have been typical of that of many others. It was at Armstrong's level of administration that the New Deal affected "average" people. Armstrong and hundreds of other women like her were the first line of relief, those in close contact with children without shoes, sick women without money for medicine, men with rags for coats. They were the ones who stretched inadequate budgets, who tried to turn policies into real help.

In We Too Are the People Armstrong devotes only two brief paragraphs to her life before she became a county administrator of emergency relief in northern Michigan, noting that she and her husband left Chicago when, after the crash, "We were almost, though not entirely, wiped out, like millions of other families." In Michigan, Armstrong's husband was active in Democratic politics and used his connections to obtain a job as a fee appraiser for the new Home Owners Loan Corporation. Political friendships also helped Armstrong find work as a relief administrator.

The only additional information about Armstrong that we have been able to obtain was provided by Stephen Harold, director of the Manistee County Historical Museum, Manistee, Michigan. He informs us that Armstrong had no children, and he has no knowledge of any manuscript materials. She did leave some of her art works to the museum. The museum's statement concerning Louise Van Voorhis Armstrong, who was born August 16, 1887, in Chicago, and died March 3, 1948, in Manistee, Michigan, includes the following:

"Mrs. Armstrong was educated in Chicago public schools and at the University of Michigan, where she took an A.B. and an M.A. degree. She subsequently attended and graduated from the Art Institute of Chicago. On April 8, 1911, she married Harry Waters Armstrong, whom she had met at the Art Institute, and made her home in Chicago, where Mr. Armstrong was engaged as a commercial artist. Mrs. Armstrong worked semi-professionally as an artist in Chicago but gave the better part of her attention to social work and writing, turning out a number of plays, some of which are still being performed. When Mr. Armstrong retired in 1932, they moved to their summer home in Manistee.... In addition to her work as a welfare administrator, Mrs. Armstrong remained active in art activities in the Manistee area, teaching and exhibiting, until her terminal illness prevented further activity."

The Library of Congress catalog lists nine plays by Louise Armstrong, one published in 1915, one in 1921, and seven in the years 1926–1929.

AFTER I BEGAN MY WORK AS Administrator, I was frequently asked: "How did you get your job? How did you go after it in the first place?" The answer is that I did not go after it. It came to me. I have not the least idea how administrators were chosen in other counties in the state, or in other states, but I can tell how I got my appointment.

On a certain sunny Saturday afternoon late in September, 1933, my husband had to appraise a house in one of the resort towns in the county. I went with him. This was the one appraising trip on which I accompanied him. That evening my great opportunity knocked at the front door. My caller was the son of our State Representative, and he was also one of the croquet players. Our conversation, as near as I can remember it, was about as follows.

He said: "Dad tried to get in touch with you this afternoon, but evidently you were out. Then he was called out of town and had to leave at once, so he asked me to see you this evening."

I said: "We were up at the Lake. What did your father want to see me about?"

"He is under the impression that at one time you had experience in professional social service work in Chicago. Is that correct?"

"Yes. Three years in a social settlement, civic recreational work, war work and various other things."

"And you have a college degree, haven't you?"

"Two of them."

"Good. Well, Dad said that if you had those qualifications, I was to ask you if you would be interested in a position with the new Emergency Relief set-up here."

Incredible though it may seem, I asked: "What is the Emergency Relief set-up?"

"Why, don't you know? Haven't you been reading the papers?"

"Oh, yes! Of course I've been reading about the Federal Emergency Relief. Is that what you mean?"

"Yes."

"It's terribly stupid of me of course, but I have thought of it only in connection with the large cities. Are we going to have it here?"

"Certainly. It's going to be everywhere in the country—in every county where it is needed."

"Goodness! This is quite exciting. It certainly would be a wonderful experience. What would they want me to do?"

"I don't know all the details, but Dad said there would be an Administrator and probably some man would be appointed to that position. Then there would be a staff of some sort. I believe they thought of you as a possible case-worker."

"I'm afraid I couldn't be a case-worker," I said. "I'd love the work, but a case-worker without a car would be utterly useless here, and my husband will have to use our car for his work. Then, as you know, I've never learned to drive, and anyway we couldn't possibly afford to buy another car."

He smiled. Everybody knew the coach. It was a town character.

"You see the point is this," he said: "The Federal Government and the State are demanding trained social workers for these jobs wherever possible, and there is almost no one in town but yourself who has had such experience. In fact, Dad couldn't think of anyone else except the Red Cross worker, and she already has a job."

"It certainly sounds interesting," I said, "but I'm doubtful about the wisdom of going into it. I haven't been employed on a regular steady job for years. I'm not sure that I should be equal to it now. It would be difficult, too, with both of us working. There's the house to think of."

"Well, would you at least be willing to come to the meeting about it?" he asked.

"Oh, yes! I'll be glad to come to the meeting. When is it?"

"We don't know yet, but it will be sometime within the next two weeks. A State man is coming to get the thing started. Father has met him. He is the Field Director in charge of about twenty counties in this section of the state. He has never been in politics. He has been prominent in social service work in Detroit, and I guess he was more or less commandeered for this work."

"Well, you let me know when the meeting is going to be and I'll come. And thank your father for thinking of me."

Our young caller left and my husband and I talked the matter over a bit. It certainly would be an experience. My salary would help too, though it would probably be small. My husband was not very much in favor of the idea because he was afraid my health would not stand it. My feeling was mixed. I was sure it would be interesting, but I was not sure I wanted it. Feeling that probably nothing would come of it anyway, I dismissed the matter from my mind and went to bed.

Sunday we were away practically all day. Monday I was very busy. We harvested the crab-apple crop and I made jelly. I do not think the conversation of Saturday night once entered my head. That night my husband went to bed about ten o'clock, but I stayed up reading. A little after eleven the telephone rang. It was our young friend who had called Saturday night.

"That State man is here," he said. "The meeting is in progress. They are at the office of the Prosecuting Attorney. Since none of the men there have met you, and Father is still out of town, they asked me if I would bring you down. They want you to come right away."

"I can't come now," I said. "My husband has been in bed for over an hour. Can't I see this man in the morning?"

"No. It's got to be settled tonight, and this State man won't make a decision until he sees you. Please do come. It's awfully important."

"But my husband has gone to bed—"

"I know! But I have no car because Dad has ours, so I can't call for you. You can pick me up and I'll go down with you—"

"But, my dear boy, Harry is sound asleep—"

"Yes, but please—please wake him up! We can't miss this!"

"All right. I'll try."

My husband was aroused, protesting, from his bed. We picked up our young friend and drove down town. On the way I learned that the local Emergency Relief Commission had already been appointed. It consisted of three men, who were to receive no salary, but who were to act in an advisory capacity, somewhat like a School Board. The three were the manager of a factory in town, a Republican, who had been campaign manager for a prominent Republican candidate on the State ticket who had been defeated; a well-to-do farmer from one of the resort sections, a former Republican who had become a Democrat; and a man who ran a string of gas stations in the northern part of the county, who had run for office on the local Democratic ticket, but had been defeated in the Primaries. I had never met any of them. When we arrived, my husband, who had dressed hastily, stayed in the car, and the boy and I went up to the office. We were admitted to the inner office. There were six men present, the three Commissioners, the Prosecuting Attorney, a man who afterwards became our accountant, and a tall, thin, homely man, with a shock of black hair tinged with gray, who rose from behind a big desk as we came in. The boy presented me to the men he knew, and one of them introduced us to the tall, homely man from the State.

He greeted me pleasantly and I noticed that he had a very kind smile. He asked me about my college training. He apparently had known some of my former professors in Social Science. He asked me about the social settlement where I had worked. I gave him the name of the Head Resident, and told him a little about my work, mentioning that it had been to a great extent with young people. We probably talked fifteen or twenty minutes. Nothing was said about a job. I did not ask for one and he did not mention the subject. Finally he asked the boy and the future accountant and me to step into the outer office, saying that he would call us back in a few moments. While we were waiting out there we heard the church clock strike midnight. In about fifteen minutes he called me back. When I had returned to the inner office, he said: "We have decided to appoint you Administrator of Emergency Relief for this county." It was a good thing I was seated before he hurled this bombshell. I was so astonished that I know I jerked back in the chair. I was much too surprised to think of it at the time, but afterwards I realized that he had not asked if I would take the position. He gave me no opportunity to consider the matter or discuss it. He simply announced that I was to be the Administrator. When I came to know him afterwards, I realized that if he had decided that I was destined, or doomed, to be the Administrator, I

Louise Armstrong

had not a chance in the world to escape my fate. One did not argue with that thin, homely man. Over a year afterwards I learned that he was the only man in the group who had wanted me to be the Administrator. The others had a man in mind for the position whom they were very insistent should be appointed. However, this man had neither college training nor social service experience, and the Field Director had refused to accept him. Of course he had never laid eyes on me before, but I had had the proper training, and he took a chance on me. I must say for the Commission that night that they treated me very courteously and gave me no inkling that I was not their choice.

I finally managed to say, "I haven't the least idea what you would expect of me in such a position."

"That's all right," he said. "I'll help you get started and you will be given complete instructions from the State Office about the details of the work. With your social service experience, you won't find this job difficult." He smiled, and dazed as I was, I again noticed that he had an unusual and very kind smile. And he added: "I didn't expect to find anyone with your background in a community of this type."

"When would you want me to start work?" I asked.

"Tomorrow." He looked at his watch. "I see it's tomorrow now. You may report to me at the hotel at nine o'clock. I won't keep you any longer now. I'm sorry I had to drag you out in the middle of the night like this, but I've been working day and night myself to get these set-ups started in all my counties. I appreciate your coming down. Don't worry about the job. I'll see you at nine."

The boy left with me. He and my husband and I went to a lunchroom on Main Street and discussed what had happened over some coffee and doughnuts. Slowly I began to think clearly again, and then I began to wonder just what I had let myself in for. I said, "I'm afraid I've been railroaded into this, and I may regret it." "It is always possible to resign," my husband suggested. But I did not like the idea of going into a thing unless I meant to see it through. The boy with us was fairly bursting with enthusiasm. He wanted to get into the work, too. He had spoken briefly with the Field Director too. Now he wanted me to take it up with him the next day, and I promised I would. . . .

I arrived at the hotel at nine the morning following my appointment. The three Commissioners and our accountant were there, also the County Clerk and a few other local political officeholders. The Field Director discussed briefly the two kinds of relief which would be given—direct relief and work relief. Work relief was entirely new to me. Later I learned that it had never been tried in a big way in this country previous to the beginning of Federal Emergency Relief. He explained that the county would have to provide an office and office equipment for us, and pay for the printing of all forms used by us, these forms being uniform throughout the State. These would be the only items of expense required of the county at present. He showed us the rather elaborate forms which were to be used for our case-records. One sheet, printed on both sides, which we called the "face sheet," was for the personal record of the relief family, containing such items as the names, birthplaces and birth dates of all members of the family, previous addresses, names and addresses of relatives, and record of previous employment. The "financial sheet" was even more important, because on it were determined the amount and kind of relief to be given the client when he was definitely accepted as a relief case. This sheet presented a complete picture of the client's financial condition. . . . He also explained the type of relief orders we later used. Until the third year in the office, no cash was ever given relief clients, except when they worked for it as regular work relief cases on Government projects, or when we were able to employ them on odd jobs, such as home nursing, which had no connection with the projects. The Field Director explained that our cases would all be on direct relief at the start until we had determined which were employable and which unemployable, and of course until work projects were presented by the county and city. . . .

We went over many other forms, including the processes of handling the funds which were to be sent in by the Federal Government and the State. The exact monthly budget we should receive would be flexible at first until we could determine the amount of need and the case-load. It was always flexible to an extent of course, since it was based on our advance estimate of our monthly need. . . .

"Don't try to absorb all this at once," the Field Director told me. "You will receive full instructions on every phase of the work in bulletins from the State office."

Louise Armstrong

At last the others left and I had a brief conference with him by myself. He told me that he would be back in about ten days. Meanwhile there were three major responsibilities for me. I must see that we had an office. It must have at least two rooms, one of which would be a private office for the Administrator. He gave me a list of names of persons who had been suggested as possible members of the staff. We should probably start with a staff of six, the accountant, four case-workers and myself. I was to have a personal interview with all the persons on the list. I was to eliminate those I thought undesirable, and to send him a written report on those I considered possible. I really should be selecting the staff, he said, but he would give them their definite appointment, thus saving any hard feeling towards me on the part of those not chosen. I mentioned the boy who had been with me the night before.

"I like that boy," he said. "I like the cut of his jib, but I doubt if it would be wise to put him on, because his father is the State Representative. We cannot have any connection with politics whatever in this outfit. However, I'll think it over."

He then told me that when he returned there would be a meeting held, at which he would explain to all the local political officeholders, and other persons in public affairs, the idea and the plan of the Emergency Relief set-up. The meeting was for these people only, and was not to be open to the public. He was not entirely in favor of this meeting, but the Commission wanted it, so he had consented. I was to arrange for the meeting and see that all the proper persons were notified by mail. I asked whom he wished included in the invitation. Well, the Mayor, the City Council, all other city officials, the ministers, the persons in charge of the leading local charities, the Poor Commissioners, and of course the Township Supervisors. . . .

The more I studied him, the more I felt that I could work with this Field Director. He was a convincing person. He impressed me as having a striking personality, though at the time I had by no means appraised him at his full value. I also noticed that he was not only very thin, but that he looked like a sick man. I learned later that he was really a dying man, doomed in the prime of life by injuries received in service during the Great War. He left for another county at noon, and I tried to shoulder the big job of getting started.

I began by trying to get acquainted with the accountant. This was rather difficult at first. He was a reticent sort of person. He was perhaps thirty-five to forty years old, of Polish extraction, and he had been employed for some years in the National Bank. He had been unemployed since the bank had crashed. He needed the job and was capable of handling it. We finally got along all right. We set out together to interview the various public officials about getting an office. We tried the City Building, the Federal Building, the Court-house. We met with no success. There was no room for us anywhere. The attitude of the men we interviewed surprised me. It was not exactly hostile, but we were greeted with complete indifference. No one seemed to care in the least whether we ever had an office or not. . . . The Relief Commissioner, who was a factory manager, lived in town, and I appealed to him for assistance in this matter. He gave it very gladly, and went around with me for further interviews. Finally, through his efforts, we did secure good space in one of the office buildings in the center of the business district, but there were many wails about its costing the county a lot of money. This was a refrain I heard unceasingly throughout my three years in the office. The expense of our office came to between forty and fifty dollars a month. Almost immediately we began receiving around twenty thou-sand dollars a month in Federal and State funds, and this amount was increased with later programs.

The accountant and I made out the list of persons to be invited to the meeting. There were about a hundred and fifty to two hundred of them. He was going to type the cards announcing the meeting, and we even had some difficulty in getting a typewriter for the job. We could not buy one, of course. We were never permitted to buy office equipment, but he finally got one somehow. After that job was done, he turned his attention to getting the other equipment needed for the office.

I looked over the list of applicants for positions on the staff, and arranged to interview them. I knew a few of them. Some of these I realized at once were unsuited for the job. One woman, who was a very good friend of mine, I knew would have hysterics at least three times the very first day in the office. With the exception of the boy who had gone to the meeting with me, those whom I decided were

Louise Armstrong

the best prospects were entire strangers to me at the time of these interviews. There were three women who seemed exceptional, and who later proved to be nothing short of gifts from heaven.

I was delighted to find among the applicants a young woman who was a registered nurse. She had also taken postgraduate courses in hospitals in Detroit and Boston. Her training would be of great value to us. She lived in one of the resort towns. She came to call on me at the house, and the moment I saw her I knew that she was a "find." She was twenty-seven years old and very attractive. She was slight, with soft brown hair, big, earnest brown eyes, and an elfish smile which dimpled her bright little face. We seemed to understand each other at once, and as I sat talking with her, I decided that perhaps all this would not be so difficult if I had a girl like that to help me. She did not disappoint me. Although she was trained for a profession which commands good pay, being unemployed she was willing to work as a case-worker for the ridiculous salary of fourteen dollars a week during the first and hardest year. Later the salary of the case-workers was raised a little. The record of her adventures on our staff would fill volumes. . . . She was with us for more than two years. During that time she married a young man in town. I have always felt that he is a very lucky man. I cannot imagine anyone more cheering, more comforting, to come home to at night than that little brown-eyed nurse.

Another applicant who impressed me favorably at once was a woman about thirty-five years old, who lived in the Finnish settlement in the northeast part of the county. She did not have the training or background we were looking for, but she did have a very vivid and convincing personality. She had been brought up on a farm in a neighboring county. She had finished high school. It was her great grief that she had been unable to go to college, but she was self-educated and she had done a good job of it. She had been active in local charitable work. She did not need this position. Her husband was in good circumstances. However she seemed to me a person with real, crackling vitality. I felt sure that she was capable and I was not mistaken. She was fairly tall and well built—an athletic type. She had a strain of Indian blood, which showed plainly in her appearance. She was not beautiful, but she was striking-looking, with warm tan skin, straight blue-black hair, a wide, flashing smile and dark eyes, and she had a sense of humor which came straight from the devil himself. She was a great success as a case-worker, and I enjoyed her immensely. The one slight flaw in her work was that she did not like the Indians. In spite of her Indian blood she was not in sympathy with them, and I soon discovered that it was better not to give her our Indian cases. She was a tireless worker and utterly fearless, the latter quality being of great value considering the type of work to which I assigned her. During the first year, and to a good extent afterwards, she handled our "Badlands," the entire eastern half of the county—a tremendous job. . . . Besides being able to cope with the rougher element, she was tactful and efficient with relief families of a better grade, and she always had a good head for thinking out plans. . . . Her adventures would furnish material for at least a dozen "best sellers."

The third case-worker, whom I recommended for appointment at this time, was a young woman about thirty-five years old, who lived in town. She had a college education. She had been a teacher for some years and also a supervisor in the grade schools, in which capacity she had visited many of the homes of the poor families in the city district. She had given up this work when she was married: there was a rule against employing married teachers in the county. Her husband was just recovering from a serious operation and he would be unable to work for some time. She also impressed me very favorably. She was of German extraction, quite tall, with reddish hair and blue eyes, and you knew the moment you looked at her that she was honest and kind and a very human sort of person. She was very efficient. There was a German thoroughness to all her thinking, and a calm, reassuring quality in her manner which immediately won the confidence of her cases. During our first terrific winter she accomplished the stupendous task of handling some six hundred cases in the city and vicinity. No human being could do a perfect job of case-work under such a load as that, but somehow she managed to take care of them to the extent that none of them starved or otherwise came to grief. When our burden was lightened by the addition of more staff workers, she proved herself capable of the most painstaking work.

These three case-workers were with us from the very start and all

Louise Armstrong

through the major part of our work, until the staff was reduced at the beginning of the WPA. During the three years I was in the office, we had a total of fifteen case-workers, though never more than seven at any one time. It would be difficult to make a choice of one among them as the best, and it is especially true of the first three whom I have mentioned, but in thinking of them I believe that this former teacher had more of the qualities which make the perfect case-worker than any of the others. She was my comfort and joy every day she was on our staff.

During this first week after my appointment, while I felt much encouraged by the good material I found available for our staff, I came more and more to have grave misgivings about the job itself. The indifference of the community was evident everywhere. I could see that we should be obliged to "build a fire under them" to accomplish every little thing. Aside from the public officials, I interviewed some of the persons connected with local charities in an effort to get some idea of what our case-load would be. They estimated that it would be from five to eight hundred families, possibly more. The higher estimates proved more nearly correct. I found these people unresponsive too. They were courteous enough, but apparently not interested. I was also beginning to have a few doubts about our Commissioners. All three of them were rather crude men with little background. They seemed to be intensely interested in the work which we were about to start, and that was in their favor. It was a pleasant change to find that someone was interested. But they had no knowledge whatever of social service procedure. They did not see, for example, why we could not begin giving out relief right and left immediately, before we had an office or a staff or even our printed forms. I urged that the already existing agencies carry on until we could start properly, and finally the old farmer saved my life in this matter. He didn't think that any of "the folks" were so "bad off" that they would starve before we could open the office. Adding up all these details, however, I could see what an uphill job this was going to be. I began to regret that I had accepted the position. The Field Director had inspired me with confidence, and several phone conversations with him that week had added to my good impression of him. I did not like to fail him, but as the day drew near for his return to the county, I had just about made up my mind to tell him that I was very sorry, but that I should prefer to be released from the job. I would of course remain and do my best until he could find someone to take my place.

The day of the meeting came. He was to arrive in the evening. I was to report to him before the meeting, and after it he would talk with the Commission, the persons whom I had suggested for the staff, and me. Fortunately I decided not to mention my intentions of resigning from the appointment until after the meeting: there would be more time to discuss it with him then. I still wanted to be a part of this great new program in which I believed so firmly, but the circumstances here were so difficult... Well, we should see. He called me up at seven, just as I finished dinner. I went to the hotel and reported our progress and lack of progress to him while he had his dinner. Then we went to the High School, where the meeting was to take place. My husband, the Commission and the prospective members of the staff were there and we all sat together. The hall filled up rapidly. It looked as if nearly everyone to whom we had sent a card was present.

I decided within the first few moments that our Field Director was not what is usually meant by a "good speaker." He had none of the grace and none of the tricks of the trained orator. His manner was very informal. Nevertheless he presented a clear picture of the conception of Emergency Relief and the plan of the county set-up. He began by reviewing the steps in the relief situation in the country which made Federal aid imperative, and which had led to the present plan to coordinate relief activities.... After briefly describing the relief set-up, he touched upon the human side of the situation. He spoke of the need of conserving not only the lives and health of our underprivileged and unemployed citizens, but also their morale, which had suffered so seriously during these years of anxiety and distress. This led to the subject of work relief, which he discussed briefly, and he urged that the community present work projects, which could be of almost any sort which they felt would be beneficial, provided that the work was of a public nature. When he had finished, he asked if there were any questions.

I would give more than I can afford to have a court reporter's

Louise Armstrong

record of the scene which followed. I had not looked forward to this evening as an exciting event. He would make his speech, perhaps a few people would ask questions, some might come forward to speak to him, and then we should adjourn to our meeting place. I did not know my fellow citizens. In less than a moment they had turned on him. Question after insolent question was hurled at him from the audience. It seemed like a planned attack. They insulted him, they goaded him, they fairly snapped at him. Even in my amazement at this spectacle, I became aware that a marvelous thing was taking place. This speaker was no ordinary man. He had suddenly become a genius. He was battling, singlehanded, against this group of "leading citizens" and "chosen representatives of the people" who where bent on humiliating him, on stampeding him, on breaking him. He never raised his voice. He showed not the slightest trace of excitement, though I could catch a steely look in his deepset gray eyes. But even in the confusion of the scene, I was conscious of watching that brilliant mind at work. I seemed almost to see that flashing intelligence dart about the hall. It was like lightning. It was like a rapier in the hand of a deft swordsman. It was here, there, everywhere— quick, sure, deadly—utterly effortless. What was this man? Who was this Cyrano de Bergerac—"alone as Lucifer at war with heaven"— fighting a hundred men?

What was it all about? Why were they fighting him? The clumsy thrusts from the audience came fast, and the speaker parried them without a split second's hesitation. It was almost impossible to determine what they were driving at. Were they attacking the man himself? Was this just a political fracas? I knew that the majority of the men present were old guard Republicans. No. That guess was wrong. A prominent Democrat was on his feet, leading the fray. Someone had just shouted: "We don't need this thing here!" Were they attacking Emergency Relief in general?

Now the speaker was parrying question with question.

"Are you able to carry the relief burden of your county without Federal and State funds?" No! Of course not. This county had just as good a right as any county to receive those funds. They wanted the money all right. That was evident. Through the jangle of complaints, I caught, "We don't want this set-up!"—and variations on that theme. Then the speaker's voice cut through—"Why are you objecting to this set-up?" A few indefinite, evasive answers greeted him. And again that quiet, firm voice: "Come out in the open! Come clean! State your objections!" There was no definite response—only continued hostile retorts. By now I had grasped the fact that it was the Government supervision they were fighting. Why? Apparently they wanted a blank check handed over to them to spend as they saw fit. And again—why? But this seemed to be turning into a personal attack on the Field Director. Finally I sensed that they were also objecting to me, though my name was not mentioned. . . . The fact that I seemed to be included in the assault registered in my mind, but that was all. It did not shock or jolt me. I was too fascinated watching the speaker perform this incredible feat of mental swordsmanship. How long could he last? Was it going on forever? I remember only one person in that audience making a single pleasant or courteous remark. That person was our Congressman. He had come in very late, he realized what was taking place, and he tried to stop it. When he rose to his feet with a brief remark or two, there was a turning point. Then, almost suddenly, the tumult and the shouting ceased. . . .

The atmosphere seemed heavy with a sort of poison as the audience rose to leave. There were many faces flushed with bottled-up rage. Somehow the attack had failed. This thin, frail-looking man, who had seemed to be at their mercy, had suddenly towered over them like a giant. They were not used to that, and he had done it so easily! My husband had barely met the Field Director, but as we made our way out of the hall he said, "He's a superman!"

We went, each in our separate cars, to the City Building, where we were to meet. There was some delay before the Field Director arrived. The future members of the staff came in, tense with excitement. The little nurse slipped her arm through mine, and squeezed my arm to her. We had met only once before, but already we seemed close to each other. "Who is that man? Tell us about him!" she gasped. "How could he do that? How could anybody do it?" As these younger people gathered about me, asking a hundred questions for which there were no answers, I knew "that man" had won our loyalty as surely as if we had been standing beside him, fighting for our lives, instead of for an idea. And where was the woman who intended to give up this job? How long ago that seemed! Falter—with leadership like that? I knew that I was in it to the end, for better or worse, as long as my services were useful. When our Field Director finally came in, I went up to him and said: "I want you to know that I'll do everything in my power not to let you down."

He interviewed the three woman case-workers and approved their appointments. All appointments received final approval at the State office of course, but the real choice was made by the Field Director. The boy was there and begged to be given a chance at the work. I realized now that we should be courting criticism by putting him on the staff, but I did not have the heart to oppose it. He was one of those boys who had had just a taste of college, and then had been obliged to give it up, and I knew how discouraged and wretched he had been for the past year with no work and seemingly no hope of any in the future. The Field Director decided to give him a chance, but he said to him: "I want you to understand that I am putting you on, not because your father is State Representative, but in spite of it." The boy felt very important in his new job, which of course was natural, considering his youth. However, also considering his youth, he was a good case-worker. He took the work seriously and he had the makings of an excellent social worker. In the third month that he was on the staff he was made an official in the State Democratic Club of young people. When the announcement came out in the paper, our Field Director thought the matter sufficiently important for a long-distance call to me. His verdict was that the boy must resign from the club or resign from the staff. He chose to resign from the staff....

By the time the personnel of the staff was settled and other matters pertaining to the work discussed, it was after midnight. We went with the Field Director to a little restaurant on Main Street, and sat there talking with him over our coffee until about two o'clock. This was the first of many long visits my husband and I had with this remarkable man who came to mean so much to both of us. We treasure every one of those visits as a priceless experience. I studied that homely but fascinating face as he sat across the table from me that night. I wondered if I could ever measure up to such an intellect as his. And who was this strange genius anyway? Was he really Cyrano?

It had seemed so, as we had watched that amazing exhibition at the High School; but I felt that he could also be many other things. He was. When we came to know him well he seemed to be a dozen men in one, and yet always himself. He had one of those beautiful Irish names, which sound like a glad voice calling out in the hills. I watched that smile. Yes, there was a touch of the Irish leprechaun in it at times. Had he really mistaken that Lutheran, with his Swedish accent, for a Catholic priest? But now the leprechaun was gone. The smile had become sad and the man himself looked very tired.

We did not speak much about the meeting. He did not seem to consider it important. I do recall his saying, "I hadn't expected that reaction. It took me completely by surprise. Was that apparent?" We assured him that it was not. "They had me backed against the wall for a few minutes," he said.

He talked mainly about the work. One of his expressions always stuck in my mind: "First, last and all the time, we are here to take care of the people who need care." The most important thing was to gain the confidence of these underprivileged people. No suffering must occur in this county which we could possibly prevent. No tragedies must happen which we could possibly forestall. We must remember, and he often stressed this point afterwards, that we were not dealing with people in a normal state of mind. We would find many of them, most of them in fact, in a highly nervous state from months of anxiety and also from undernourishment. When they seemed unreasonable, as many of them would, we must remember this. . . .

The next day I tried to think about the meeting at the High School in the cold light of reason. I had left the hall the night before feeling that I could never again have an atom of respect for this particular group of my fellow citizens. They had turned the meeting into something very like a brawl. Gentlemen and ladies—(yes, there were ladies present)—did not do such things. This man had come to them as a representative of their Government. He was an emissary not only of the State, but, more remotely of course, of the Federal Government, and they had chosen to insult him. Even if I had taken an instant, personal dislike to this Field Director himself, I should have respected his position, and treated him courteously for that reason, if not merely on general principles. Was their behavior due to an inheritance from the lumber days? Those old lumber barons, who used to take out a Government claim on a "forty" and then cut timber from every adjacent "forty" within their reach, had not welcomed Government officials either. . . . Thousands of dollars of Government money were going to be poured into this half-populated and half-starved county. Not only would the poor be made less miserable, but every merchant in the county would benefit, and through the work projects every citizen would have the benefit of better roads, better schools and other public improvements. Why didn't they have flags waving on Main Street, and the town band out to welcome the man who was bringing them this largesse, instead of figuratively biting and scratching him? . . .

They wanted the money. There was no doubt about that. It was not until considerably later that we began hearing the outcry about the sinful waste of "the taxpayers' money." But they did not want any outsider telling them how they could spend it. As nearly as I could figure out, that was where the shoe pinched. Later, I learned from an old resident that there had been a riot in town the day the first street paving was started. I heard of the violent opposition of the taxpayers when the Public Library was proposed. It was evidently characteristic of them to resent any interference from outside, even if it was beneficial. They no doubt resented me because I was a city woman. They did not consider me one of them and hence I was all wrong. But was that audience at the meeting really representative of the community? It consisted of persons who held office, and other positions of more or less authority, but a good many prominent citizens, even among the Hill folks, were not there. And what of the other citizens who were not Hill folks? What about those laborers and those shabbily dressed old people who had stood in line with me during the run on the bank? What about those farmers, those men in boots, who had marched on the Courthouse? Would they have thought for themselves if they had been there, or would they have been dominated, as they always had been in the past, by the few persons in power? I thought of the Presidential Election. Those citizens had spoken then in no uncertain terms. I decided that my fellow citizens were indeed a subject for thought, and I wondered if I should ever get to the bottom of their behavior motives. Should I ever discover just what really was wrong with this community? It must have been nearly two years later when a relief client summed it up in one brief sentence. She was a comparatively recent resident in the county, a gentle, kindly, hard-working Negro woman, who had come up from the deep South. She said to me in her soft voice: "Ah cain't unde-stand dese folks up heah. Dey's grouchy-hearted." That was it. They were grouchy-hearted. Why? When I left her I pondered on the cause of the malady. Was it poverty? Poverty would explain some of the cases, but some of those worst afflicted did not suffer from financial poverty. Perhaps it was poverty of intellect—poverty of soul. . . .

As soon as our office opened there was a deluge of applicants, male and female, who wanted jobs on the administrative staff. No one could see why any special training was needed for the work. All you had to do was to sit behind a desk and write out relief orders. We did secure several very fine staff members through these applications, but most of the applicants were hopeless and some of them were funny. . . . However, among the applicants there were two men each of whom had two college degrees, and several men and women who had one college degree. The two men with two degrees, and several of the others, later became members of the staff. . . .

I was quite happy and excited when I arrived a little before nine and unlocked the office door on the day that it was to open. Everything was in order and it looked very businesslike. Three of the case-workers and the accountant had been sent to a neighboring county to observe the various procedures of the work in an office which had been opened before ours. The city case-worker and I were alone, and she was out on errands most of the time. I had the lists of men from the Re-employment Office, and I had intended to devote my time to going over them, sorting them by townships, and so forth. I never touched them.

The avalanche began almost at once. In less than half an hour the main office began filling up with the old people, the sick people, the widows and the like, who had been receiving aid from the County Poor Commission. I took them, one at a time, into my office, took their names and addresses, and got a brief picture of their situation. All were assured that our case-worker would call on them within a

Louise Armstrong

day or two, and that they would be cared for. I interviewed over forty applicants that day. There was something strange about these poor people: Nearly all of them, especially the old people, came in apparently terribly frightened. Some of them were trembling so that I could actually see them shake, and at first they could hardly speak. Their fear rapidly disappeared, of course, under kind treatment, but I could not help wondering why they were so frightened in the first place. I did not think that there had been time for the enemies of Emergency Relief to spread around a campaign among them to the effect that we were ogres. I am a small, blond, harmless-looking woman, and I did not believe that anyone had ever found me in the least terrifying. This was also contrary to my social settlement experience. I had never seen anyone trembling and cringing there. Our neighbors had always come to us confidently, sure of a friendly welcome and courteous treatment. Well, if you try to make friends with a stray dog and it cowers away from you, you usually conclude that someone has abused it. I could only decide that somewhere along the line someone had been at least harsh, if not actually cruel, to these old people. It was certainly unlikely that the church ladies or the Red Cross worker had ever been unkind to them. I began to wonder about the Poor Commission. . . .

At last the day was over. I looked over the forty-odd application slips I had made out, and sorted them out into four neat little piles for the case-workers. It seemed somehow a great moment, for me, the first time the four workers gathered about my desk to get their assignments: the little nurse, her big, brown eyes so serious; the former teacher, quiet, perhaps saddened by thoughts of the pathetic home she had just seen; the handsome dark woman, eager, alert, like a race horse waiting for the start; and behind them the boy, with the look of a crusader on his young face. I believe that moment was a thrill for all of us. We were off. The big adventure had begun. We were part of the great machinery of the New Deal.

PART THREE

In the Workplace

VERA

BUCH

WEISBORD

"The road to Communism was the only road out . . ."

Vera Weisbord, as she aptly titled her autobiography, led "a radical life." A committed communist, she agitated for dramatic changes in American politics and society. She also spent decades attempting to organize leftist labor unions, especially among textile workers.

Born in 1895 to a New York working-class family of German origin and headed by a father who was a wood engraver, Weisbord attended Hunter College as a scholarship student and won national prizes for her fluency in French. Tuberculosis stalled a budding career as a high school languages *teacher. Between 1916 and 1918 she spent most of her time confined to TB sanatoriums. A friendship formed in 1917 with a fellow patient, a woman telegraph operator, changed her life. The woman, whom Weisbord knew by the pseudonym "Bob," was an ardent communist. Weisbord became a convert. By 1920 she had joined the fledgling American Communist party.*

Instead of teaching French to adolescents, she embarked on a life of false names, police arrests, strike actions, and efforts to win members for the radical United Front Committee of Textile Workers and, after 1928, the National Textile Workers Union. In 1925, while organizing a strike among woolen workers in Passaic, New Jersey, she met Albert Weisbord, a fellow communist and organizer. They became lovers and finally married in 1938 "to console" Vera Weisbord's mother. During the twenties the couple worked together, both as party functionaries and labor organizers. In 1929 Vera Weisbord became involved in a series of violent and ultimately unsuccessful attempts to organize cotton workers in Gastonia, North Carolina.

As Weisbord notes in this section from her autobiography, A Radical Life, *the Gastonia strikes began the thirties for her. They were to be extremely difficult years. Battles between Stalinists and Trotskyists, disagreements over the degree of control to be exercised by Moscow over the American party (CPUSA), and debates about the kinds of "Popular Front" alliances to be made by communists with socialist, liberal, and progressive groups often led to chaos. Albert Weisbord was only one of several communist leaders expelled from the CPUSA as rival groups warred for control. In 1930, along with Vera, he founded a splinter group, the Communist League of Struggle, but it never won many adherents. As Vera Weisbord recounts, these conflicts, added to her own ill health and unemployment, made the entire decade one of struggle.*

SOURCES: Anyone interested in reading Vera Weisbord's entire autobiography would be well advised to place it within the context of the history of the Communist party in the United States. The excerpt included here becomes much more interesting if read along with the best book on American communism during the Depression, Harvey Klehr's *The Heyday of American Communism: The Depression Decade* (1984). See also Peggy Dennis, *The Autobiography of an American Communist: A Personal View of a Political Life, 1925–1975* (1977).

THE SAME TRAUMA-INDUCED memory lapse that had blotted out most of my speaking tour of the summer of 1929 prevents any recollection of my reunion with Albert, of what he was doing then, or of where we located. Albert thinks he was in New Jersey, but surely after the seven-month separation we would have wanted above all to be together.

I can recall my teacher friends in New York telling me that with the publicity of the Gastonia trial, my pictures in the papers, and people talking about me in the high schools, there was little chance of employment for me in the public school system. With many small plants in New York and Brooklyn, a job in a knit goods factory was still possible, even though jobs in general were getting scarcer. Luckily, I had had the foresight the winter before to protect myself by an assumed name. What boss in a New York factory would ever associate the quiet, reliable, competent Merrow operator known as Anna Miller with the notorious Southern agitator Vera Buch?

Out of the dimness of that period two scenes emerge. In one of them some people, Party members, a small room somewhere in New Jersey.... Behind the table in front Fred Beal speaking; of his words only these can I recall: "Albert Weisbord deserted his post in the South...." I learned then the meaning of the word "dumbfounded." Did I jump to my feet, did I shout, "That is a damn lie!" No, I was literally stricken dumb with astonishment, with disbelief....

With Herbert Hoover as President the country at the end of 1929 was entering into the great Depression. On October 29, following the failure of an Austrian bank, the Credit Anstalt Bankverein, came an unprecedented stock market crash, then panic and a run on the banks. The events affected not merely the workers but the middle class: small manufacturers, storekeepers, and professional people, who after years of work, having saved up some thousands of dollars, found themselves at one stroke left penniless. While we ourselves were not personally involved, headlines and pictures in the newspaper conveyed stunned shock and anguish, followed by hysteria, stampeding, and injuries. Remembering previous depressions, people had been asking, "How long will this one last?" But now the calamity created an atmosphere of apprehension; it was becoming clear this was no ordinary depression, but a crisis of capitalism on a global scale.

For Albert and myself these months were among our most important and critical; it was the time of our separation from the Party. A year before how indignantly would we have repudiated any suggestion that we might ever leave it! Yes, we who were so devoted, so totally committed. Not in the least had we changed our basic opinions; the road to Communism was the only road out for the working class, in fact for all humanity. . . .

All during the summer of 1929 Albert had maintained his confidence in the Comintern itself. He had in fact sent an appeal to Moscow denouncing the frame-up that had been designed to get rid of him and demanding a trial and the right to appear personally before the Russian leaders. He even wrote a statement to the Party secretariat on June 19, 1929, saying that "the CI [Communist International] called upon every party member to finish what the CI had begun: the elimination of the present leadership fundamentally vitiated by petty-bourgeois politician tendencies and rotten diplomacy and for the creation of a leadership actually tested in the fire of proletarian struggles."

It was through the *New York Times* that he learned his loyalty was rewarded with expulsion by the CI. . . .

It was not possible for the membership to know all the maneuvers and decisions in Moscow by which the leadership of the American Party was being shuffled around. We ourselves had seen enough and experienced enough to feel complete lack of confidence in all the American leaders. Our original view that the Party could be so influenced by mass work as to create a new leadership had been shown to be unfounded. It was upon this conclusion that we drew up a statement of resignation from the Party, charging the leaders with total involvement with and domination by Moscow and utter incompetence in building the American Party.

We never had cause to regret our decision. This did not mean, however, that the transition was easy. In our devotion we had cut off practically all ties with non-Party people. It was necessary now not merely to build a new life but to learn new ways of thinking. We decided as a fundamental policy to get jobs in some basic industry and live among the workers. Under an assumed name, Albert found an opportunity in a Ford assembly plant located in Newark, New Jersey. So we moved there. We stayed first with a Party family, renting a bedroom with kitchen privileges.

Albert's first job was as a stevedore loading automobiles in their cases onto barges at a wharf on the Passaic River. From there they were transported to Newark Bay to be loaded on ships for overseas. It was a heavy, dangerous job. The Ford plant worked an eight-hour, five-day week and paid twenty-five dollars a week. These were unusually good hours and pay for those times, but everybody knew Ford got his money's worth. Albert was a healthy young man, never had had a seriously sick day (though he did have tension headaches sometimes in Passaic), and had built up a good muscular system by athletics in his youth. Still, he would come home exhausted every day and would spend the weekend recuperating.

For me the brief period till I found a job was pretty unsatisfactory. After the long separation, there seemed to be no opportunity for personal communication of any sort. The struggle for survival was uppermost; there was no time to talk, and, indeed, as far as the political situation was concerned, there were too many unknown factors for us to be able to find clarity. And what of Gastonia, our great experience? Was there no time to speak of that, to analyze it, to achieve an historical perspective? Like the Passaic strike, when it ended Gastonia was thrust into some limbo of the mind, the ordeal perhaps too great to stand revival. I recall at that time frequent dreams of being pursued by unknown enemies. With the withdrawal into a merely personal life, something of my old insecurity had returned.

Soon, however, I obtained a job in an important textile mill, the Clark Thread Company, a Scotch firm long established in Newark that made ONT (Our New Thread). The plant employed five thousand people, many of them women. Like some medieval castle, it had massive high walls of gray stone, with turrets posed at intervals on top...for what purpose, to conceal machine guns? Two wide gates stood open between 6:45 and 7:15 a.m., as seven was the hour for beginning work. Arriving there once at 7:20, I had to go into a little gate house at the right to fill out a pass, which I had to take first to my building superintendent to be countersigned, then to my department foreman, the lost time being deducted from my pay.

Within the walls were many large buildings spread around a cobblestone courtyard. I had to climb big flights of stairs to get to my department, where enormous spinning frames made in Birmingham, England, perhaps thirty feet long and seven feet high, were ranged down a long room. Some ten or twelve new "girls" were receiving instruction from a forelady. Finding myself on the outer fringes of the group, I couldn't see how the knots had to be tied in the "ends," and I believe throughout my employment there I tied them the wrong way. Rows of threads close together, moving upward over the frames, were the object of one's attention. Each of the new girls had to attend to about twelve feet of frame. The thread would break and the ends had to be quickly tied; that was the job, not hard but demanding. Standing for long periods was always hard for me. Backache quickly developed. My fatigue was great. For the noon hour there was no place to eat, not even a chair to sit on (such luxuries as plant cafeterias and coffee breaks being unheard of in those days). The older workers had their own little folding camp chairs on which they sat to eat a lunch brought from home. The newcomers went out to some slop joint in the neighborhood.

Saturday at eleven-thirty the power was shut off. We then had to spend a full half hour cleaning the machinery. Textile work always produces dust as the friction of the machinery erodes the cotton fibers. We had to clean an inch-high layer of dust from all the parts of a big complicated machine, using swabs of cotton waste which lay in piles on the floor. Under the dust was the black grease that protected the machinery. It was a filthy task. Because some of the women were on piecework, this half-hour every week was just a present they had to hand over to the company. The pay for learners was fifteen dollars, for experienced workers twenty to twenty-five dollars.

I had not been long at Clark Thread Company when we made a change in our domestic arrangements; we rented a room with a Negro family, the Newcombs, who owned a small cottage at the edge of a Negro quarter. Part of our general plan was to make contact with the black people; this seemed a modest beginning. The room was big and cozy, with a carpet and cretonne curtains; at the two sunny windows were plants and a rocking chair. We had not been ten minutes in the room unpacking when the landlady's little boy knocked on the door. His mamma said, could we lend her five dollars? Foreseeing a bad precedent, we simply told him we didn't have five dollars.

As soon as I had gotten somewhat used to the job at Clark, I began to think of organizing in the department where I worked. Here were employed possibly fifty women, the majority old-timers; some of them had even come from Scotland with the company. A few approaches to them showed them to be unresponsive, even hostile. Some of the beginners intended to remain. Poor as the job was, it gave promise of being steady if you could stick to it. As the beginners were all discontented with the low pay and conditions, they listened to me. Within a couple of weeks, feeling I had made enough progress, I told the women I had a contact with a union in New York which might send someone out to help us organize.

With that I wrote two letters, one to the office of the NTWU in New York, the other to the organization committee of the Party (District 2 included New Jersey). I described fully the Clark plant, its location and layout. I drew a ground plan showing where the exit was and gave the time the workers came out. Then I suggested they put out a leaflet, send in some people to get jobs in different departments, and assign an organizer to cooperate with me in an attempt to organize the plant. Fully expecting a response and waiting daily to see a leaflet crew when I got out from work, I allowed a week to pass.

Because it was remotely possible my letters had gone astray, at the end of ten days I dispatched two similar letters. Again no reply, none whatever. I was forced to conclude that rather than cooperate with Vera Buch, rather than give her a chance to function effectively among the workers, my ex-Party would pass up an opportunity to penetrate a big textile plant right at their doors, a half-hour away from downtown to New York. Alone now in the plant, with no contact outside I could do little.

Meanwhile our arrangement with the Negro family terminated unexpectedly. Coming home from work one Saturday afternoon, I found a group of strange people outside the house. We had always noticed that our hosts seemed to have a lot of friends; people were always dropping by. Now the Newcombs were arrested for running a numbers racket. Later, when Albert got home, we obtained the services of a lawyer and got the arrestees out on bail. We felt, though, that it was inadvisable to continue living there. (It was lucky we weren't home when the raid took place.) We decided to move to Jersey City, nearer to Albert's job than most locations in Newark. I quit the thread mill job, for which I no longer had any motivation.

Our location in Jersey City was a pleasant furnished apartment; a large room with a bed and dresser in an alcove; three big windows on a quiet street, in a closet at the back a sink, a little electric stove, and cupboards. And I spent time in that place, for we had decided I was to take a month off to read the three volumes of Marx's *Capital*. So now every morning at eight o'clock or even earlier I would sit down at the table and remain hunched over my task for most of the day. As I progressed through this tremendous work, so detailed yet so profound, so completely thorough and all-inclusive in its analysis of the functioning of the capitalist system as it was in Marx's day, I seemed to find at last that truth which I had been seeking all my life. Marx's system did not touch on the old questions of the immortality of the soul or man's relations to the sidereal universe, but since such problems are in all likelihood unsolvable, I found enough inspiration in comprehending the objective world in which I lived; here at last was my key to that world. Reading Marx wasn't easy; I had been so long away from study, for months having read little except the newspaper, that at first mere concentration was hard. There was nothing, however, that could not be understood with enough effort, and steadily I progressed to the end.

The fragmentary and unfinished Volume III, edited by Engels, was disappointing, and it left a keen sense of the limitations of all human efforts, even the greatest of which must be defeated in the end by death. Of course such a massive work as Marx's *Capital* was not something to remember; it was rather to be referred to often and constantly applied to current developments, economic and political, national and international, with a gradual deepening of one's understanding of Marx's thought and the laying of a firm basis for the interpretation of events.

Albert was gradually upgraded in the Ford plant. From the loading dock he progressed to a job of closing packing cases containing completed cars; the wood had to be sawn to size and nailed in place, the nails being held in the mouth. Everything had to be done with the greatest speed; it was another hard and exhausting job. Later he was put on a slushing job; machine parts had to be loaded into baskets, this heavy load lifted up to a container where the parts were flushed with oil before being packed to be sent abroad. He sustained a few accidents on these jobs, luckily none too serious. Finally his good service and reliability, perfect attendance, and ability to keep up with the pace of work were rewarded by his being made a stock picker, a less arduous and more interesting job that enabled him to get around the plant and meet more of the workers. Really he had accomplished a feat of survival rare in the Ford plant, where only two or three out of one hundred men lasted that long.

Our life was now a secluded and narrow one; the prevailing hostility excluded us further from contact with Party members. Albert did, however, go into New York one Sunday, returning with a copy of the Cannon group newspaper, *The Militant*. I remember my shocked reaction: "What, you're reading that . . . that *sheet?*" Strangely enough, though we were ourselves expelled, we looked upon the other groups thrown out of the Party as untouchable. Albert replied that we simply had to investigate all opinions and begin to reorient ourselves to political life. It was not long afterward that we had a visitor in our hideout, no less than James P. Cannon himself [the Trotskyists' leader].

Discussion brought out first that Albert was not a Lovestonite* as had been charged. It also began to open our eyes to the violence that had been done to Leon Trotsky, who a few years before had been forcibly expelled from the Soviet Union and taken in exile to Alma Ata, a remote place in Asia (actually beyond the Pamir Mountains, so far that it was near the borders of China). Merely faint echoes of slander had reached the American membership. Trotsky's eminent record since 1905 had been erased from Russian histories; his name was anathema. We learned now of Lenin's Testament asking for the removal of Stalin as general secretary of the Russian Party and suggesting Trotsky in his place. Max Eastman, a liberal writer, was beginning to translate Trotsky's many writings.

While we were grateful for the information concerning Trotsky, we were not persuaded to join Cannon's group. Perhaps the chief deterrent was Cannon himself. He was considered in the Party not merely to be an unprincipled factionalist like the others but to be inefficient as well. In all those months of turmoil in Passaic that had brought innumerable arrests, not once did James Cannon appear in the field. His paper, the *Labor Defender*, gave very poor coverage of the strike. (In the New Bedford strike his defense policy was in effect strike-breaking.) Cannon would go out once a year for a tour of the few [International Labor Defense] branches that existed. This he called a "refreshing plunge among the masses," as though he were jumping into a swimming pool. He was a fairly large man of thirty-five with reddish sandy hair, shifty blue eyes, a high-pitched voice, and a rather theatrical manner. Some compared him to a preacher.

Cannon's visit with us was brief; he did not argue or attempt to persuade. It is possible he came only to probe, or if he had hopes of winning an adherent, he may have sensed from Albert's coolness there would be no support for him in our quarter. He touched only briefly on the history of his relations with Trotsky, and he did not attempt to exaggerate his following in New York, saying they had only a small group too weak to attempt mass work.

*Jay Lovestone, general secretary of the Communist Party, U.S.A. for a time in the 1920s, was expelled from the party in 1928 by order of the Kremlin. He founded his own Communist party and years later became an architect of the American labor movement's anti-communist foreign policy.—EDITORS.

Not long afterward came another pilgrim to our humble retreat: Jay Lovestone of the majority group, which now functioned as a separate entity with more members than Cannon had. It was amusing to see people who had had no use for Albert while we were all in the Party now coming practically hat in hand to our door. Lovestone fared no better than Cannon. It probably would have been difficult if not impossible for these Party leaders to realize that they themselves were the chief reason for our leaving the Party.

Lovestone was a young man, only about two years older than Albert. Tall, blond, not sluggish like Cannon but energetic and quick, he spoke fast and incisively. His contention was that his new grouping *was* the Party, since he had the majority recognized by the Comintern. Of course all his followers were not in the new group: many had remained with Foster-Browder; others had simply dropped out. He said he had hundreds of members and a functioning apparatus and was putting out a paper, *Revolutionary Age*. Lovestone offered Albert a chance to speak at their coming convention, to which Albert replied that if he spoke it could only be to criticize and attack the majority group. Lovestone left soon after that and we heard no more from him.

A final unexpected visitor there in Jersey City was my father, who came out one evening from New York. Long afterward Papa told me he had every intention that time of "telling us off," of "giving us a piece of his mind"—all this of course in relation to the lack of an official piece of paper in our marriage.

Ill feeling had prevailed in my family for years on this question. It all traced back to the one visit home Albert had made with me in the fall of 1926 after he had left Passaic. On that trip he insisted I acquaint my family with the fact of our living together. It was harder than Albert could imagine for me to break through the barrier my mother had built up between herself and her children on any matter concerning sex. I put it off until the very last minute. At last at ten o'clock I blurted out, "Albert and I are married. We'll stay in my room," and we went up to bed. When I came down early the next morning, Mother confronted me.

"Just when did you get married?" she asked.

It had to come out now. "We're not married. Albert is married to somebody else, so we're just living together."

She didn't say a word, but I could see her heart beating fast under her dress. Nellie's hair was all gray now, though her cheeks still showed a little color. In her gray-blue eyes that avoided mine was the look one sees sometimes in the eyes of those who have not known passion, an incongruous look of virginity. Later she sent me a letter stating I could come out there, "*but alone.*" She never thought her daughter would do a thing like that, she said.

But now in Newark Papa evidently had a change of mind. We had a friendly chat over coffee cups; Albert and he seemed to get along well together. The soberness and happiness of our relationship must have been apparent to any sane mind, and if there was such a mind in my family, it was Papa's.

My Marxian vacation over, I returned to the little knit goods factory in the New York garment district where I had been employed briefly after leaving Gastonia. It was more than a year now that Albert had worked in the Ford assembly plant. As a stock picker he was one of the solid inner core of workers and was not laid off for the Christmas–New Year period as most of the plant was for inventory. He made an effort to organize the plant, but met with the same failure of the Party to cooperate as I had experienced in the Clark Thread Co. Accordingly, he reached the conclusion, in which I concurred, that it was time he got back to political life. We had saved up some money and could ride for a while. So Albert quit his job and we returned to New York, locating in a small furnished room downtown. Because we ate our meals out, I was free from housework and had my evenings. Albert gave full time now to study of whatever material was available in order to find a new political orientation and above all to make contacts.

One of the results of the splits that divided the Communist movement into three sections [Trotskyites, Lovestonites, Fosterites] was that many members, bewildered by the rapid changes and the many unexplained decisions from Moscow and disgusted by the turmoil and unprincipled direction of the movement, had simply dropped out. These were the people to be reached, as well as those who had been expelled. To attend any official Party meeting in those days would have meant physical attack ("renegades" were definitely not tolerated). However, in the ferment of the political life of which

Fourteenth Street was the center there were meetings of the two other groups, also of the Socialists, occasionally the IWW or anarchists, neutral forums, and so on. Interested people were to be found also in the cafeterias, where the unemployed would congregate to chew on political questions by the hour over a cup of coffee.

Albert was coming to feel he had to set up his own political group. There seemed to be no alternative; to join an existing group was impossible since we didn't agree with any of them. What were we to do, be annihilated, drop out altogether from political life? I remember suggesting at one point that we might consider, for a while at least, working within existing mass organizations until we could get more of a following or until the situation clarified. To this Albert had a conclusive answer: what was most necessary now was to provide a correct political line; for this we must put out a paper, and to do that we had to have a group. He was his old self once more, a dynamo waiting to be attached to a mechanism, his mind teeming with ideas, talking incessantly as he worked out his thoughts, absolutely sure of himself.

It was not long before he had gathered around himself a group of like-thinking people. The conception we had of our group was not merely one of theory but of action. In fact, it was clear that there could be no theory of the working class struggle worthy of the name without participation in the mass actions of the workers; activity and theory were inevitably intertwined. Had we been willing to accept as members all those who agreed in principle, our group would have been much larger, but as actual members we would take only those who agreed to take part in whatever actions were possible and donated regularly ten percent of their wages. The others were considered sympathizers who would donate money as they wished, attend public meetings, help distribute the paper, and provide a certain moral support as friends.

The question arises: why did Weisbord not draw a following out of the Party as the other leaders did? For one thing, the others were part of Russian groupings, which in itself carried prestige and protection. Also, in the Party Lovestone and Cannon spent most of their time winning adherents for their factions. Weisbord gave full attention to mass work, making no effort to build a personal following.* Our union was a new one, and there had not been time to build a base through it. In Passaic there were Party members among the textile workers, but they were attached to the foreign federations, which claimed their principal loyalty. As for the Cannon group, they survived chiefly through Trotsky's support and prestige; they were thus a parasitic group much like the Fosterites supported by Stalin. The Lovestonites, attached to Bukharin, with all their superior numbers and apparatus achieved little and in a few years crumbled apart.

On March 15, 1931, we launched a new organization which we called the Communist League of Struggle, combining two historic names: Karl Marx's Communist League and Lenin's early organization, the League of Struggle for the Emancipation of the Working Class. Soon we started publishing the *Class Struggle*. I was associate editor. The paper was at first printed, but that proved beyond our means financially, so we bought a secondhand mimeograph machine and ground out the sheets by hand. All members participated in getting the paper out, and the sympathizers helped to distribute it. The first issue of the paper contained a thesis written by Albert Weisbord and adopted after thorough discussion by the group. The CLS announced itself as an internationalist group adhering to the basic principles of the International Left Opposition, headed by Leon Trotsky. We were a Marxist group, involved in American life, understanding and utilizing the laws of motion that flow from the internal contradictions of capitalism. We stood for the close connection of theory and practice, for leadership based on participation in mass struggles, for a vanguard party.

We were what was then called a "splinter group." The workers' movement was indeed fragmented. We were pelted from the right and from the left; the U.S. government tried to deprive us of mailing privileges, which was to be expected; the Cannon group always

*Keller and Dawson went with Lovestone, Murdoch with Foster. Jim Reid of Providence, Rhode Island, not a textile worker but a dentist who had been made president of the union because of years of devoted service, had solidarized himself with Weisbord to the extent of signing the telegram sent to Moscow protesting Albert's ouster. However, Reid was an older man, perhaps not equal to the rigors of the political struggle, and eventually dropped out.

referred to us disparagingly and finally raided our headquarters and stole our Marxist library. The official Party people physically attacked our members who attempted to distribute leaflets at their meetings. It was a steady warfare paralleling the theoretical bombardment in the press.

For a headquarters our group rented a sort of loft in a building at 212 East 9th Street, near Third Avenue. Well I remember when we went to look at this place, Albert and I and a couple of other comrades. It was a very large room occupying a whole second story, windows in front, entrance at the rear, and a tiny office partitioned off in back. A large round iron stove was the only provision for heat. It looked so poor, so barren. As the comrades cheerfully viewed the place and discussed its advantages, a cold grayness came over me, a presentiment: this cannot succeed. Of course I said nothing; it really was a good headquarters and the price was low. Overcoming my hesitation, I devoted myself completely to the new enterprise. The comrades built a set of wooden benches and bookshelves; all who had books of a Marxist nature donated them to the group. Later on in 1933 we were able to move to a better location on Second Avenue.

I had shifted my place of work to a factory in Brooklyn where I could in a way feel more at home because some of the workers knew me as Vera Buch. The regular working day at that time was nine hours; in the busy season one, two, or even three hours of overtime were added at only the regular rate of pay. With this fifty-five or sixty-five hours of work, the accumulation of fatigue was great. Exhaustion took its toll in sickness; there were always some machines vacant. It was hardest after five o'clock. How slowly that clockhand moved! After a while the aches and pains were replaced by numbness, one worked on as an automaton, the hands moved to put the pieces in place, to guide them through the machine, the knee pressed the pedal; shoulder seams, sleeves setting, collar, underarm seams—on and on, on and on. One was now really only a part of the machine, all thought gone, feeling reduced to one dull general ache, until at last it was 8:30 or 9:00 p.m.—quitting time! The young girls would laugh and giggle in the elevator. There was a need for release, to feel human again, to overcome this numbness that weighed one down.

There were two busy seasons a year and two slack; in the slack seasons most of the shop would be laid off, only a few relatives or bosses' favorites being kept on. In those periods I would sometimes pick up a job in another trade. Once I worked on pocketbooks. Another time I answered an ad for an operator on blouses. So many women applied for that miserable twenty-dollar-a-week job, crowding the stairs and pushing into the office, that the boss, wild-eyed, shouted, "Get out!" and shoved us all out of the room, locking the doors. Whether he hired anyone or not I didn't know, but surely at least two hundred applicants were there. So it was in the depression.

Under direction of the CP bureaucrats the knit-goods workers in the National Textile Workers Union were shifted into the Needle Trades Workers Industrial Union, which was the Party union in the needle trades at that time. The excuse for this move was that with the depression many cloakmakers and ladies' garment workers, union people, were finding employment in the knit goods, which was expanding with the invention of rayon yarn to make dresses and suits of knitted material as well as sweaters and bathing suits. In practice the move helped further to break down the NTWU. A small committee functioned for the organization of the knit-goods trade consisting chiefly of Party members working in the shops with a few others, of whom I was one. There was also an anarchist named Louis Nelson, who always treated me with respect. It was hard indeed after a long day's work to stay up for these committee meetings devoted to reports on shop conditions and discussion of ways and means to build the union. We all had to fight off sleep and fatigue. I remember the efforts to keep my heavy eyelids from closing.

Sometimes we called public meetings for the workers. While in the committee meetings I seemed to be accepted as one of the group, at the open workers' meetings it was a different story. Evidently the Party people had been instructed to attack me in public, to see to it that I couldn't build any influence. I would take the floor only to make some concrete proposal in relation to the workers' interests. And each time I spoke four or five of these Party people would jump up in succession to denounce me. I was a Lovestonite, a Trotskyite, a careerist, an intellectual who was using the workers for her own purposes, and so on. I would be given three minutes to reply. What could I do? Their tactics disrupted the union work and probably drove some workers away. There were times when I thought I might do better to stay away altogether, but that was just what they wanted. I couldn't capitulate.*

Who were the people around us in our group, the Communist League of Struggle? As New York was a financial and commercial center with variegated light industry, the only members from basic industry were a group of seamen. We also had a railroad worker, three cooks, a baker, a butcher, two teachers, a garage mechanic, some taxi drivers, a laundry worker, several office workers, one knit-goods worker (myself), one mechanic in the Brooklyn Navy Yard, one plumber's helper, and a number of unemployed youth. We had a German family who had belonged to a left socialist German group (the *Allgemeine Union*). We had a Welshman, formerly a coal miner, an English seaman, an Australian seaman, a young Russian only a few years in this country, and one Negro from Patterson, so that our group was to a limited extent international. Though the original founders of the group were chiefly male, eventually some women were drawn in. . . .

The CLS ran a regular weekly forum, at first held at our headquarters on East 9th Street, later in the Labor Temple at 14th and Second Avenue. Current events and political questions were discussed. Attendance often ran to one hundred or more. One of the forum's notable events was advertised as a debate between A. Weisbord and A. J. Muste on the program of the CPLA (Conference for Progressive Labor Action, Muste's group). Muste was also scheduled to debate William Z. Foster the following week. When Foster heard of the projected debate with Weisbord, he threatened to cancel his debate with Muste. So in place of Muste, Louis Budenz debated Albert.

At another time Albert debated Arthur Garfield Hays, a prominent liberal and my attorney in Gastonia. The subject was "Democracy or Communism, Which Way Out for the American Workers?" We also ran classes in our headquarters. I taught Marx's *Capital*, volume I. Albert gave volumes II and III. I also contributed frequently to the paper. As the Depression continued, it became less and less possible

*Eventually in 1935 we called a general strike in the trade. It was fairly successful, with the result that we became Local 155 of the ILGWU, with Louis Nelson as president.

to get other work in the off seasons of the knit goods; thus I had weeks of free time.

During those years since my mother's rejection of Albert I still maintained some contact with my family, going out to the country once in a while. Albert thought I should break altogether, but to me this seemed uncalled-for. How could I forget my mother's sacrifices to give me an education, her devotion to me in my early years? In spite of the Depression my father had managed to improve his situation; using his native talent for drawing, he had worked himself into poster designing. Now he was the artist in a small firm printing theatrical posters, was made foreman of the plant too. He would sometimes help out with the wood engraving. There was plenty of good food and Mother was saving money, something she had always wanted to do; perhaps she was at last free from financial worry. They had put in a bathroom and bought some shrubs for the front lawn. Otherwise the house was the same, the rooms generally untidy. I used to spend my holidays there housecleaning and, in the right seasons, working outdoors.

Having lost her job, my sister had appealed to our parents to let her come and stay with them. Years later Papa admitted that was one of the big mistakes of his life. She never left. The antagonism between Ora and Papa remained. He had to endure her slurs on weekends when he was there, and he would break out once in a while. For me she had jibes about Communism and my unmarried state. Ordinarily I tried not to get into conflict with her, but once she made such an insulting remark about Papa that I couldn't stand it and I hit her, dealing her a couple of blows and feeling very mean as I did so. She retaliated by going to the county sheriff and swearing out a warrant against me. I had to make myself scarce there for a long time afterward. . . .

From 1931 on, [Albert] devoted a good part of his time daily to research in the 42nd Street library, and he began the writing of *The Conquest of Power*.*

In 1932, thinking to establish a closer relationship with Trotsky, the group raised money to send Weisbord to confer with this leader,

*2 vols. (New York: Covici Friede, 1937).

who was then in exile in Prinkipo, Turkey. In the course of his visit of three weeks with the great Russian, Albert eventually made a favorable impression because thereafter Trotsky contributed articles to our paper and was eager for us to unite with the CLA (Cannon group). We did try to arrange for a series of discussion meetings with them, but when the time for the first meeting came, not one of them showed up. . . .

Albert's trip included also a one-month stay in Germany at the time Hitler was coming to power. Albert lived there with a worker's family in Berlin, learning German well enough to give a talk in the language. In Paris he had an interview with a leader of the French Trotskyists, and he spent some time as an observer in Spain, which was involved in revolution. From that time on we had correspondence with and received publications of various left European groups. During Albert's absence I put out the paper as usual.*

Tired of furnished rooms, I rented a secluded nook in a rear building on Avenue A, just south of 14th Street, a little two-room, cold-water flat, only eight dollars a month. It had sun and cross-ventilation, two west windows in the kitchen-living room overlooking a big courtyard, one window in the bedroom getting the East River breezes. There was no bathroom; the public bath nearby, a clean place with plenty of hot water, sufficed. A toilet between two flats was shared. I bought a small gas heater, some secondhand furniture, and fixed up the flat attractively. There were the usual set washtubs, over them a two-burner gas plate, cupboards above, and a sink in the corner.

The neighborhood was chiefly Italian. Pushcarts with cheap vegetables and fruits swarmed on First Avenue. Some of the peddlers were unlicensed and always kept an anxious eye out for the cops, ready to push off. Occasionally there were funerals, with people marching after the hearse and a band playing soul-touching dirges. And sometimes at night from the courtyard below my little flat would come a wine-rich male voice pouring out romantic Neapolitan songs in Italian. I would always think, "I'll remember this," but with the morning every trace of the song would be gone.

*The editor of the Greenwood edition gives me credit: "While he [Weisbord] was away, Vera Buch ably carried on the journal."

Vera Buch Weisbord

Some gypsies lived in the store in the front building, a large family, the men generally absent by day, the women with their big, dirty, colorful skirts and seductive dark eyes waiting for palm-reading customers. One of them was very pregnant. I passed her sitting by the door one morning as I left for work. When I returned twelve hours later there she sat in the same spot, her face wan and drawn now, her belly collapsed, while from the store inside came the wail of a newborn infant.

Moments of anguish which the mind shrinks to recall . . . instincts may be strong, overwhelming common sense as well as political expediency. Poor foolish me, I had always wanted to have a baby. I was getting on in my thirties. I didn't have much time. I remember Dolores' reaction—she must have visited me once in the rear flat— "To all this, to add the care of a baby!" Well, I tried. The pregnancy was confirmed in the osteopathic clinic where I was being treated for my lower back trouble. They didn't charge a fee but had a plate at the entrance where you put your quarter or fifty cents or dime, and if you had nothing it was all right. The two women doctors were solicitous, encouraging. "She must have the best care at the end." There was a nursery in the neighborhood where I could leave the baby while I worked.

One day in the headquarters, I began to spot. I told Albert what would happen and went home. I had to go through it all alone. He came at last, found me in the blood-soaked bed. He got a doctor, who tried to cheer me up: "Every woman has at least one miscarriage." They took me to Bellevue Hospital, to the charity ward. Long rows of beds, with women of all ages. . . . Some of the nurses did more than their share for there was a help shortage. Others spared themselves, were callous. Once they trundled a lot of us out into the hall on stretchers "for x-rays." We waited a long time in the chilly, drafty hall. Then they just took us all back in. It was Christmas time, and they had a tree for us there in the ward. . . .

With everything else I had to do, somehow or other during that period of the early thirties I managed to write a novel. Always I had this urge to write. To one who had read so many novels and stories a novel seemed a natural expression. There was some urge in me that was not to be satisfied by political work or by the contributions I made to the *Class Struggle*. That novel, which I called *But Unbowed*, was an attempt to express the life of our CLS and of poor people during the Depression. I took a group of people who happened to live in a rear house like mine, a few others tangentially associated with them, some incidents that tied them together, much detail of life during the Depression, and behold—a novel.

My life was complicated, my difficulties increased by the fact that my health had deteriorated. A slight thing at first, it had been worsening: some pelvic difficulty, pain and inflammation at times, and discharge. We had no money for a doctor, so I went to one of the free clinics that functioned in the New York hospitals. They would have half a dozen women lined up on the tables, their feet in the stirrups, knees bent, without even a sheet thrown over them, waiting for the doctors to examine them. I don't really recall whether any treatment was given; at any rate, I was getting worse. Finally we located a doctor sympathetic to the movement who would treat me without payment. It seems I had incurred a strep infection in the abortion two years earlier. That rapid pulse detected in Charlotte [North Carolina] may have been a first symptom. My uterus was full of pus. I was given suppositories and douches that were supposed to lead up to an electric cautery of the cervix.

I also had at this time a heart disturbance, first noticed in Detroit, called paroxysmal tachycardia. I had occasional attacks of violent, uncontrolled beating of my heart, which was not considered dangerous but was distressing to experience. The Party physician in Detroit had advised, "Comrade Buch should never have to work very hard."

In 1935 began my first bout with arthritis, just in the foot and ankle, but I found myself again in a clinic, where they strapped the foot so that I could walk. When I asked the doctor, "How long will this last?" he said, "Two years," which prognostic proved to be correct.

Yes, Anna Miller's life was a hard one, but there were compensations. There was a camaraderie in the shop; the very act of working day after day with the same women at their machines on the long table created a certain familiarity, and conversation was not prohibited provided we kept up a steady pace of work. And there would be jokes and confidences exchanged. Evenings, of course, I would go over to the headquarters. Sometimes there were meetings, sometimes work on the paper, or else I just sat around talking with the comrades. Sundays, weather permitting, we would go out hiking. We would take the subway to Van Cortland Park, then hike to Hunter's Point, where there was a beach on Pelham Bay. We would go swimming in summer, carry lunch along, and hold discussions too. Those days in the open air compensated a little for the long hours at the machine. An occasional trip to Staten Island on the ferry was a big treat. The Depression brought people closer together; the common misfortune leveled differences, cooperation took the place of competition, and, as money was lacking for diversions (movies, shows, trips), people learned to get satisfaction out of being with one another. There was time now too for reading, for study, for thinking.

At least in those days prices were low and rents were low in the poor neighborhoods. There were cafeterias set up by MacFarlan, a humanitarian, where one could eat a small meal for as little as five cents; stewed raisins, one cent, stewed wheat berries and other cereals, one cent. A Child's restaurant on Fourteenth Street had a weekly bargain of "All You Can Eat for 60¢." We used to save up for that, dreaming of it all week. But I always lost out; never could I eat much more than usual without great discomfort for hours afterward; gorging could be only a fantasy for me.

It was no longer possible to have illusions; this was no ordinary depression. As the bread lines of the Salvation Army and other private charities grew, as hunger became a common phenomenon, people were beginning fearfully to ask, "What is going to become of us?" During 1931 the city belatedly had opened a relief station. It was, however, on a limited scale, for single men only. Unemployed men begging for food and sleeping on the streets at night had become a problem. At the relief station they were given fifteen cents to sleep in a flophouse; there was a bread line where, after long standing, a bowl of weak soup and a hunk of bread could be obtained once a day. Many were keeping themselves alive on that. During the summer of 1932 the applicants swarmed in such numbers to the station that the officials in desperation closed the place for a few days.

Truly capitalism had reached a low ebb. Under President Herbert Hoover the country went from bad to worse. Production fell and fell, banks were failing on all sides, the millions of unemployed were multiplying.

Then came a dramatic change. When Franklin D. Roosevelt took over with the resounding message, "We have nothing to fear but fear itself," with a coterie of advisers behind him, suddenly a new and strong leadership appeared. Daily new powers were handed to the President, and legislation from Washington setting up all sorts of bureaus never heard of before became the order of the day. The NIRA (National Industrial Recovery Act) attempted to put capitalism on its feet again by regulation; the WPA, the PWA, and the CCC (Works Progress Administration, Public Works Administration, Civilian Conservation Camps) were born. The domestic market had to be restored. So the able-bodied unemployed were put to work, either on massive public works (PWA dams, roads, bridges, etc.) or on make-work, "doodling" things such as clearing away rubbish, beautifying the parks, etc. (WPA). With a little money in their pockets people could spend again. Massive loans and subsidies to business and to farmers started the factory wheels turning and the farmers raising grains and animals.

That the powers of the President were being extraordinarily increased, that the public works might be really war preparations, that all this regulation of business and of people's lives was paving the way for Fascism, the final stage of capitalism, was not so easily recognized. Capitalism was being saved; that was the main thing. As for the poor, at last public assistance, or dole, was organized.

Now at last if you had no job, no money, and no food, you could go somewhere for help. You "got on the relief." And we too got on the relief. Well I remember that huge gymnasium of a public school somewhere downtown. The first hurdle was to get through the mob at the door. Then you joined the long lines waiting at some half dozen windows for a clerk to take down your pedigree. After the preliminary questioning you were sent to a room upstairs for another going over. Finally you would be told to wait at least a week until an investigator came to interview you in your home (but you were supposed to be completely destitute, penniless, before you applied!). At least there was modest help; if you were approved, they paid your rent and gave you a check for groceries which could be used in only one store. Supplemental foods were handed out from special stores—once in a while a big slab of butter or some cabbages or potatoes. The canned beef from Argentina was really good. You were required to report every two weeks to the office, waiting interminably each time. . . .

As the years of the Roosevelt Administration progressed, it became clear America was entering an entirely new period. The first social legislation such as workmen's compensation was enacted in 1935. It was becoming plain that the day of immediate revolution was not yet at hand. The threat of Fascism was in the air, and we pointed out the germs of it in all the Roosevelt regulations, especially in the greatly increased powers of the President.

The threat of war too lay ahead.

Our group made little headway; the difficulties were always overwhelming. We were tired of the endless debates in the Fourteenth Street cafeterias that were the chief object in life of New York radicals. We began looking toward Chicago, center of basic industry and heartland of America, as to a mecca where our ideas might be sown in more fertile ground. "Westward Ho!" became once more a magnetic slogan. The question was discussed for some months among members and sympathizers. Some were tied to jobs, others to family obligations, some perhaps were glad of an excuse to drop out. Finally we sifted out those loyal and courageous people who were ready to go, made arrangements for those left to continue the work in New York, and westward we went, a close-bound handful of people illumined by hope and illusions, to Chicago.

ELLA

REEVE

BLOOR

"I never saw anything like the militancy of those farmers..."

      Like Vera Weisbord, Ella Reeve Bloor
gained national notoriety as a communist labor organizer during the thirties.
But Bloor, a much older woman, came to the Communist party along a more
circuitous route.

    Born in 1862, the eldest of ten children in a Dutch family whose ancestors
had settled on Staten Island, New York, in the eighteenth century, Ella Bloor
became interested in reform as a follower of her uncle Dan Ware, an ardent
abolitionist and freethinker. In 1880, when she was not yet nineteen, Bloor
married his son, Lucien Ware. During the next fifteen years she not only gave

birth to six children but also became an active temperance campaigner and an agitator for the rights of workers to organize. Lucien Ware, unlike his father, did not approve of his wife's activities. Increasingly estranged, they divorced in 1896.

Freed from Ware's disapproval, Ella Bloor embarked on a lifetime career as a radical organizer. Another brief marriage to Louis Cohen, a socialist, produced two additional children but also ended in divorce in 1905. In 1906 Bloor journeyed to Chicago, funded by the Socialist party to investigate conditions in the meat-packing industry. She traveled with Richard Bloor, another socialist. The party, fearing scandal should it become known that an unmarried couple were working as a team, insisted that she sign her letters as Mrs. Ella Bloor. Although she never married Richard Bloor, and in fact claimed that they were not romantically involved, Ella Bloor, who had previously been known as Ella Ware and then Ella Cohen, retained his name for the rest of her life.

By the thirties, Mother Bloor, as she came to be called, had spent more than four decades organizing for the Socialist and Communist parties and for several labor unions, including the Cap Makers and the United Mine Workers. Furious that some of her fellow socialist leaders had supported American entrance into World War I, Bloor resigned from the Socialist party in 1918 and became a founding member of the American Communist party in 1919. In 1930, on the eve of her seventieth birthday, she met and married Andrew Omholt, a North Dakota farmer and communist organizer. For the next twenty years, until her death in 1951, she remained married to Omholt. A self-described "farm wife," she continued to travel the country for the Communist party well into her late eighties. The following excerpt from her autobiography, We Are Many, describes the efforts she and Omholt made between 1932 and 1934 to organize farmers into a United Farmers' League.

SOURCES: No full-length scholarly biography of Mother Bloor exists, but several of her radical allies wrote admiring, often unreliably romantic, accounts of her life. See, for instance, Anne Barton, *Mother Bloor: The Spirit of 76* (1937); Elizabeth Gurley Flynn, *Daughters of America: Ella Reeve Bloor and Anita Whitney* (1942); and William Z. Foster, *History of the Communist Party of the United States* (1952). See also Thomas Edwards and Richard Edwards' brief account of her life in *Notable American Women*, 85–87. Ella Reeve Bloor's papers are housed at Hollins College.

IN SEATTLE I RECEIVED A TELE-
gram from the Central Committee of the Party asking me to take
charge of the Party's 1932 election campaign, in North and South
Dakota.

Andrew Omholt was the Party's candidate for Congressman and
Pat Barrett for Governor. I went into the campaign with all the zeal I
possessed. Our campaign brought the program of the Communist
Party to many of these farmers for the first time. We made full use of
the North Dakota law providing that each party could post bulletins
at every crossroad, with five-word slogans for each party. Our slogan
was very direct: "Communist Party—Workers, Farmers, Unite."

Along with the miners and textile workers, the farmers were a
depressed section of the population all through the boom years. In
the decade between 1920 and 1930, there was a crisis of "over
production" (with millions starving), farm prices falling below the
cost of production, and the number of farms decreasing by 150,466.
During the year ending March 1, 1930, 20.8 out of every 1000 farms
were lost through forced sales, foreclosures or bankruptcy. Hoover
refused effective farm aid. His makeshift Agricultural Marketing Act
was administered by a Farm Board made up of bankers, and prices
continued to drop. The Party's practical proposals for farm relief
started many of the farmers thinking along new lines.

The Party was first to advance the demand for a sharp cut in the
unreasonable spread between the low prices paid to the farmer and
the high prices paid by the consumer. Other important proposals by
the Party were support for these demands: "No more foreclosures.

No evictions. No deficiency judgments. The farm family holds the first mortgage!" The Party also advocated cash relief for those in distress through no fault of their own, and close cooperation between the farmers and organized labor.

This campaign in North Dakota is personally memorable to me because of my marriage to that pioneer North Dakota farmer and good Communist, Andrew Omholt. He was district organizer of North and South Dakota and Montana, and we campaigned together, visiting towns as far as 700 miles from the headquarters in Minot, North Dakota.

After the election campaign was over, we helped organize the farmers into the United Farmers' League, an organization which paved the way for the great Farm Holiday movement. The Hoover depression had hit with particular severity the farmer on the dry plains of the Dakotas and the Great Lakes region of cut-over timber lands ruined by the lumber barons. The United Farmers' League appeared in this region to fight for the homes, equipment and livestock of thousands of farmers who had exhausted their resources.

Once, in Frederick, we were called on by a farmer named Lutio who was about to be evicted by the bank from the family home where he had brought up seven children. The U.F.L. got together about seventy cars and drove down there. We told the sheriff and the banker they couldn't evict the Lutio family. The banker gave ten days' grace; then the new tenant would move in. We told him the Lutios would make room for the new tenant, but would keep on living there too. They had no place to go and no money. A week later I was asked to come down again, to explain to some 60 or 70 new people who had joined the U.F.L., as a result of our visit, how they should function. We held a big meeting before the cooperative gasoline station. The banker's seventeen-year-old son rounded up hoodlums to break up the meeting. They catcalled and booed me. But we had mobilized a group of powerful young Finns, and I announced, "You can stay here all night, but we're going to have this meeting." Presently the hoodlums disappeared. A big Finnish woman whispered to me, "They've gone to get the fire engine and hose." But I wasn't worried. I had seen our husky Finns detach themselves from the crowd and follow them. When the hoodlums reappeared with the fire engine and hose, there was a tug of war; somehow the hose got slit, and it was the hoodlums who got the wetting. We had our meeting, and the Lutios were not evicted.

In 1931, the first of four successive years of drought, there was a severe grasshopper plague in the Dakotas. The Red Cross workers sent out from eastern cities to administer relief had very little understanding of the farmers and their needs. If a farmer drove up to the relief station in a battered old Ford, the Red Cross worker would say, "You can't have any relief if you can afford to drive here in a car." "But I had to drive twenty miles to get here," would be the answer. "Why didn't you use a horse?" "My horses are dead in the fields."

One very helpful action at that time was the following: North Dakota farmers took truckloads of lignite coal, very plentiful all over North and South Dakota, to exchange for hay. But when farmers in Red River Valley sent word to the United Farmers' League that they had a lot of potatoes, and if the men dug them we could have them to distribute, the Red Cross refused to let us ship the potatoes we dug where we knew they were needed. However, our strong organization finally prevailed and directed the farmers to meet the carloads of potatoes wherever they were sent.

During the 1932 Presidential campaign which resulted in Roosevelt's election and in which Foster and Ford were the Party candidates, the big militant milk strike then going on in Iowa came up for discussion at a meeting of the Central Committee of the Party in New York. With crops a little better, prices for farm products had reached a record low. Strikes, which the farmers called "holidays," by which they meant a moratorium for evictions and foreclosures, were sweeping the farm areas, with Iowa as the storm center. Feeling that something must be done by our Party in recognition of the importance of the milk strike, I suggested that [my son Hal] should be sent out with me to Iowa to encourage the farmers. Milo Reno, president of the Farmers' Holiday Association, had called the governors of seven states together in Sioux City, Iowa, to discuss moratoriums for farm debts. We feared his purpose was to break the strike, so successfully carried on by the farmers, and in which they had the cooperation of the workers of nearby cities, since the farmers gave the milk to the children of the unemployed instead of throwing it out when they stopped trucks trying to make deliveries to the big trusts.

We wired Hal to come to Des Moines, and met him there. After holding a big meeting in Des Moines, Hal, Rob Hall, who had joined us, and I drafted a set of resolutions for the Sioux City conference, dealing with such problems as the low price of milk at the milk sheds, and the spread between that and the price paid by the consumer; and a call for a convention of real dirt farmers in Washington to carry their problems direct to their congressmen. The meeting of governors was to take place in Sioux City next day and we were determined to get the ear of those farmers coming to town to tell the governors what they wanted.

We got up early the next morning and drove all day to Sioux City, some two hundred miles away. The papers featured statements by Milo Reno that the strike was over, which we knew was not true, because the pickets were as lively as ever on the roads, and no milk was passing through. The governors had arrived and had put up at the largest hotel. A few days before, a county sheriff, near Sioux City, deputized over a hundred men to stop the pickets by force. But instead of the deputies stopping the unarmed pickets, it was the pickets who, with bare hands, took charge of the deputies, disarmed them, removed their coats, and sent them back in their shirt sleeves to Sioux City.

About 10 o'clock in the morning Hal, Rob Hall, and I drove out to the park where 10,000 farmers were already assembled. Towards noon the number swelled to about 15,000. They were milling around, apparently with no plans or leadership. I went up to one keen-looking farmer and asked, "Where are your leaders? You are Holiday members, aren't you?" "Yes, we are Holiday members, but I don't know whether or not we have any leaders. If we have, they must be up with the governors in the hotel." His tone was sarcastic. "Well," I said, "I am national organizer of the United Farmers' League of North Dakota, and have brought greetings from North Dakota. They are willing to cooperate in this strike in every way." The farmer's eyes popped. "Woman, can you speak?"

"A little."

He just took me by the shoulders and lifted me up on a table and said, "Shoot!"

In about a minute the farmers were around me in a solid mass, and I talked as I had never talked before. I told them not to listen to the governors' instructions to stop their fight just as they were gaining the victory, but to seize this opportunity to tell the governors their needs. They wanted me to go on and on and finally asked me to lead their parade.

That parade was something to remember. A cowboy band led it, followed by farm boys on horseback, and after them the prize truck. In it stood forty men, straight and proud, representing picket line Number 20—which had never let a truck go by. Behind Number 20 came the marching farmers. I was hoisted up on top of the truck cab. Perched up there precariously as we rode through the streets of Sioux City, I kept waving to the crowds with one hand, and trying to hold on with the other. I had often felt ready to die for the miners, but this time I was sure I was about to die for the farmers! The parade had a thunderous reception. Workers lining the streets shouted: "Boys, we are with you. We'll help you, and you help us!" We halted before the governors' hotel, and the farmers called out, "Come on, governors, send out your soldiers, we are ready." We could see them peeping out from behind the curtains and knew they were good and scared of these farmers.

Before the meeting had disbanded at the park, I had said, "Why not hold a meeting right in the hotel, draft resolutions to the governors, and tell them in an organized fashion what you want and why you want to continue the strike?" So now they marched right into the hotel auditorium, elected a chairman, and passed all the resolutions unanimously. The meeting ended with a call to the convention in Washington, and election of a committee to present the resolutions to the governors. The governors at first contemptuously refused to see the committee and didn't give in until about 9 o'clock. Late that night the newsboys ran through the streets shouting, "Extra! Extra! The farmers have the governors on the spot!" The resolutions, printed in the papers, made a great stir. The next day the farmers went on with their strike. We went out to their picket lines in the middle of the day. The women brought cooked dinners to the men, setting tables right by the roadside. We were invited to eat with them. Every time a milk truck came along, the men stopped eating, made the truck driver turn around and go back, and then

255
Ella Reeve Bloor

returned to their dinners. They asked me to stand on the table and talk.

That night we visited another picket line. Here they had cleared a big space at a cross-roads, erected a temporary platform draped with flags, and wanted me to talk. Having no leadership from their own organization they were hungry for encouragement. As a farmer's wife from North Dakota, they accepted me as one of their own.

This was followed in Iowa by the period of the "penny sales," when the militancy of the organized farmers kept them on the land until they got their moratorium. At sheriff's sales, the farmers gathered, bid ten cents for a cow, ten cents for a plow, ten cents for the house, etc., allowing no other bids. Having bought the farmer's property, they gave it back to him again.

In Lamar, Iowa, thirty miles from Sioux City, a well-liked farmer was behind in his interest payments to an insurance company. The company lawyer came with the judgment note enabling the insurance company to put in a bid for the farm and take it over in case the farmers did not bid. The news went around like lightning. Two truckloads of Unemployed Council members joined the thousands of farmers assembled at the court house. They told the sheriff that he would not be able to sell the man out. "I must," he said, "or I will lose my job." Then they went to the lawyer and asked, "Have you got a judgment note?" "Yes," he told them. "You are not going to use it to bid with," they said. "I must," he cried, "or I will lose my job." The farmers took him out of the court house and stood him under a tree, and asked, "Will you write a telegram to your company and tell them to withdraw the note?" He said, "No, I can't do it." One old farmer said, "Get the rope." They didn't intend to use the rope, but they had one handy, threw it over the limb of the tree and repeated: "Will you send the telegram?" "Give me a paper and pencil!" He wrote: "Withdraw the note. My neck is in danger."

Another method the farmers used successfully to prevent evictions was the "silent protest." In Sioux City, the farmers packed the court room every month on the day set for the public sale of foreclosed farms and small homes. As he read each item on his list, the county treasurer would pause for bids. But the farmers there to save their neighbors' farms would just stand silently with grim smiles on their faces, and no bids would be made. Once a man ventured to bid, and the farmers quietly closed in on him and heaved him out with their shoulders, hardly moving, just pushing him along until he went through the door. Groups of unemployed workers came too to stand there with the farmers in case they were needed. At the end of December, the county treasurer said in disgust, "I've done my duty, but there's not a bid in the lot of you. The sales will be postponed until spring." The farmers never failed to appear to make their silent protest. It was the most convincing demonstration I ever saw of the power of solid, persistent organization.

Even after the moratorium law on farm debts was passed in Iowa, the judges kept on selling farms illegally. The farmers gathered in protest, were met by troops and some terrible fights occurred. One judge at Lamar who ignored the moratorium bill was taught a lesson by the farmers who took him out of his office one day and made him walk a mile in his B.V.D.'s.

I never saw anything like the militancy of those farmers. They were wonderful. Only on one occasion a few of them threatened to get out of hand. The National Guardsmen sent to Lamar were just high school boys—some of them farmers' sons. The night after their entry into Lamar, we heard a tramping up the stairs, and a bunch of hot-headed farmers came into our office saying, "How many men can you give us? What arms have you got?"

"Wait a minute, boys," I said. "We haven't any guns, you know."

"We can't stand having those young boys come and interfere with our rights—we're going to do something about it."

We made them sit down and talk it over. We told them we were preparing leaflets calling on Milo Reno to organize a big meeting of the Holiday Association in Des Moines, and rallies before the court houses in various counties to protest to the Governor against violations of the law and sending in the National Guard. We got them to see this was a better way than to go out and start a fight.

Within a week soldiers had raided our office, taken away baskets full of our papers, thrown our people into jail, arrested and held incommunicado a harmless old man who was distributing our leaflets. Andy and I were away at the time. They had planned to arrest us for inciting to riot when, as a matter of fact, it was we who had stopped a riot!

By the end of 1932 our work among the farmers had broadened out to such an extent that we were able to hold a highly successful Farmers' Emergency Relief Conference in Washington in December, 1932.

My son Hal was asked to help call such a conference by the Farm Holiday Committee in Sioux City. Some Nebraska Holiday members carried the news of the proposed conference back to their offices and it was enthusiastically supported. The call was quickly endorsed by Pennsylvania, New England and Alabama farm organizations, and became a real national conference. Working with Hal on the conference preparations were Lem Harris, Rob Hall, Otto Anstrom, and other active, intelligent young men who were familiar with the problems of the farmers.

Two hundred and forty-eight delegates from twenty-six states, representing thirty-three organizations and unorganized farmers attended the conference. It took place at the same time as the big march of the unemployed to Washington. The unemployed were being held outside the city by Hoover's police, and some were getting pneumonia and dying of exposure. The farmers' protests to their Congressmen were an important factor in finally getting the unemployed marchers into the city. The farmers themselves were treated courteously by their Congressmen, and even given a police escort into the city.

The farmer delegates visited their Congressmen, then came back and reported to the conference. One after another was told, after hearty handshakes, "I'm all for you, boys, but there's nothing we can do here." It was a good education for them. Twelve of us who were delegates from North Dakota were taken to lunch by Senators Nye and Frazier and Congressman Sinclair. When we got back the others jokingly accused us of having been bought. "Don't worry," we told them. "It was only a fifty-cent lunch!"

Delegations called upon the President and the Vice-President. The delegation to Vice-President Curtis included a Negro. Before being admitted, their pockets were flipped by a guard. Then they were lined up single file to shake hands. Curtis refused to shake the

Negro's hand. The farmer who followed after him didn't put out his hand. Instead he said:

"Mr. Curtis, if you won't shake hands with our Negro delegate, I guess I don't want to shake your hand."

A plainclothesman hustled him off saying, "You ought to have your block knocked off."

One of the high points of that convention was the arrival of the sharecroppers' delegation from the South. They arrived a day late. Many of the farmers were living in tourist cabins down on the Potomac, only some of which were heated. The white farmers rushed to offer their heated cabins to the Negro delegates from the South, who they thought would suffer from the cold. The sharecroppers got a tremendous ovation at the convention. An Alabama sharecropper reported on the desperate conditions in his state, telling about the extreme poverty and the struggle for even the most elementary rights. A tactless delegate asked, "Tell us about the terror in the South," whereupon the speaker, who had lived for months under its shadow and was now near exhaustion from a sleepless and foodless journey, collapsed. We had to protect these sharecropper delegates from any publicity whatsoever, as their very lives were endangered by their attendance.

The conference raised demands for a moratorium on farm debts, and mapped out a program for militant action to improve farm conditions, including a struggle to prevent foreclosures, evictions and loss of farm property.

The convention voted to organize the Farmers' National Committee for Action, and to publish a weekly paper. The F.N.C.A. was a broad, united front movement taking in all kinds of farm organizations. I was asked to superintend the organization of the committee in five states—Montana, North and South Dakota, Iowa and Nebraska. Moving my headquarters to Sioux City, Iowa, I took up my work as secretary of the Farmers' Committee in these five states, Andy becoming organizer for the Sioux City district.

Following the Washington conference similar conferences and mass demonstrations took place in Nebraska, South Dakota, Iowa, and elsewhere. We who were on the Farmers' National Committee of Action Executive Committee attended Farmers' Holiday and Farmers'

Union State Conventions as delegates. One memorable occasion was at the State Agricultural Fair grounds in Lincoln, Nebraska. Several of us had been made fraternal delegates—among others Lem Harris who had become national secretary of the F.N.C.A. He had just returned from a visit to the U.S.S.R. and had secured from Julien Bryan, well known lecturer, his motion picture of collective farms. The Washington Conference had received these pictures enthusiastically, and Lem took it for granted the Nebraska farmers would be interested. But the backward element there tore down the screen. Next morning a man whom I knew was no farmer but a postman and a notorious Republican politician proposed a resolution condemning "that man" for bringing pictures of the Soviet Union to the conference. He shouted, "The farmers of Nebraska don't want to see, hear or know anything about Russia!" He was quickly seconded and the chairman was about to ask for discussion. Seeing the resolution about to be stampeded through, I climbed up on a table and cried at the top of my lungs, "Wait a minute, brothers, before you do anything like this. Don't you realize that at this very moment the President and Congress are considering recognition of the Soviet Union and all over our country people are advocating this move? What will they think of you farmers of Nebraska if you pass a resolution like this?" They stopped to think, because these men had voted for Roosevelt and were opposed to Hoover and his Farm Board. "And where does this resolution come from?" I went on. "From a farmer? No! From a Hoover postmaster!" I got applause and the vote, too.

The main thing we urged at these conferences was legislation to protect farmers from foreclosures. In Iowa the Lieutenant Governor pledged such legislation to the farmers who crowded in at a joint session of the House and Senate, with other farmers singing outside. At the conference at Pierre, South Dakota, farmers marched into the Capitol and presented their demands right on the floor.

In November, 1933, we held the second big F.N.C.A. conference in Chicago, heard reports of the success of the penny sales from many sections, and organized national legal defense work for farmers. The conference went even further than the Washington Conference by raising the demand for cancellation of secured farm debts of small and middle farmers, along with the stand against forced sales and auctions of impoverished families. It called for cash relief for destitute farm families, lowered taxes, measures to increase farmers' purchasing power, and abolition of oppression of Negroes. Here, with agricultural worker delegates present, we first brought vigorously to the fore the problems of agricultural workers. Our idea was to break down the antagonism between small farm owners and the agricultural workers. We made a special point of bringing the workers and farmers together at this convention, as in all our work. To drive home the point of workers' and farmers' unity, we wound up the convention by hiring a large auditorium for our final session, where thousands of Chicago workers cheered the farm delegates. The central section was reserved for the 702 farmer delegates from thirty-six different states. That meeting was a real demonstration of solidarity.

Next year, 1933–34, I was in Nebraska, bringing a message of encouragement and hope to these farmers triply stricken by drought, the dust storms that went with it, and low prices for farm products. It always seemed to me the farm women were the greatest sufferers. The choking, dust-filled air burns throat and eyes. It seeps inexorably into the houses, which have often been thrown out of plumb by high winds, leaving gaping chinks. Food, bed-clothing, furniture are all covered with a thick deposit, making it impossible to keep homes clean and tidy in the manner that these brave farm women would wish. Even their small and indispensable vegetable gardens are lost. Many a farm woman has carefully watered her small vegetable garden every evening in the hope of raising a few fresh vegetables only to have a hot dry wind blow a sand-blast which slithers the leaves and stops the growth of the plants. The combination of calamities to which these families were subjected would seem overwhelming, and yet they were in no sense beaten. We organized large groups of Nebraska farmers and found them just as militant as the farmers of Iowa.

MERIDEL

LE SUEUR

"In these terrible happenings you cannot be neutral now . . ."

Like Ella Reeve Bloor, Meridel Le Sueur *was a disillusioned socialist who won notoriety as a Communist party labor organizer during the Depression.*

Born in 1900 in Murray, Iowa, Le Sueur grew up in a socialist home. Her stepfather, Arthur Le Sueur, was the mayor of Minot, North Dakota, from 1912 to 1914. Her mother, Marion Wharton, was extremely active in Socialist party politics. Prominent radicals such as Eugene Debs, Emma Goldman, and Big Bill Haywood were their personal friends.

Claiming that the Socialist party harbored too many posturing intellectuals and did too little for the working class, Meridel Le Sueur joined the Communist party in 1924. It was a decision she never repudiated. During the twenties and thirties she financed her organizing activities with a second career as a successful novelist and short-story writer. Her fiction appeared in such large-circulation magazines as the Dial, Scribner's, *and* American Mercury. *At the same time, such radical publications as* New Masses *and the* Daily Worker *carried her labor journalism.*

Like Anzia Yezierska, Le Sueur never made precise distinctions between fiction and autobiography. The stories in her best-known collection, Corn Village, *often focus on the adventures of a Midwestern radical strikingly similar to the author herself. The more autobiographical* Salute to Spring, *from which the following selection is taken, sometimes mixes real and fictional characters. The following account, however, of Le Sueur's participation in the 1934 teamsters' strike in Minneapolis, is, as far as we can tell, a straightforward piece of personal reporting.*

SOURCES: Literary scholars have in the past few years rediscovered Le Sueur. In addition to the books cited above, see Meridel Le Sueur, *Ripening* (ed. by Elaine Hedges) (reprint ed. 1982). For information about Le Sueur's life, see Linda Pratt, "Woman Writer in the CP: The Case of Meridel Le Sueur," *Women's Studies* 14 (1988), 247–264. See also Robert Shaffer, "Women and the Communist Party, USA: 1930–1940," *Socialist Review* 9 (1979), 73–118, and Neala Schleuning, *America: Songs We Sang Without Knowing: The Life and Ideas of Meridel Le Sueur* (1983).

MERIDEL LE SUEUR

Minneapolis, 1934

I HAVE NEVER BEEN IN A STRIKE before. It is like looking at something that is happening for the first time and there are no thoughts and no words yet accrued to it. If you come from the middle class, words are likely to mean more than an event. You are likely to think about a thing, and the happening will be the size of a pin-point and the words around the happening very large, distorting it queerly. It's a case of "Remembrance of Things Past." When you are in the event, you are likely to have a distinctly individualistic attitude, to be only partly there, and to care more for the happening afterwards than when it is happening. That is why it is hard for a person like myself and others to be in a strike.

Besides, in American life, you hear things happening in a far and muffled way. One thing is said and another happens. Our merchant society has been built upon a huge hypocrisy, a cutthroat competition which sets one man against another and at the same time an ideology mouthing such words as "Humanity," "Truth," the "Golden Rule," and such. Now in a crisis the word falls away and the skeleton of that action shows in terrific movement.

For two days I heard of the strike. I went by their headquarters, I walked by on the opposite side of the street and saw the dark old building that had been a garage and lean, dark young faces leaning from the upstairs windows. I had to go down there often. I looked in. I saw the huge black interior and live coals of living men moving restlessly and orderly, their eyes gleaming from their sweaty faces.

I saw cars leaving filled with grimy men, pickets going to the line, engines roaring out. I stayed close to the door, watching. I didn't go in. I was afraid they would put me out. After all, I could remain a spectator. A man wearing a polo hat kept going around with a large camera taking pictures.

I am putting down exactly how I felt, because I believe others of my class feel the same as I did. I believe it stands for an important psychic change that must take place in all. I saw many artists, writers, professionals, even businessmen and women standing across the street, too, and I saw in their faces the same longings, the same fears.

The truth is I was afraid. Not of the physical danger at all, but an awful fright of mixing, of losing myself, of being unknown and lost. I felt inferior. I felt no one would know me there, that all I had been trained to excel in would go unnoticed. I can't describe what I felt, but perhaps it will come near it to say that I felt I excelled in competing with others and I knew instantly that these people were not competing at all, that they were acting in a strange, powerful trance of movement together. And I was filled with longing to act with them and with fear that I could not. I felt I was born out of every kind of life, thrown up alone, looking at other lonely people, a condition I had been in the habit of defending with various attitudes of cynicism, preciosity, defiance, and hatred.

Looking at that dark and lively building, massed with men, I knew my feelings to be those belonging to disruption, chaos, and disintegration and I felt their direct and awful movement, mute and powerful, drawing them into a close and glowing cohesion like a powerful conflagration in the midst of the city. And it filled me with fear and awe and at the same time hope. I knew this action to be prophetic and indicative of future actions and I wanted to be part of it.

Our life seems to be marked with a curious and muffled violence over America, but this action has always been in the dark, men and women dying obscurely, poor and poverty marked lives, but now from city to city runs this violence, into the open, and colossal happenings stand bare before our eyes, the street churning suddenly upon the pivot of mad violence, whole men suddenly spouting blood and running like living sieves, another holding a dangling arm shot squarely off, a tall youngster, running, tripping over his intestines, and one block away, in the burning sun, gay women shopping and a window dresser trying to decide whether to put green or red voile on a manikin.

In these terrible happenings you cannot be neutral now. No one can be neutral in the face of bullets.

The next day, with sweat breaking out on my body, I walked past the three guards at the door. They said, "Let the women in. We need women." And I knew it was no joke.

At first I could not see into the dark building. I felt many men coming and going, cars driving through. I had an awful impulse to go into the office which I passed, and offer to do some special work. I saw a sign which said, "Get your button." I saw they all had buttons with the date and the number of the union local. I didn't get a button. I wanted to be anonymous.

There seemed to be a current, running down the wooden stairs, towards the front of the building, into the street, that was massed with people, and back again. I followed the current up the old stairs packed closely with hot men and women. As I was going up I could look down and see the lower floor, the cars drawing up to await picket call, the hospital roped off on one side.

Upstairs men sat bolt upright in chairs asleep, their bodies flung in attitudes of peculiar violence of fatigue. A woman nursed her baby. Two young girls slept together on a cot, dressed in overalls. The voice of the loudspeaker filled the room. The immense heat pressed down from the flat ceiling. I stood up against the wall for an hour. No one paid any attention to me. The commissary was in back and the women came out sometimes and sat down, fanning themselves with their aprons and listening to the news over the loudspeaker. A huge man seemed hung on a tiny folding chair. Occasionally someone tiptoed over and brushed the flies off his face. His great head fell over and the sweat poured regularly from his forehead like a spring. I wondered why they took such care of him. They all looked at him tenderly as he slept. I learned later he was a leader on the picket line and had the scalps of more cops to his name than any other.

Three windows flanked the front. I walked over to the windows. A red-headed woman with a button saying, "Unemployed Council," was looking out. I looked out with her. A thick crowd stood in the heat below listening to the strike bulletin. We could look right into the windows of the smart club across the street. We could see people peering out of the windows half hidden.

I kept feeling they would put me out. No one paid any attention. The woman said without looking at me, nodding to the palatial house, "It sure is good to see the enemy plain like that." "Yes," I said. I saw that the club was surrounded by a steel picket fence higher than a man. "They know what they put that there fence there for," she said. "Yes," I said. "Well," she said, "I've got to get back to the kitchen. Is it ever hot?" The thermometer said ninety-nine. The sweat ran off us, burning our skins. "The boys'll be coming in," she said, "for their noon feed." She had a scarred face. "Boy, will it be a mad house?" "Do you need any help?" I said eagerly. "Boy," she said, "some of us have been pouring coffee since two o'clock this morning, steady, without no letup." She started to go. She didn't pay any special attention to me as an individual. She didn't seem to be thinking of me, she didn't seem to see me. I watched her go. I felt rebuffed, hurt. Then I saw instantly she didn't see me because she saw only what she was doing. I ran after her.

I found the kitchen organized like a factory. Nobody asks my name. I am given a large butcher's apron. I realize I have never before worked anonymously. At first I feel strange and then I feel good. The forewoman sets me to washing tin cups. There are not enough cups. We have to wash fast and rinse them and set them up quickly for buttermilk and coffee as the line thickens and the men wait. A little shortish man who is a professional dishwasher is supervising. I feel I won't be able to wash tin cups, but when no one pays any attention except to see that there are enough cups I feel better.

The line grows heavy. The men are coming in from the picket line. Each woman has one thing to do. There is no confusion. I soon learn I am not supposed to help pour the buttermilk. I am not supposed to serve sandwiches. I am supposed to wash tin cups. I suddenly look around and realize all these women are from factories. I know they have learned this organization and specialization in the factory. I look at the round shoulders of the woman cutting bread next to me and I feel I know her. The cups are brought back, washed and put on the counter again. The sweat pours down our faces, but you forget about it.

Then I am changed and put to pouring coffee. At first I look at the men's faces and then I don't look any more. It seems I am pouring coffee for the same tense dirty sweating face, the same body, the same blue shirt and overalls. Hours go by, the heat is terrific. I am not tired. I am not hot. I am pouring coffee. I am swung into the most intense and natural organization I have ever felt. I know everything that is going on. These things become of great matter to me.

Eyes looking, hands raising a thousand cups, throats burning, eyes bloodshot from lack of sleep, the body dilated to catch every sound over the whole city. Buttermilk? Coffee?

"Is your man here?" the woman cutting sandwiches asks me.

"No," I say, then I lie for some reason, peering around as if looking eagerly for someone, "I don't see him now."

But I was pouring coffee for living men.

267
Meridel Le Sueur

For a long time, about one o'clock, it seemed like something was about to happen. Women seemed to be pouring into headquarters to be near their men. You could hear only lies over the radio. And lies in the papers. Nobody knew precisely what was happening, but everyone thought something would happen in a few hours. You could feel the men being poured out of the hall onto the picket line. Every few minutes cars left and more drew up and were filled. The voice of the loudspeaker was accelerated, calling for men, calling for picket cars.

I could hear the men talking about the arbitration board, the truce that was supposed to be maintained while the board sat with the Governor. They listened to every word over the loudspeaker. A terrible communal excitement ran through the hall like a fire through a forest. I could hardly breathe. I seemed to have no body at all except the body of this excitement. I felt that what had happened before had not been a real movement, these false words and actions had taken place on the periphery. The real action was about to show the real intention.

We kept on pouring thousands of cups of coffee, feeding thousands of men.

The chef with a woman tattooed on his arm was just dishing the last of the stew. It was about two o'clock. The commissary was about empty. We went into the front hall. It was drained of men. The chairs were empty. The voice of the announcer was excited. "The men are massed at the market," he said. "Something is going to happen." I sat down beside a woman who was holding her hands tightly together, leaning forward listening, her eyes bright and dilated. I had never seen her before. She took my hands. She pulled me towards her. She was crying. "It's awful," she said, "something awful is going to happen. They've taken both my children away from me and now something is going to happen to all those men." I held her hands. She had a green ribbon around her hair.

The action seemed reversed. The cars were coming back. The announcer cried, "This is murder." Cars were coming in. I don't know how we got to the stairs. Everyone seemed to be converging at a menaced point. I saw below the crowd stirring, uncoiling. I saw them taking men out of cars and putting them on the hospital cots, on the floor. At first I felt frightened, the close black area of the barn, the blood, the heavy moment, the sense of myself lost, gone. But I couldn't have turned away now. A woman clung to my hand. I was pressed against the body of another. If you are to understand anything you must understand it in the muscular event, in actions we have not been trained for. Something broke all my surfaces in something that was beyond horror and I was dabbing alcohol on the gaping wounds that buckshot makes, hanging open like crying mouths. Buckshot wounds splay in the body and then swell like a blow. Ness, who died, had thirty-eight slugs in his body, in the chest and in the back.

The picket cars kept coming in. Some men have walked back from the market, holding their own blood in. They move in a great explosion, and the newness of the movement makes it seem like something under ether, moving terrifically towards a culmination.

From all over the city workers are coming. They gather outside in two great half-circles, cut in two to let the ambulances in. A traffic cop is still directing traffic at the corner and the crowd cannot stand to see him. "We'll give you just two seconds to beat it," they tell him. He goes away quickly. A striker takes over the street.

Men, women, and children are massing outside, a living circle close packed for protection. From the tall office building businessmen are looking down on the black swarm thickening, coagulating into what action they cannot tell.

We have living blood on our skirts.

That night at eight o'clock a mass meeting was called of all labor. It was to be in a parking lot two blocks from headquarters. All the women gather at the front of the building with collection cans, ready to march to the meeting. I have not been home. It never occurs to me to leave. The twilight is eerie and the men are saying that the chief of police is going to attack the meeting and raid headquarters. The smell of blood hangs in the hot, still air. Rumors strike at the taut nerves. The dusk looks ghastly with what might be in the next half-hour.

"If you have any children," a woman said to me, "you better not go." I looked at the desperate women's faces, the broken feet, the torn and hanging pelvis, the worn and lovely bodies of women who persist under such desperate labors. I shivered, though it was ninety-six and the sun had been down a good hour.

The parking lot was already full of people when we got there and men swarmed the adjoining roofs. An elegant café stood across the street with water sprinkling from its roof and splendidly dressed men and women stood on the steps as if looking at a show.

The platform was a bullet-riddled truck of the afternoon's fray. We had been told to stand close to this platform, so we did, making the center of a wide massed circle that stretched as far as we could see. We seemed buried like minerals in a mass, packed body to body. I felt again that peculiar heavy silence in which there is the real form of the happening. My eyes burn. I can hardly see. I seem to be standing like an animal in ambush. I have the brightest, most physical feeling with every sense sharpened peculiarly. The movements, the masses that I see and feel I have never known before. I only partly know what I am seeing, feeling, but I feel it is the real body and gesture of a future vitality. I see that there is a bright clot of women drawn close to a bullet-riddled truck. I am one of them, yet I don't feel myself at all. It is curious, I feel most alive and yet for the first time in my life I do not feel myself as separate. I realize then that all my previous feelings have been based on feeling myself separate and distinct from others and now I sense sharply faces, bodies, closeness, and my own fear is not my own alone, nor my hope.

The strikers keep moving up cars. We keep moving back together to let cars pass and form between us and a brick building that flanks the parking lot. They are connecting the loudspeaker, testing it. Yes, they are moving up lots of cars, through the crowd and lining them closely side by side. There must be ten thousand people now, heat rising from them. They are standing silent, watching the platform, watching the cars being brought up. The silence seems terrific like a great form moving of itself. This is real movement issuing from the close reality of mass feeling. This is the first real rhythmic movement I have ever seen. My heart hammers terrifically. My hands are swollen and hot. No one is producing this movement. It is a movement upon which all are moving softly, rhythmically, terribly.

No matter how many times I looked at what was happening I hardly knew what I saw. I looked and I saw time and time again that there were men standing close to us, around us, and then suddenly I knew that there was a living chain of men standing shoulder to shoulder, forming a circle around the group of women. They stood shoulder to shoulder slightly moving like a thick vine from the pressure behind, but standing tightly woven like a living wall, moving gently.

I saw that the cars were now lined one close-fitted to the other with strikers sitting on the roofs and closely packed on the running boards. They could see far over the crowd. "What are they doing that for?" I said. No one answered. The wide dilated eyes of the women were like my own. No one seemed to be answering questions now. They simply spoke, cried out, moved together now.

The last car drove in slowly, the crowd letting them through without command or instruction. "A little closer," someone said. "Be sure they are close." Men sprang up to direct whatever action was needed and then subsided again and no one had noticed who it was. They stepped forward to direct a needed action and then fell anonymously back again.

We all watched carefully the placing of the cars. Sometimes we looked at each other. I didn't understand that look. I felt uneasy. It was as if something escaped me. And then suddenly, on my very body, I knew what they were doing, as if it had been communicated to me from a thousand eyes, a thousand silent throats, as if it had been shouted in the loudest voice.

They were building a barricade.

Two men died from that day's shooting. Men lined up to give one of them a blood transfusion, but he died. Black Friday men called the murderous day. Night and day workers held their children up to see the body of Ness who died. Tuesday, the day of the funeral, one thousand more militia were massed downtown.

It was still over ninety in the shade. I went to the funeral parlors and thousands of men and women were massed there waiting in the terrific sun. One block of women and children were standing two hours waiting. I went over and stood near them. I didn't know whether I could march. I didn't like marching in parades. Besides, I felt they might not want me.

I stood aside not knowing if I would march. I couldn't see how they would ever organize it anyway. No one seemed to be doing much.

At three-forty some command went down the ranks. I said foolishly at the last minute, "I don't belong to the auxiliary—could I march?" Three women drew me in. "We want all to march," they said gently. "Come with us."

The giant mass uncoiled like a serpent and straightened out ahead and to my amazement on a lift of road I could see six blocks of massed men, four abreast, with bare heads, moving straight on and as they moved, uncoiled the mass behind and pulled it after them. I felt myself walking, accelerating my speed with the others as the line stretched, pulled taut, then held its rhythm.

Not a cop was in sight. The cortege moved through the stop-and-go signs, it seemed to lift of its own dramatic rhythm, coming from the intention of every person there. We were moving spontaneously in a movement, natural, hardy, and miraculous.

We passed through six blocks of tenements, through a sea of grim faces, and there was not a sound. There was the curious shuffle of thousands of feet, without drum or bugle, in ominous silence, a march not heavy as the military, but very light, exactly with the heart-beat.

I was marching with a million hands, movements, faces, and my own movement was repeating again and again, making a new movement from these many gestures, the walking, falling back, the open mouth crying, the nostrils stretched apart, the raised hand, the blow falling, and the outstretched hand drawing me in.

I felt my legs straighten. I felt my feet join in that strange shuffle of thousands of bodies moving with direction, of thousands of feet, and my own breath with the gigantic breath. As if an electric charge had passed through me, my hair stood on end, I was marching.

LUCY
RANDOLPH
MASON

"These ten- and eleven-hour days . . . burned my conscience . . ."

Lucy Randolph Mason traveled the country during the thirties as a representative of unions affiliated with the Congress of Industrial Organizations. In striking contrast to other women organizers included here, Mason was not a radical, nor did she rise to union leadership from the shop floor. She represented another tradition in labor organizing. Mason came to her long career as a prominent public relations representative for the CIO from a background of middle-class social reform activities.

Born in 1882, Lucy Mason was a member of a socially well-connected

Virginia family. The names Randolph and Mason linked her to two of the state's First Families, but Mason's own parents had little money. Instead, Lucy and Landon Mason were committed social activists. Landon Mason, an Episcopalian minister, was a Southern progressive, a champion of civil rights for blacks, the abolition of poll taxes, and better public medical care. His wife agitated tirelessly for prison reform. The Mason family was a large and close one. When her mother died in 1918, Lucy Mason, as the family's unmarried daughter, quit her job as industrial secretary of the Richmond Young Women's Christian Association to care for her aged father.

As the pages excerpted here from Mason's autobiography, To Win These Rights, *inform us, Landon Mason died in 1923, freeing his daughter to resume her career as a social reformer. She returned to full-time work for the Richmond YWCA until 1932, when she accepted a position as executive secretary of the National Consumers League. As an officer of another reform organization with an agenda parallel to that of the YWCA, Mason continued to lobby for better conditions for working women, for minimum wage laws, and for social security legislation. She frequently traveled to Washington to testify at congressional hearings.*

During a joint congressional hearing in 1937, in which she supported the proposed Fair Labor Standards Act, Mason met CIO president John L. Lewis. He asked her to join the Textile Workers' Organizing Committee of the CIO, and Mason agreed. Already in her late fifties, she embarked on a new career as a union organizer. As she notes in the following passages, her job as a public relations representative did not allow her to remain in a comfortable office, sending out information and brochures. Rather, until her retirement sixteen years later, Mason traveled the South, promoting the union cause.

As these excerpts clearly indicate, Mason courted danger, not just the good will of Southern politicians and editors. She continued as a CIO troubleshooter until failing health forced her retirement in 1953, but the decade of the Depression was to remain the most dramatic and important of her life.

SOURCES: An excellent new biography of Mason is John Salmond's *Miss Lucy of the CIO: The Life and Times of Lucy Randolph Mason* (1988). See also Nancy Ann White's essay in *Notable American Women*, 461–462. Lucy Mason's extensive papers are housed at the Rare Book and Manuscripts Division, Duke University Library, Durham, North Carolina.

"Unto the Least of These"

Both mother and father had a strong sense of social responsibility. It was part of their religious conviction. Their deep concern for human welfare led them into many unusual contacts. Father would respond to calls for help from poverty stricken families who had no connection with our congregation. I remember his carrying a bushel of coal on his back, from a store to the home of a destitute family, one winter day when an eighteen-inch snow had stopped all traffic. That was typical of his way of answering calls for help. In times of epidemics such as scarlet fever, he went wherever he was needed, often sitting up all night with some ill or dying person. . . .

Mother had a Bible class Sunday afternoons in the State Penitentiary, located in Richmond. Many of the men she met there came to our house when they were released. Some of them stayed with us while looking for work. They used the third-floor bedroom next to mine, but none of us ever had any fear of their doing harm. Through these contacts, mother discovered the atrocious cruelties that were perpetrated within the prison walls. . . .

One morning Mother received through the mail a newspaper clipping about a young girl who had killed her baby and tried to kill herself. She had been committed to jail. Mother never knew who eased his conscience by mailing her that clipping, but she went immediately to the jail and was permitted to see the girl, who was in a desperate state of mind. We knew where Mother had gone and were not surprised when a phone call came from her at supper time saying she must spend the night in the cell with the girl, who still threatened to kill herself.

Mother and Father practiced what Jesus said when he described the final test that made men fit to inherit the Kingdom of God. They took in and fed the stranger; they refreshed the spirit of the thirsty; they gave clothes to those who lacked them; they visited the sick; and they went to those in prison. They knew they served God as they cared for His children, remembering the Command "Love thy neighbor as thyself." . . .

Cooperating with Labor Unions

When I first became "union conscious" I do not know. I suppose it grew out of my concern because of the industrial accidents that happened to so many of the working people I knew, the long work days in Richmond's factories, laundries, stores, and everywhere else. These ten- and eleven-hour days were not only bad for the people who worked them, but disrupted normal family life. They burned my conscience and during my long life I have spent a lot of time laboring to shorten hours of work for both men and women.

It early became apparent that the best paid workers were union members, and they had an eight-hour day, with half of Saturday off. So it seemed natural that my sympathies and hopes should turn toward the unions. I remember that when I was still a stenographer there was a street railway drivers' strike and I avoided riding on street cars for the duration of the strike. There was a lot of snow and sleet that winter, and traveling on foot was not easy. . . .

In the spring of 1932 I had a letter from Mary W. Dewson, chairman of the executive committee of the National Consumers League, asking if I would consider a call to fill the office of general secretary. Mrs. Florence Kelley, who had been the first and only secretary of the League, had died and a successor was being sought. I accepted with humble joy, feeling too small for the work, but impelled to go into it. I had known Mrs. Kelley for years and greatly admired her. Mary Dewson (affectionately known as Molly) was a well-liked acquaintance whom I had met at various national conferences.

The League has had an honorable history. It was founded by churchmen of Christian and Jewish faiths, and by social workers and other public-spirited men and women. It was a newly formed organization when Florence Kelley went from Chicago to New York in 1899 as its secretary. Its purpose was to expose and fight sweatshop conditions in industry through "investigation, education and legislation."

Mrs. Kelley in 1909 attended an international conference on minimum-wage laws held in England, where such legislation was in effect. Ever after that she worked with unremitting vigor for minimum-wage laws in this country. When I was with the League I often called it the "consumers' conscience," for that is what Florence Kelley actually accomplished—she made people aware of the evil conditions under which goods were made, sold, and distributed, and made them feel responsible for doing something about them.

Mrs. Kelley was the daughter of a steel manufacturer who was thirty years in the U.S. House of Representatives. She used to recall that her father had given her an injunction she must live up to: "My generation has created industry," he would say, "your generation must humanize it." She spent her consecrated life doing just that.

One of Mrs. Kelley's most stalwart co-workers was Mary W. Dewson, a great woman who accomplished notable things and yet rarely got into the limelight. From the time I met Molly at a National League of Women Voters conference in Baltimore, soon after woman suffrage was gained, we had a bond in common—labor legislation for the amelioration of working conditions, and women's responsibility as citizens to bring this about.

After I had gone with the Consumers League, Molly told me that Mrs. Kelley had suggested me as her successor not long before she died. Two of her reasons were that my background would help me work effectively in the South, where working conditions were poor and labor laws few and weak; and that I was consecrated to improving the lot of working women.

Mrs. Dewson deserves a volume about her service to the best elements in the Democratic Party. She is a woman of honesty and great ability. The issues before the country were always the paramount fact with her—not the personalities of the candidates. After her work in directing the women's division in a considerable area during the 1928 presidential campaign, she was made chairman of the Democratic National Women's Division in the first Roosevelt campaign and did a notable job. Mrs. Roosevelt and Molly were friends of long standing and worked closely together in that campaign. I am indebted to Mary Dewson for introducing me to Mrs. Roosevelt, who I think is the world's greatest woman, and one of its few greatest citizens. She was one of the Consumers League's vice presidents and partly because of that I was to see her fairly often in the future. A gain for women made by Miss Dewson was the fifty-fifty participation by women on all Democratic Party committees. After some years of working on this, she saw that her urgings had prevailed and the matter was, in her words, "cinched in the nominating Convention of 1940." Molly Dewson was the first woman to be vice-chairman of the Democratic National Committee.

When I went to live in New York in September, 1932, the Great Depression was at its worst. The New York papers told what was happening. Stories of unemployment, short working weeks, starvation wages, and human want and misery were prevalent. For instance, in a downtown industrial district in New York a garment manufacturer advertised for skilled workers at ten dollars a week. The police had to break up the riot as a thousand women struggled to be up front and have a chance at a job.

In Cleveland, Ohio, a merchant advertised for ten experienced salesladies at eight dollars a week. The mob that formed outside his store was so great that the pressure of women against one another resulted in the smashing of a plate-glass window. Some women had to be taken to the hospital.

The sweatshop type of garment manufacturer got wages down to five or six dollars a week, with no pay for beginners. In the garment plants, textile mills, and tobacco factories of the South, wages were unbelievably low and completely inadequate to support workers and their families.

We decided that the National Consumers League should publicize conditions in every way possible. We called a conference on labor standards, sent out questionnaires in all directions and asked social agencies to give us all the facts they could. Information poured in. Mrs. Emily Sims Marconnier, the able associate secretary of the League, found free-lance writers who got material from our office and made it the basis for magazine stories. Labor unions helped us gather facts and publicize them.

During the formative period of the NRA Codes in the summer of 1933, I spent a good deal of time in Washington and frequently spoke before code commissioners for the consumers' interest in good labor conditions and wages. In industries with a considerable amount of union organization, the unions took care of getting witnesses before the commissioners. I appeared chiefly in those unorganized industries whose workers had no means of making effective presentations—they were called the "sweated industries," denoting low wages and often poor working conditions, but mainly overwork and underpay.

The first code to be heard was that of the Textile Industry. For finally that industry was seeking national wage and hour control. I spoke on the need of such controls and for higher standards than the manufacturers had asked. When I had finished my twenty-minute talk, the commissioner in a courteous way asked if I would answer some questions—which I was delighted to do. He asked me what the textile people would do with their money if wages were raised. I said they would spend it; they would get more and better food; shoes for the children so they could go to school in cold weather; the women in the family—and men and boys too—would get some better clothes to wear to church and on the street. They might go to a movie once in a while; and even buy an old car and some gasoline to go to see their people. If fact, I said, the workers would do with their higher pay exactly what President Roosevelt hoped they would—spend it and put the money into circulation. This was greeted by roars of laughter and much hand-clapping. The northern textile manufacturers beamed upon me, most of the southerners scowled.

I remember particularly the code hearing on crushed stone, sand, and gravel, obviously a low-wage industry according to the testimony. It was claimed that the majority of the workers in this industry in the South were Negroes, ignorant and unskilled, who, if they made more money, would work only two or three days a week and then get drunk and throw away their money.

One of the southern employers said that if these colored workers should get wages of 25¢ an hour it would *demoralize the economic and social status of the whole South!* Again, I made the statement for higher wages, and answered a number of questions. Some of the younger southerners came up after the hearing and said they entirely approved what I had said, for competition in low labor standards was not only bad for individual workers but for their industry and for the whole southern economy.

At the NRA code hearings in Washington I met many outstanding union men and women. Also in New York my work took me to meetings which were attended by labor's representatives. Prominent among them were Sidney Hillman, president of the Amalgamated Clothing Workers, and Jacob S. Potofsky, then the union's vice-president, now its president. Also David Dubinsky, president of the International Ladies Garment Workers Union, and many of his staff. These two great unions of men's and women's garment workers had so completely organized the older portions of their industries that strikes were things of the past. Labor-management peace was maintained by settling differences through mediation, conciliation, and arbitration— around the conference table, not on the picket line.

Meanwhile, Molly Dewson had forgotten how tired she was when the Roosevelt campaign of 1932 ended, and had gone to work reviving interest in Minimum Wage Legislation. Benjamin V. Cohen, one of the most brilliant of Roosevelt's legal staff and drafter of much New Deal legislation, put his mind on a model "fair wage" law for states that would not be thrown out by the Supreme Court. Seven states passed such laws in the following sessions, and the Supreme Court sustained them.

Tom Corcoran and Ben Cohen also prepared the Fair Labor Standards Act which Senator Black introduced and had passed in the Senate, but when difficulties arose in the House, Frances Perkins, Secretary of Labor, had her counsel work on a new and much shorter act. This bill passed the House and was the basis of the bill which became law. The Fair Labor Practices Act of June, 1938, was a result of much that had gone before. The Act set up a basic eight-hour day and forty-hour week, with a definite sum for a national minimum wage. It also provided for increasing the minimum wage for an industry through industry committees of employers, employees, and the public.

About the end of June, 1937, I had gone to Washington to speak before the Senate Committee on Labor in behalf of the Fair Labor Practices Bill. Mr. John L. Lewis appeared as a witness for the bill and was the first speaker. I had met him briefly once at a dinner meeting in honor of Frances Perkins, newly appointed Secretary of Labor. In connection with the purchase of his home in Alexandria, Mr. Lewis had met my brother-in-law, Taylor Burke, President of Burke and Herbert Bank. The banker and union leader liked each other and had become friends.

I admired Mr. Lewis' brilliant leadership of the industrial union movement and took the opportunity to speak with him while we were waiting for the hearing to begin. He was cordial and spoke highly of Taylor Burke. I was staying with the Burkes, and that evening, I expressed an often felt desire to go back South to live, where I could work with organized labor and interracial groups. I was particularly concerned with the status of Negroes in the new unions.

My sister laughed and said, "Why not try John Lewis?"

Her lightly spoken words rang a bell for me. "Ida, you are joking," I said, "but that may prove to be the smartest thing you ever said to me."

The result was that the next evening Taylor called Mr. Lewis and suggested a talk with him, to which Mr. Lewis responded by dropping by in less than an hour.

It was a delightful evening. Mr. Lewis is a remarkably well informed man and interesting conversationalist. He was impressed by the idea that I might work in the South as a publicist and public relations representative for the CIO and particularly in behalf of the Textile Workers Organizing Committee. He practically settled the matter then and there, but said that inasmuch as Sidney Hillman was director of the organizing drive in the Textile Industry, I must see him before the matter could be concluded. He said he would speak to Mr. Hillman, and after that I should see him.

When I returned to New York I found Mr. Hillman out of town, but talked on the telephone with Jack Potofsky, his right-hand man in the Amalgamated Clothing Workers, and asked if I might see him. As soon as Mr. Potofsky realized that I wanted to work in the field of public relations and publicity for the CIO in the South, he said: "Do you mean you will live and work in the South all the time?" When I said yes, he answered: "You don't need to see me about that. I heard you talk about unions when you spoke in St. Paul's Church in Richmond. I told you then that you ought to stay in the South all the time. I am all for this. I will tell Sidney we ought to put you down there and he will be for it too."

Soon after, Mr. Hillman and I did have a talk and he said that I would be working under him as southern director of organization for textiles and clothing, and under Mr. Lewis as president of the CIO. He said, "John is generous and I am stingy, so you'd better deal with him when it comes to salary."

Mr. Lewis spoke to me about my salary and I told him what my last two salaries had been with the YWCA and the National Consumers League—$3600 and $5000 respectively. I said I was willing to have a salary from the CIO of $3600. Mr. Lewis replied, "You will get $5000." I protested that this was too much for working people to pay me. He replied that he was not willing to pay me less than I had been receiving with the League.

I went to work for the CIO in July, 1937, and three months later I sent in my first salary and expense account with the salary at $300 a month—$3600 a year. In about 1945 when there was a general salary increase, I accepted $4000 a year.

The important concern to me was that my services might be worth something real to the industrial union movement. Every day of this new life was an adventure—every assignment in the field a challenge. Meeting and talking with the union folk was the inspiration, and coming back to the office to tell the story was the fun. My rewards were in the commendation my fellow workers gave me....

The Movement

Where Jimmy Cox and I first met, I don't remember. It was in August of my first summer with the

CIO. We must have met in Atlanta or in some union gathering where he had gone looking for help. The meeting resulted in my driving to the small city of Tupelo, Mississippi, in the heart of Congressman John E. Rankin's territory.

Jimmy was a worker in a run-down, obsolete, small cotton mill in bad financial shape. The mill had been deteriorating for some time, I was told. Its stockholders had not received dividends for a long time. The commission man who handled selling the mill's goods was the only one connected with the plant who made any money on it—it was said he had bought the mill and got his profit out of commissions for selling its goods. It seemed about the worst possible place to try to organize.

Jimmy knew that the CIO was doing a lot for southern workers, and he did not know anything about the finances of that little mill. He thought that if only a union could be organized the situation could be worked out. Wages and working conditions were bad—there was plenty to make the people desperate and ready to try anything. The result was a strike which took most of the people out of the plant, but was now disintegrating. The owner closed the mill. Some of the people drifted away to try their luck elsewhere.

Townspeople spread the rumor that if Jimmy could be gotten rid of the strike would end, the mill open, and people go back to work.

The background in Tupelo was most unfavorable for labor unions. Congressman Rankin had worked hard for the Tennessee Valley Authority for the simple reason that it meant cheap electric power for his own town and state—he wanted industries for Tupelo. He had fought every piece of progressive labor legislation promoted by the New Deal. The National Labor Relations Act had aroused his utmost fury and he had said that if it became law the streets of southern towns would run red with blood. He failed to say that if blood was shed, it would be the blood of the workers—not that of management, police, or the public.

There was a garment plant in Tupelo that made women's garments and the employees had become interested in a union. Up in Memphis, what newspapers called "a society girl," Ida Sledge, social worker by training, helped in efforts to organize a local union of the International Ladies Garment Workers. Somehow the garment workers in

Tupelo heard about her and asked her to come help them. It resulted in Ida's going to Tupelo to organize the women garment workers into the International Ladies Garment Workers Union.

Already I had heard of Ida's adventures. Her first was an early-morning visit in her hotel room from a number of women from the garment factory, whom the management had persuaded to form a small mob when the morning shift came on. They made her hustle into her clothes and walked her out of town, all the while threatening her with her life if she came back. Later in the day Ida returned to the hotel.

A few days later a delegation of "best citizens"—young men from the social and business circles of Tupelo—entered her hotel room at night. When she tried to use the phone to get a newspaper friend in Memphis, she was told the wires were disconnected. Again she had to hustle into her clothes, fling the rest into a suitcase, and get out. This crowd took her to the railroad station and saw that she took the next train—with dire warnings as to what would happen if she came back.

(During this time I had been on my way to Tupelo in my blue coupe.)

Strangers were not welcome in Tupelo. At the post office I got out to inquire my way to the street number that meant Jimmy's home in the mill village. The dignified, elderly man to whom I spoke gave me a suspicious and hostile look.

Ida was sleeping across town in the spare room of a nice young couple. She used part of a room in Jimmy's house for her office, with her typewriter on top of a trunk. When I arrived I saw that the house was in wretched condition, had but two fair-sized rooms, a tiny back porch with running water—no bath. The bedroom had two double beds, the other room was kitchen, sitting room, and storeroom. Furnishings were sparse. The family made me have the evening meal with them and I observed that Ida brought along a good part of it.

Excitement began late Saturday afternoon. There was a special meeting of the cotton mill union people, from which Jimmy returned to tell us that the people had voted to continue the strike. Within an hour the village was rife with rumors that a mob was going to take Jimmy out and hang him that night. Union men came to warn him to leave town. A friend brought him a pistol, which I persuaded him to return—since it was a sure way to suicide for Jimmy to be seen handling a pistol.

I tried to see Claude Clayton, city attorney, but his mother told me he had gone fishing and would not be back until midnight. I left a note to him with her, in which I urged his help. I had never met Mr. Clayton, but Ida and Jimmy believed he would take steps to protect them if he could be found. He had warned Tupelo's best citizens that if any one interfered with her again he would go to all limits in prosecuting, "let the chips fall where they may."

Next day, Sunday morning, I found Mr. Clayton at home and we had a long talk. It seemed that when he got in late the night before he read my note and went straight to the chief of police. Special officers were put on around the mill village. But the night was quiet. Mr. Clayton thought the attacks on Jimmy and Ida were over.

Saturday night, Ida and the two sweet little girls and I stayed at the home where Ida had a room. Jimmy wanted to stay at his home and face the enemy alone, but I told him that if he did, I would sit up all night on the front porch. That was too much for his chivalrous soul and we got him off to the home of friends.

About two weeks later, I had a wire from Ida saying that a group of men from the garment plant (instigated by the employer of course) had picked up Jimmy on the street and taken him out into the country on a lonely road. They said they were going to drag him to death, tied to the car's rear axle.

They actually put the rope around his neck. They beat and kicked him so badly he had to go to a hospital for some days. Jimmy had a fluent tongue and believed in his cause. He asked to be heard before they killed him, and whether from conscience or from fear of the law, they let him go after he promised not to return to Tupelo.

Huntsville is a pretty little North Alabama town, set in a green and rolling country, not far from Tupelo. Its chief industry is textiles, and at times there have been four mills operating, with a total of several thousand employees. I have never had a chance to see its "social and cultural life"—for my frequent encounters with the editor of the *Huntsville Times* could hardly be called on the social side.

Whenever I was suddenly called to Huntsville because of some emergency situation, it was a question of getting there as fast as I could, spending my time with the local union people and the representatives of TWOC, and seeing some of the citizens the union people wanted me to talk with. Then I would go back by Birmingham and spend some time with the newspaper editors on the subject of conditions at Huntsville and the progress of CIO unions in the South.

Because of events which took place in connection with the Dallas and Merrimack Mills, they are the subject of this story, without reference to the other two mills in Huntsville with which things were going quietly.

Some of the local unions in Huntsville had been there for several years before the general cotton textile strike in 1934. They were among the oldest locals in the South—but they did not have written and signed collective bargaining agreements arrived at by negotiation. Indeed, it seems to have been some advance when management would sit down across the table and admit that the union representatives did in truth represent the union workers. Recognition was the first step, negotiation—or discussion of all points—the second, and a written, signed agreement the third. Probably the struggle between union and management in these two cases was greatly aggravated by the lack of any defined and signed contract between the parties. The first real contract with the Dallas Mill came in October, 1938, and with Merrimack several months later.

The Dallas Mill was part of a chain of twenty-one mills when this story began. Steve Nance had negotiated a verbal agreement in the spring of 1937. That summer the company got the Roper Company, a firm of efficiency engineers, to make a study which resulted in eliminating a great many people, increasing the work-load for those employees who remained, and cutting real wages.

The new agreement terms and their actual effect on the workers caused considerable altercation. Finally the mill closed in November, 1937, and remained closed until around the first of April, 1938, when management wanted to open it. But instead of calling back the workers who had been in the mill when it closed (most of them union members) management claimed they had no employees; that the

November dismissal was permanent. The Mill management requested the State Employment Service to supply the needed workers. The union insisted that the former workers, as members of the union, had an agreement with the mill when it closed and should be called back. But the company stood firm.

Naturally, a strike was called by the union which picketed the mill to keep the new people out. The Dallas manager was a man from Georgia, said to be hard and bitter against the union. Some of the citizens of Huntsville were enlisted on the side of management in trying to break the union.

A citizens' committee was formed and one of the most active opponents of the union was the editor of *The Huntsville Times*. In April, 1938, the editor threatened the union people that the mills would move away, and that they would find themselves black-listed wherever they went. I quote a few lines from one of these editorials:

> You may go to Chattanooga or Birmingham, New York or Chicago, BUT THERE ARE NO JOBS THERE FOR YOU. . . . If application is made to another mill elsewhere, the story of this city will be familiar, until your dying days!

I used to see this editor when I went to Huntsville—he was always personally polite, but I never saw a more acid person than he was when he talked of unions. He used to call the TWOC a snake and said it must be killed at once and never allowed to raise its head again.

As the deadlock continued, the Dallas management announced they were going to open the mill and start work. The union replied that it would picket the mill to see that only former employees went in. Management then asked the Governor to send in militia to protect the new employees and get them into the mill. The Governor said the trouble should be settled by conciliation and arbitration, which was his consistent stand during the altercation. The union also demanded arbitration, with Governor Graves as the arbitrator. The company flatly refused to be a party to arbitration, saying they would stand on their right to employ whom they wanted.

Suddenly the citizens' committee announced that a cavalcade of automobiles would leave Huntsville on April 20 and proceed to the

Governor's office in Montgomery to petition him to send troops to Huntsville and break the strike. At this point, Roy Lawrence called me up and asked me to go at once to Huntsville.

But before going to Huntsville I went to Birmingham, arriving by train on the morning of the nineteenth and proceeding at once to the editorial office of the *Age-Herald*. Then I was with editors of *The News* and finally of the *Post*. I began at the top but was careful to see the next top man in each case. All three papers had been having heavily slanted editorials in favor of sending militia to open the mill.

My total talking time in these editorial offices was just over six hours in one day, and I was armed with a long column containing my story of the situation in the Dallas Mill. The *Age-Herald* printed that in full. Next day those three papers had strong appeals for what the union had asked loud and long—"conciliation and arbitration." I got the same favorable editorial slant from the *Montgomery Advertiser*—by long distance telephone call. That was the best job in changing editors' opinions that ever I did.

Next morning, Bill Mitch, then state director of the CIO, drove me in his car to Huntsville. We met the citizens' cavalcade enroute to Montgomery—horns blowing, men shouting and already triumphant. But they went home very flat, very quiet—we met them straggling back, their line of march all broken. The Governor had given them a courteous reception—offered conciliation and arbitration—at which the unruly crowd had shouted and jeered and booed.

In due time the Dallas mill opened and the union had not been killed.

Meanwhile, some time in 1938 the Textile Workers Organizing Committee had negotiated an agreement with the Merrimack Mill. Borden Burr, the mill attorney, however, had been successful in keeping the management from signing, so there was no contract. When this verbal agreement expired there was a long strike. It lasted more than a year and caused great suffering among the people.

When cold weather came in the winter of 1938, the Merrimack Mill continued its severe policy of evicting mill village workers, putting them out in groups. I have before me a "Partial Report on Eviction Survey, Merrimack Mill Village, November 19, 1938," made by the "Women's Emergency Committee on Evictions and Welfare."

This committee personally canvassed the situation. There was an incredible amount of destitution, overcrowding, and undernourishment. One house with four rooms contained fifteen people, with four beds for all of them. A man with a daughter near death in the hospital requested a few days' postponement of eviction, but was refused. The girl died the day the family was evicted.

The report showed that real estate and business interests were involved in a widespread conspiracy to drive the evicted people out of the community—yet the workers' average time of employment in the mill was fourteen years per person. The families had lived from two to twenty-three years in the houses from which they were evicted.

I was in Birmingham November 23, 1938, to hear Mrs. Roosevelt speak in the city auditorium to the Southern Conference for Human Welfare. The Merrimack local appointed a delegation to attend this conference, hoping that Mrs. Roosevelt would tell the President of their plight. Late that afternoon, Roy Lawrence asked me to meet with him and the Huntsville delegation. We had a conference and decided to try to ask Mrs. Roosevelt to meet us right after her address, before she left for her night train to Warm Springs. She would be with the President in the morning.

Mrs. Roosevelt had many appointments and I could not find her until she had gone on the platform where she would speak. So I wrote her a note, asking if she would meet with the delegation, Roy, and me, in the rear, left wing of the platform as soon as the meeting was over. I told her where I would be standing, when she read my note.

I waited until the question period, then sent my note in when it would be one of many coming to Mrs. Roosevelt. Characteristically, she looked up and in an instant our eyes met and she smiled and nodded yes. When the meeting was over I ran up to her and we went to the left wing, with a mob trying to follow us. When the police understood the situation they helped us and we joined hands to make a circle around Mrs. Roosevelt, so that it would be possible for the Huntsville men to tell their tragic story.

I'll never forget that sight. Mrs. Roosevelt, tall, lovely, gracious, shaking each work-hardened hand and bending her head to catch what each man said. They made their requests—for army tents for shelter to keep their families from sleeping outdoors, investigation of their plight, and aid from federal agencies. To all, Mrs. Roosevelt said, "I don't know what the President can do. I will tell him all you have told me. I know he will do what he can, but remember there are many limits to his power to help."

Then when she swung away from the group to go to her train, she caught my arm in hers and while I apologized for asking her time and attention, she said it was all right, and that she only hoped the President could devise something when she told him the situation.

Next morning, Thanksgiving Day, I drove back to Huntsville with Yelverton Cowherd, Dr. Witherspoon Dodge, of the TWOC staff, and Bill Mitch. We gathered in the hotel room of one of the men and discussed further steps. Union men crowded in and out. They were elated over Mrs. Roosevelt's promise to take this story to the President.

Paul Styles, a field investigator for the National Labor Relations Board, came in and told us that he had been called from the NLRB office that morning and told to go at once to Huntsville. The message said the President had that morning requested the NLRB top office in Washington and the Department of Labor to send investigators immediately into Huntsville in order that they might inform him of the situation there as quickly as possible.

It happened that two conciliators from the Department of Labor and Styles from the Regional NLRB had actually been in Huntsville when these orders came, because the crucial nature of the situation had led to their being assigned there during the emergency. Paul Styles was a native of Huntsville.

The personal appeal to Mrs. Roosevelt—her report to the President and his immediate action—greatly aided the Merrimack people. The evictions immediately stopped, relief was given, and it became possible for the National TWOC to rent an empty hotel for the evicted families. In the end a contract was secured.

The manager of the Merrimack Mill told a Conciliation Bureau representative that "if everybody had stayed out of Huntsville" he could have handled the situation by evicting the people, who would then have left Huntsville. This man had boasted of getting rid of "undesirable workers" (union members) by similar methods in Gastonia, North Carolina, some years before.

This "everybody" who had interfered with his plan, of course, included the President of the United States and his wife. . . .

Another union which had appeared on the southern scene in the early days of the CIO was the Amalgamated Clothing Workers of America. Already in 1935 a contract had been negotiated at Friedman–Harry Marks in Richmond, Virginia, which was to be significant because it was Amalgamated's first contract that became lasting in the South. It was also one of the three cases in which the National Labor Relations Act was upheld by the Supreme Court of the United States.

The man who had organized the workers at Friedman–Harry Marks was the Reverend Charles Webber. . . . One of my more exciting experiences in the Amalgamated's service began a few years later with a letter from Bernard Borah, southern director for this union.

"Our organizers have been driven out of Blank three times," wrote Borah. "The last time, Ed Blair was taken out of his hotel by a mob of citizens and warned not to come back lest he get much worse treatment." He went on to say that the third time he had sent in a woman, Mrs. Eula McGill, but she fared no better. The mob went to her hotel room, made her pack hastily, and told her to get out and stay out, or it would be hard for her. My good young friend, with whom I had worked in many situations, ended his letter, "I wish you would go in there and see what can be done."

So I set forth in my Plymouth as soon as possible. Upon arrival I parked my car in front of the courthouse and went across the street to see the bank president. It was he who had taken leadership in fighting organization of the town's recently built garment factory.

The tall, handsome young banker was in the cashier's cage and as I approached he gave me a friendly greeting—probably mistaking me for a new depositor. We talked about the lovely country and the weather and how I had enjoyed my drive. I confided that my brother-in-law was a bank president in Alexandria, Virginia. When I told him my occupation the transformation was instantaneous. His smile froze, the muscles of his face tightened—enmity replaced cordiality.

"We don't want the CIO around here," he said, and proceeded to tell me what he thought of the CIO and all its unions, works, and ways. I reminded him of federal laws, such as the National Labor Relations Act, which guaranteed the right of workers to organize, and also the rights of free assembly and free speech. All of this was piffle to the banker.

"If the government in Washington under this crazy New Deal passes laws that this town disapproves, the thing for us and other towns to do is to ignore them," he declared. "We are law-abiding people in this country, we don't need any police to protect us. We sleep with our doors open, but we have a pistol on the table beside our bed and know how to use it. Vigilantes perform a useful service and are often brave and effective men."

"We don't know anything about civil rights," the banker continued, "but we know how to protect our own rights. The Labor Board is unfair and should be disregarded until Congress wipes it out."

Though I went at once to call on the judge (also on the anti-union committee) the banker must have already phoned him, for he was looking suspicious. When I told him my mission, the judge pounded his desk and said, "I'm not going to talk to anybody about this damned CIO. I am against it and am going to do all I can to get it out of here." He hurried into another room and banged the door behind him.

So I went to the mayor's office—but he was in the state capitol many miles away. I had good luck in his office for I found his brother, an intelligent young lawyer who knew the need for unions, and had been counsel for farmers' cooperatives in that region. He told me what I suspected already. The town had given a substantial subsidy to the northern company that built the garment factory. He did not think the union could get anywhere until a large addition to the plant was completed and paid for.

While we were talking the telephone rang and I could hear the judge's voice roaring out the story of my visits to him and the banker. He wanted to ask the mayor what could be done about my presence in town. My friend told the judge that he saw no occasion for alarm over my being there, and as a lawyer he thought there was nothing the judge or others could do about it—also that he thought I would not be there long. When he put down the telephone he shook his head and smiled at me.

The young man advised me not to be in town when night fell, but well on the way to my destination. He did not think the citizens' committee would interfere with me, but tension was high and you could not tell what might happen.

The newspaper editor was away, but I talked with two of his associates. Later I had a letter from a fine young Methodist minister who regretted that I had not discovered him as he was unhappy about the lawless behavior of the citizens' committee. Nevertheless, I was forced to write this visit down as one of my less successful ventures.

In the summer of 1938, Dick Anderson of the Mine, Mill & Smelter Workers (then CIO), appeared at the CIO offices in Atlanta and asked for public relations help at Ducktown, Tennessee. There was a strike by the copper miners on the Ducktown side of the stream, but the men in the smelting plant on the Copperhill side were AF of L members. I had to attend a meeting at Highlander Folk School and promised to drive on from there through Cleveland, Tennessee, to Ducktown.

After a late getaway from Highlander I arrived at the end of the hard finished road at Cleveland at night fall. My road on to Ducktown ran close to the little river that flows between Copperhill and Ducktown. I did not know that the fairly broad stream on my right was only a few inches deep. The winding road kept me hugging the outside track and the river was uncomfortably close as I took the sharp curves in the dark.

Arriving on top of the mountain, I was soon in Ducktown and found the hotel. There Anderson was waiting for me and we went to my room to talk things over and give me a picture of the situation so that I could go right to work the next morning. Anderson had a list of persons he wanted me to talk with, mostly in Copperhill, which was much more of a town than I had expected.

The most sensible and fair person I met in Copperhill was a prominent doctor. He told me about the copper mines and the high death rate of the miners with what the townspeople called "miners' tuberculosis." Really a form of silicosis. The doctor was righteously indignant over the bad conditions of the mines leading to a shockingly high death rate. He wanted the miners to organize so that they could collectively secure better working conditions. There was no hope any other way.

The doctor gave me some names, some of whose owners I saw and found friendly. Some I could not find and others were antagonistic and could see only dangerous devils in the CIO. The silicosis they shrugged off—it always had been that way and always would be.

At the Copperhill furniture store I saw an unusual sight—coffins were lined up on one side of the store. I expressed surprise at this unusual combination of furniture and coffins in the front part of a store. "Well," said the proprietor without any resentment, "these men need coffins more than anything else because of the miners' tuberculosis—it is mighty bad around the mines."

Someone told me the druggist might be sympathetic since he had the opportunity to know how devastating the "miners' tuberculosis" was. But when the druggist stepped forward cheerfully and I told him my reason for being there, he turned and hurried up the back steps. The next man I saw was friendly and told me that the druggist and other leading business men were, at the time of my call, meeting upstairs in the drugstore to decide what they could do to keep the CIO out of the mines.

To anyone who has never seen the devastated valley between the two small cities it is hard to visualize the raw, red earth, the shallow little river wandering between the hillocks of mud in its bed, and the lack of green anywhere. It was fumes from an earlier smelting process which, by destroying all vegetation, had caused the special desolation of the Copperhill-Ducktown area.

Late in the afternoon I went back to the hotel and Anderson took me to a union meeting. I can still see the thin, yellow faces and sunken chests of men whose lives were eaten away each day as they worked.

The striking miners were greatly in need of food. I promised to try to get a carload of surplus products to carry them through the immediate situation. I wrote out a long telegram to Milo Perkins, then in charge of surplus products, and got it off at once. Then I followed up the telegram by a letter. In a few days a carload of surplus food went to the local office of the Tennessee Department of Public Welfare with the request that the food be dispensed to the striking miners.

The CIO lost that strike, but I have heard that the men finally succeeded in organizing with the AF or L. I hope that they found some relief from their distressing situation.

That second night at Ducktown, Anderson took me around with him checking on the pickets at the various entrances of the mines. As we were about to set out he ran back and got his pistol, which he put in the car pocket saying, "I'd better have that because somebody might want to get me."

We drove out to the Hiawassee Dam which lay between two high promontories with the valley between them, drained of its river. Floodlights shone glaringly on the great natural cut between the banks, and steam shovels carried on their noisy and efficient job. It was a titanic, amazing scene. Whenever I have seen that particular dam since then, I still see its beginning.

That dam and its significance to the life of that area consoled me after my Ducktown visit, for it meant to me the use of land, water, and power in the service of people, as contrasted with the seared devastation of the Ducktown area.

MARY
HEATON
VORSE

"People can no longer live on what they are getting..."

*Like Meridel Le Sueur, Mary Heaton
Vorse combined careers as labor journalist, union activist, and fiction writer
with notable success in the twenties and thirties. In common with Lucy
Randolph Mason, Vorse was a well-born social reformer who committed herself
full-time to labor organizing relatively late in life.*

*Born into a rich New England family in 1874, Vorse traveled widely and
studied in a French art school before marrying a newspaperman, Albert Vorse.
Backed by her money, Mary and Albert Vorse returned to Europe, where
Albert intended to write the great American novel. Instead he spent most of*

his time engaged in compulsive philandering
well-reviewed novels. After two children and e
Vorse had had enough. In 1910 she left her hus
ship on the Atlantic, she received word of his u
hemorrhage.

Back home in America, the young widow a
her furious family disinherited her. She moved
into a Greenwich Village world populated by
radicals. Vorse became an editor of the socialist
same time her reputation as a novelist began t
married Joe O'Brien, a socialist and free-lanc

Between 1912 and 1915 the couple travel
labor reporters. It was a "joyful" marriage tha
also tragically brief. In 1915 O'Brien died sud
Mary Heaton Vorse had been widowed.

When the Depression struck, Vorse was in h
she had financed her labor journalism and supp
magazine fiction and novels. She was one of A
read by millions. At her death in 1962, Vorse
many hundreds of short stories. In a great nu
character was a strong woman, battling grea
was such a woman, but she wrote movingly o
efforts to combine the life of a writer, labor
three.

Mary Heaton Vorse wrote an autobiography
in 1935, but it covers only the years betwe
those interested in following her activities
journalism provides an unintended autobiog
cluded here present Vorse's accounts of the grea
of 1934 and the Flint auto workers' strike of
in the New Republic. *Labor historians gen*
sit-down strike in Flint the most significant
in the twentieth century.

SOUR

extensively among selections of Mary Heaton Vor
Heaton Vorse, *Rebel Pen: The Writings of Mary Heaton*
included here have been taken. Dee Garrison no

d the best biography of Vorse, *Mary Heaton Vorse: The Life of an American Insurgent* See also Leslie Gould and Carol Hurd Green, "Mary Heaton Vorse," in *Notable Women*, 712–714. Vorse's papers are housed at the Labor History Archives, Library, Wayne State University, Detroit, Michigan.

MARY HEATON VORSE

Textile Trouble

T HE STREETS ARE STILL DARK, oblong of the mills is gray and silent. From a distance comes noise of the sea. There are already men standing in threes and n street corners. It is New Bedford the morning after Labor e day set for the big textile strike—"The first strike of its kind history of the labor movement of America," as the organizers een telling the workers in the mass meetings throughout the

strike is in the nature of a showdown. It was fathered by the p and stretchout and mothered by evasions of the code, by the rd of Section 7a. People can no longer live on what they are They can no longer exist under the conditions under which ork. Too many skilled workers have been discharged and byed as "learners"—one means of avoiding the minimum-wage Too many workers have been forced to do three people's work day. In the past five years less and less of every dollar earned mills has gone to the worker.

time of anxiety. Are "they" going to come out? Will there be for the mills? I'm striking and you're striking, but are the Our mill is striking but what about the other mills? And if we New Bedford, what about the rest of the towns in New

England and what about Manchester and Lowell and Lawrence? What about Passaic and Paterson?—These are the things the workers are thinking as they watch the crowd on the street become larger, as the streets get bright. The small groups have flowed into each other; the streets are filled. The Hathaway mill stares empty-windowed at the mounting crowd. On the mill side there is no one. A guard at the gate, a few policemen, very few, no imposing display of armed force—as yet. On the side away from the mill, every language in the world is spoken: French, Portuguese, and Italian predominate. Everybody is good-tempered, even jolly.

No one has gone in. There is no picket line. There does not need to be. All the workers are out on the street opposite the mill. There are no scabs against whom to picket the mill. These mills in the South End are out 100 percent. Organization is no new thing to the New Bedford workers. They have gone through many a struggle. In 1928, the big good-natured Portuguese women who look like full-blown peonies snatched clubs from policemen's lifted hands and hit back. The black-eyed little French Canadians fought like wildcats. We wonder if the North Side is holding as well and hurry over there. The two manufacturing sections of New Bedford are far apart. We drive past sleeping, old-fashioned houses, past the business section. Down the steep street near the Wamsutta mills the workers are gathered. Here one sees an old-fashioned type of worker. Middle-aged prissy Americans, they hold themselves apart from the foreign worker but they are out here striking in the street for all that. Some people tell you four people have gone in. Others say they have counted seven, a handful. It's the same in the Nashewena mills—it's the same in twenty-five mills in New Bedford. A 100 percent strike—only the three great tire-fabric mills have not come out, Firestone, Goodrich, and Fisk.

People begin to drift away slowly. Everyone is relieved, everyone seems happy. It seems more like a fiesta than a strike. There is just time to eat something before the mass meeting in the park. Yesterday William Beatty had made a fighting speech. He refused in a roundabout way the unity proposals of the National Textile Workers' Union, the left-wing, Communist-dominated union which before the National Recovery Act was strong in New Bedford. This union has already

299
Mary Heaton Vorse

formed a merger in Paterson. The local United Textile Workers' leaders will not hear of it.

Today's meeting is short. There are three messages from the organizer Sylva; one a new one. "Don't think of yourselves as New Bedford workers—your fight is the fight of all the textile workers of America. It is as wide as the land." The next is "Trust our president. He will see we get justice." Yes, the steelworkers were told that and the automobile workers—one knows the result and a heavy feeling of defeat comes over me as I look at the hopeful people in their holiday mood. Dressed as for church instead of for work. The third message is concrete: "We're out 100 percent except the tire fabrics. We've got to get them out. Everybody go over to Fisk and Goodrich and picket; *now*."

The meeting breaks up. We go over and now they come in groups. Men and girls, old and young, hundreds and hundreds of them streaming over to the great factories, and filling the streets in front. Mr. Beatty and Mr. Sylva lead a small picket line on the mill side. On the opposite side the gay crowd calls to the workers who throng to the windows. There are few police.

The papers come out with screaming headlines starting a Red witch-hunt. They say the left-wing textile leader, Ann Burlak, is in hiding. But we have seen Ann Burlak quietly attending the meeting. Ann Burlak, secretary of the National Textile Workers' Union, will be arrested. What for? Oh, anything will do.

We read the papers on our way to Pawtucket and Fall River. The papers say that yesterday, Labor Day, in the big mass meeting the independent unions in Fall River voted not to come out. The Associated Press reports Pawtucket working as usual. But in Fall River the dreary, the workers are buzzing excitedly in the street. The mills are tied up. The United Textile Workers have struck 100 percent and they have the loom fixers. So the mills are tied up, perhaps over 60 percent.

The Pepperell mills are being picketed by a gay band of young girls. There are silent mills in Fall River from whose windows stovepipes protrude as in Moscow in 1921. There is where fly-by-night sweatshops operated. Other mills have been torn down. Piles of gray stones lie about.

In Pawtucket a lively meeting is going on. The union hall is full of

weavers and spinners. The place hums with life. A national organizer, Elizabeth Nord, is making a comprehensive talk. She is slender,
young, full of fighting spirit. Later she tells me thousands are out.
The Associated Press story has been contradicted. She calls for
pickets for a mill out of town where they make Fruit of the Loom.
The real story will be the coming out of those mills not already on
strike. In the South they have called out the militia. The tone of the
evening papers is more sensational.

Back in New Bedford we hear there is trouble near the tire
factories. A large crowd has gathered in an open square nearby. It is
after ten. Mr. Beatty has stopped picketing. Fifteen thousand people
have been down around the tire-fabric mills this evening. The police
have been reinforced by the khaki-clad motorcycle cops, who hoot
their sirens as they tear past, by members of the liquor squad, by the
traffic police. For the first time there is tenseness. Thousands of
workers are in the open space, near the mills. They are pale under
the high arc lights. The day which began quietly has been one of
mounting excitement. It is as if one could see and feel the massed will
of the workers who are out directed toward the workers who have not
yet come out.

The young socialist editor of the local labor paper mounts a gray
outcropping of rock and makes a speech about everyone's being on
tomorrow's picket line. A Negro near us calls out, "How about the
night-shift? What about a picket line now!" They form a picket line,
the editor in front. The crowd swarms forward behind him. At the
street by the mill they are stopped. The police bar the way to the
mill, the crowd pushes on under the pressure of those behind. Stones
are hurled—the chief orders the workers back. The crowd breaks.
Motorcycle police and police wagons herd the crowd down the street,
but their action might well be a lesson to the police of other cities.
There have been no beatings and no arrests.

Wednesday morning mass picketing was barred in front of Fisk and
Goodyear on the South Side and on the North Side in front of
Firestone.

Wednesday noon one picket alone walks up and down, up and
down, in front of the Goodyear plant. It is none other than Mr.
William Beatty. Up and down he walks on his endless patrol. No

workers are allowed within the police lines. The New York correspondents are sharply questioned. There is a squib in the paper about a car with a New York license supposed to contain "outside agitators" and "literature." It contained its owner, Mr. Waldo Frank. The morning papers also contain statements from the managers of the three factories that they expect no trouble. Not a chance in the world of these contented workers striking. We walk along by the mill. A group of a dozen men are leaning on a wall facing the mill. "Staying out?" we ask.

"Yeah, we're twisters from Fisk. We're staying out," they grin. We drive blocks around the enormous mill, then down one side where there are only a scattered handful of police. We see the street lined with an excited crowd.

Girls are pouring out of the back entrance of the Fisk factory. The crowd is applauding.

"Are you coming out?" we ask.

"Sure thing," they chorus.

"Many of you?" "We're 'most all out." "Yes, only the boss men left." The word goes from mouth to mouth.

"Fisk has struck! Fisk has struck—the fabric workers are out!"

The word has gone out over the wire to Washington, "Fisk is out." The tire-fabric factories are all closed. The first victory.

The Emergency Brigade at Flint

About the time that the pressure of the crowd waiting to get into the injunction hearing was tearing off the hinges of the courtroom door, word came to union headquarters that there was fighting in the Chevrolet plant.

Anyone experienced in strike atmosphere could have told at the mass meeting on Sunday night that there was something in the air. The meeting, which was addressed by Father J. W. R. Maguire and Mrs. Cornelia Bryce Pinchot, was no ordinary mass meeting. It was an assembly of men and women who are on the march. It was almost impossible to get through the good-natured crowd. Every seat was taken. Workers were packed close against the wall. They thronged the stairway while Father Maguire was talking to the overflow.

One felt that this special meeting was the molten core of this historic automobile strike. Here was a strike whose outcome might influence the labor movement for many years. Its success or its failure did not concern automobiles alone. It took in its sweep steel, coal, rubber, electrical workers. The fate of the whole labor movement was bound up in it. It had emerged from the frame of unionism and had become a contest now between industrial leaders, like the duPonts, Morgans, Sloans, and a president and administration favorable to organized labor. Here in this hall was the burning center of this momentous strike. Failing immediate settlement, action of some sort was inevitable.

The action came. All that week the Chevrolet workers had been holding meetings about the discharge of workers for union activities. Now there was a sit-down in the Chevrolet plant. Plant Manager Lenz would not meet the union to iron out the trouble. First he agreed to do this, then he withdrew. This is one striker's story of what happened:

"A hundred of us started walking through the plant calling a sitdown. The company police and thugs sprang up from nowhere. They kept them shut up in the employment office and sprung them loose on us. In a moment there was fighting everywhere. Fighters were rolling on the floor. They had clubs and we were unarmed. They started shooting off tear gas. I saw one fellow hit on the head and when he swung backwards he cut his head on the machinery. He started to stagger out. Two of the thugs knocked him down again. I let go on a couple of thugs. You kind of go crazy when you see thugs beating up men you know."

There were about eighteen casualties in all. Two of them had to be taken to the hospital. Most of them came up to the room in the Pengelly Building, where there is a nurse, a striker's wife, in attendance all the time. The room was soon full of bleeding men, the table heaped high with crimson gauze. None of the casualties happened outside the plant. All the injuries occurred inside, showing who made the trouble. Union headquarters say they have definite proof that there are 500 thugs from a strike-breaking detective agency in St. Louis scattered in the plant. At the present moment the majority have barricaded themselves in Plant No. 8 of Chevrolet.

The Women's Emergency Brigade had come back from their first march past the plant. One of the women I knew was wiping her eyes, which were smarting with tear gas. Around her clung the acrid smell of gas. "They were fighting inside and outside the factory," she said. "The fighting would have been much worse if it hadn't been for us. We walked right along with our flag at our head. The gas floated right out toward us. But we have been gassed and we went right on."

Someone speaking admiringly of the Women's Brigade said, "Gee, those women can sure break windows fast!" But they didn't want to break them. "We had to break windows, I tell you, to get air to the boys who were being gassed inside. We don't want violence. We just want to protect our husbands and we are going to." These women were veterans of the battle for Fisher No. 2, known in Flint as "Bulls Run" because the police ran away. I have seen women do yeoman service in strikes. I have seen some pretty good women's auxiliaries in my time, but I have never before seen such splendid organization or such determination as there is in the women's auxiliary of Flint.

Who are these women? They are strikers' wives and mothers, normally homebodies. Ma and the girls in fact. They are most of them mature women, the majority married, ranging in age from young mothers to grandmothers. In the auxiliary room there are always some children playing around. A big crowd comes after school to find out what Ma's doing, more come in after movies, and there's always a baby or two.

I should judge the majority of the brigade have been to high school, and all are neatly and carefully dressed. There isn't a flaming-eyed Joan of Arc among them. One and all are normal, sensible women who are doing this because they have come to the mature conclusion it must be done if they and their children are to have a decent life. So they are behind their husbands as long as there is need, with the same matter-of-fact capability—and inevitability—with which they get the children off to school.

Today their job was "protecting their men." I went down to the Chevrolet plant with two of them. The workers had now captured Plant No. 4. The street was full of people; there were about twenty police behind the bridge and the high plant gate. The police were quiet and unprovocative so the crowd of pickets was good-natured. The sound truck was directing operations as usual.

The use of the sound truck is new to me in strike procedure and it is hard to know how a strike was ever conducted without it. As we came down past the policemen a great voice, calm and benignant, proclaimed that everything was in hand, the plant was under control. Next the great disembodied voice, really the voice of auburn-haired young Roy Reuther, urged the men in the plant to barricade themselves from tear gas. Every now and then the voice came, "Protection squad. Attention! Guard your sound car. Protection squad, attention!"

Then the voice addressed the workers who crowded the windows of the lower levels. At the top of the steep flight of steps were other workers, lunch buckets under their arms, waving at the pickets in the street, and still more workers fringed the roof. The sound truck inquired if they were union men. They shouted, "Yes." The crowd cheered.

The measured, soothing voice of the sound truck boomed: "Word has come to us that there are men in the crowd anxious to join the union. Go to the last car, you will find the cards ready to sign. If you have no money for dues with you you can come to Pengelly Hall later." The sound car strikes up "Solidarity," the men at the top of the steps, on top of the plant, in the street, all sing. A woman's voice next. She tells the crowd that the women have gone to the auxiliary hall to wipe their eyes clear of the tear gas and will soon be back. "We don't want any violence, we don't want any trouble. We are going to do everything we can to keep from trouble, but we are going to protect our husbands."

The Chevrolet plant covers eighty acres and has twelve departments. Plant No. 4 is the key plant, because it makes the motors. Without Plant No. 4 Chevrolet cannot make cars. This plant is set in a hollow, below a little hill about five hundred feet long. Down this hill presently came a procession, preceded by an American flag. The women's bright red caps showed dramatically in the dark crowd. They were singing "Hold the Fort."

There was something moving to all the crowd to see the women return after having been gassed. A cheer went up; the crowd joined in the song. The line of bright-capped women spread themselves out in front of the high barbed-wire-protected gate. Some of the men who had jumped over the gate went back, amid the cheers of the crowd.

I went to the top of the little hill where a string of men were coming out of the back of the building.

"Are you going home?" I asked.

"Home? Hell, no! Half of us are sitting down inside, and half of us are coming out to picket from the street."

"How many of you are for the sit-down?"

"Ninety percent," a group of them chorused.

It is getting dark, the crowd has grown denser. A black fringe of pickets and spectators is silhouetted against the brilliant green lights of the plant windows. "Protection squad! Guard your sound car!" the voice warns solemnly. I go with members of the women's auxiliary to Flint No. 2 to get salamanders and material for a shack for the night picket line. The women are going to stay all night.

There is plenty of excitement in union headquarters a mile and a half away, a meeting is being held. You can hear the cheers as you push up the crowded stairway. Presently some of the Women's Emergency Brigade come in to warm up; the night is bitter. "The Guard has been called out," they report. "We met the soldiers going down as we came back." Why has the National Guard been brought out? I have been in scores of crowds where trouble hung on the edge of a knife. This crowd in front of Chevrolet No. 4 was not so terrifying as a Christmas crowd. After the first fighting was over there was not even the semblance of trouble.

I was at a union meeting at the Cadillac-Fleetwood Hall in Detroit, where a pale organizer started his speech with emotion, saying, "Your hardsweated wages are being used to pay hired thugs and gunmen!" This was Organizer Mayo, who, with three other organizers, had been surrounded by a mob in a hotel in Bay City. They appealed for police protection, which must have been meager, since the organizers were kidnapped in Saginaw. Mayo escaped and made his way to Detroit. The other organizers were sideswiped by the thugs' car on the outskirts of Flint and are still in the hospital, one in critical condition.

It is not only in Flint that one gets the impression of a vital movement. In all the union meetings I have attended there is this sense of direction of workers knowing what they are doing and where they are going. Here at this meeting in Detroit were reports from the picket captains; the welfare committee, which had been in Lansing and had succeeded in cutting red tape for strikers under relief; the "chiselers'" committee, which goes to various merchants to get donations of food; the recreation committee; and the strategy board, which is always in contact with the central strategy board of the union in Detroit. There is also a women's auxiliary, which cooks the food, goes on picket duty, and so forth.

The vitality of this movement shows itself by the many spontaneous cultural movements that are springing up on all sides. Inside Fisher Body Nos. 1 and 2 the sitters are going to classes run by the union. Since last Monday the plants have been turned into workers' educational institutions. Classes conducted by Merlin D. Bishop include parliamentary procedure, public speaking, and collective bargaining. The workers are writing their own plays. There are two groups of strikers who want to put on incidents of the strike in a living newspaper. Classes in journalism and workers' writing classes have been started with a graduate student from the University of Michigan journalism school as an instructor. This is a strike, Model 1937.

AFTERWORD

HISTORIANS HAVE LONG ARGUED ABOUT THE ROLE OF THE INDIVIDUAL
in history. Their positions have ranged from the thesis of Thomas
Carlyle, who held that remarkable individuals determine the main
trends in history, to the Marxist view of G. V. Plekhanov, who
asserted, "Owing to the specific qualities of their minds and characters, influential individuals can change the individual features of
events and some of their particular consequences, but they cannot
change their general trend, which is determined by other forces."[1]
Sidney Hook, in *The Hero in History*, distinguishes between the
"eventful" person who harnesses historical forces (Mikhail Gorbachev
has been called an "eventful" man), and the "event-making" person
who, through the power of his or her own personality, generates
historical forces.

Most historians see the roles of individuals in terms of a blend of
the person and the times. In this regard we may note that in 1982,
846 historians, placing presidents on a scale of Great, Near Great,
Above Average, Average, Below Average, and Failure, ranked Lincoln first, Franklin D. Roosevelt second, and Washington third.[2]
These presidents attained greatness amidst the three most perilous
passages in our domestic history: the Revolution, the Civil War, and
the Great Depression, which, respectively, threatened the loss of

independence, disunion, and economic (and possibly political and social) collapse. In sum, the three greatest presidents had the opportunity to become great.

Presidents, needless to say, are elite figures. For our purposes we may point out that the Great Depression also provided an opportunity for ordinary people—especially women—to display, in their own way, greatness. Lillian Cantor Dawson, a social worker in the 1930s, recalled finding jobs as taxi drivers for three hundred medical doctors who were grateful for the chance to earn a pittance. There were, she continued,

> a hundred stories like that; but I don't think men could have done what they did if they hadn't been backed by their women. The women carried such a load. I came to believe in those years that the female of the species is entrusted with the perpetuation of life at her own expense. Perhaps nature compensates for this burden in a way: women develop the strength to survive anything.[3]

One ought not to forget estimable ordinary women in the midst of our selections from the writings of exceptional women who had an opportunity in the 1930s to show greatness. Many things came together to set the stage for their activities. Long-term developments in women's work patterns and the professions led to the growth of fields such as social work. The heritage of Progressive reform, in which women had played vital roles in the settlements and the social justice movement, provided crucial continuities to the 1930s. The return to power of the Democrats under the twin tutelage of Franklin and Eleanor Roosevelt also encouraged women's progress, as did the burgeoning of the labor movement. Yet one factor, which assured Roosevelt's election and occasioned the spectacular growth of unions, above all others shaped the experiences of women (and men) in the 1930s: the Great Depression. Into the void created by this massive economic dislocation stepped a group of talented and committed women. As participants in the dramatic changes in American politics and culture in that depression decade, they tell stories that add to our understanding of the New Deal as well as political and women's history in the twentieth century.

Before closing this presentation of the words of these women of valor, we may, with the help of historian Susan Ware, consider the experience of women in general in the 1930s as it relates to several long-run developments. First, women's labor in the home often replaced the purchase of goods and services outside the home, enabling many families to make do rather than do without. "This substitution represented a break from the general trend toward more labor-saving devices in the home and the removal of family functions to other social and economic institutions." Needless to say, this trend resumed after the Great Depression.

Second, as noted in our introduction, "most Americans, men and women, overwhelmingly supported traditional family roles." The Depression, Ware observes, "reinforced traditional ideas by giving women larger roles to play in holding their families together." More-over, she argues, "the roots of the Feminine Mystique of the 1940s and 1950s are clearly visible in the preceding decade."

Third, noting that women's proportion of the work force increased in the 1930s from 22 to 25 percent, with more married women going to work despite widespread opposition, Ware notes "the long-range shift in the female work force from young single women to older, married women workers." The beginning of this changeover is usual-ly assigned to World War II, but "the trend was well under way by the Depression."

Fourth, Ware points out that "feminism did not die in the decade either, but it was in a period of transition." The dominant feminists of the Progressive era were gone; women who had come of age in the Progressive era were active in public life, but they were not militant feminists; women who had come of age in the 1920s and 1930s showed little concern with feminism. Still, in the 1930s "older women and some younger ones (notably on the political left), kept the feminist standard flying, providing continuity and laying the groundwork for the revival of feminism thirty years later."[4]

As for our women of valor, the efforts demanded by their immedi-ate task of combating the Depression contributed substantially to at least two developments of long-run importance: the creation of the welfare state and the rise of organized labor. Their interests and accomplishments reinforce Ware's assertion that "Instead of a bleak

and desolate time for women, the 1930s emerge as a rich, if sometimes contradictory, period of twentieth-century women's history."[5]

NOTES

1. G.V. Plekhanov, *The Role of the Individual in History* (Moscow, 1944), 41.
2. Robert K. Murray and Tim H. Blessing, *Greatness in the White House: Rating the Presidents, Washington through Carter* (University Park, Pa., 1988).
3. Jeanne Westin, *Making Do: How Women Survived the '30s* (Chicago, 1976), 186–187.
4. Ware, *Holding Their Own*, 198–200.
5. *Ibid.*, 201.

A NOTE ON THE EDITORS

Bernard Sternsher is Professor of History at Bowling Green State University. He grew up in Fall River, Massachusetts, and studied at the University of Alabama and Boston University. He has written *Rexford Tugwell and the New Deal* and *Consensus, Conflict, and American Historians*, and has edited *Hitting Home: The Great Depression in Town and Country; The New Deal: Laissez Faire to Socialism*; and *The Negro in Depression and War.*

Judith Sealander is Professor of History at Wright State University. She grew up in Fayetteville, Arkansas, and studied at the University of Arkansas and Duke University. She has written *As Minority Becomes Majority: Federal Reaction to the Phenomenon of Women in the Work Force, 1920–1963*, and *Grand Plans: Business Progressivism and Social Change in the Ohio Miami Valley, 1890–1929.*